RYAN FERRIER ★ DEVAKI NEOGI ★ JEREMY LAWSON

CURB STOMP ™

BOOM!
STUDIOS

BOOM! STUDIOS

CURB STOMP, January 2016. Published by BOOM! Studios, a division of Boom Entertainment, Inc. Curb Stomp is ™ & © 2016 Ryan Ferrier & Devaki Neogi. Originally published in single magazine form as CURB STOMP No. 1-4. ™ & © 2015 Ryan Ferrier & Devaki Neogi. All rights reserved. BOOM! Studios™ and the BOOM! Studios logo are trademarks of Boom Entertainment, Inc., registered in various countries and categories. All characters, events, and institutions depicted herein are fictional. Any similarity between any of the names, characters, persons, events, and/or institutions in this publication to actual names, characters, and persons, whether living or dead, events, and/or institutions is unintended and purely coincidental. BOOM! Studios does not read or accept unsolicited submissions of ideas, stories, or artwork.

A catalog record of this book is available from OCLC and from the BOOM! Studios website, www.boom-studios.com, on the Librarians page.

BOOM! Studios, 5670 Wilshire Boulevard, Suite 450, Los Angeles, CA 90036-5679. Printed in China. First Printing.

ISBN: 978-1-60886-777-6, eISBN: 978-1-61398-448-2

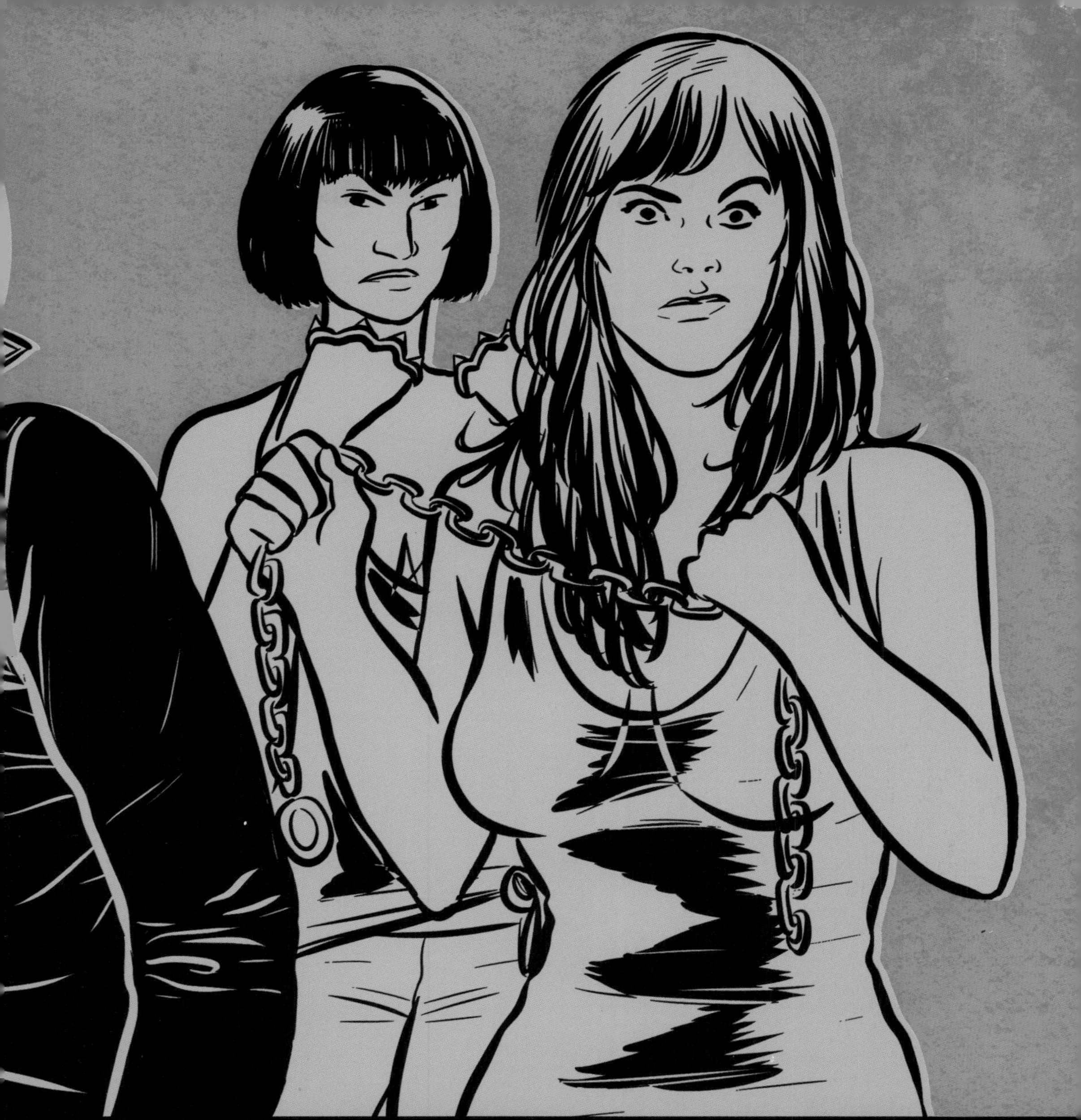

CURB STOMP™

CREATED BY
RYAN FERRIER & DEVAKI NEOGI

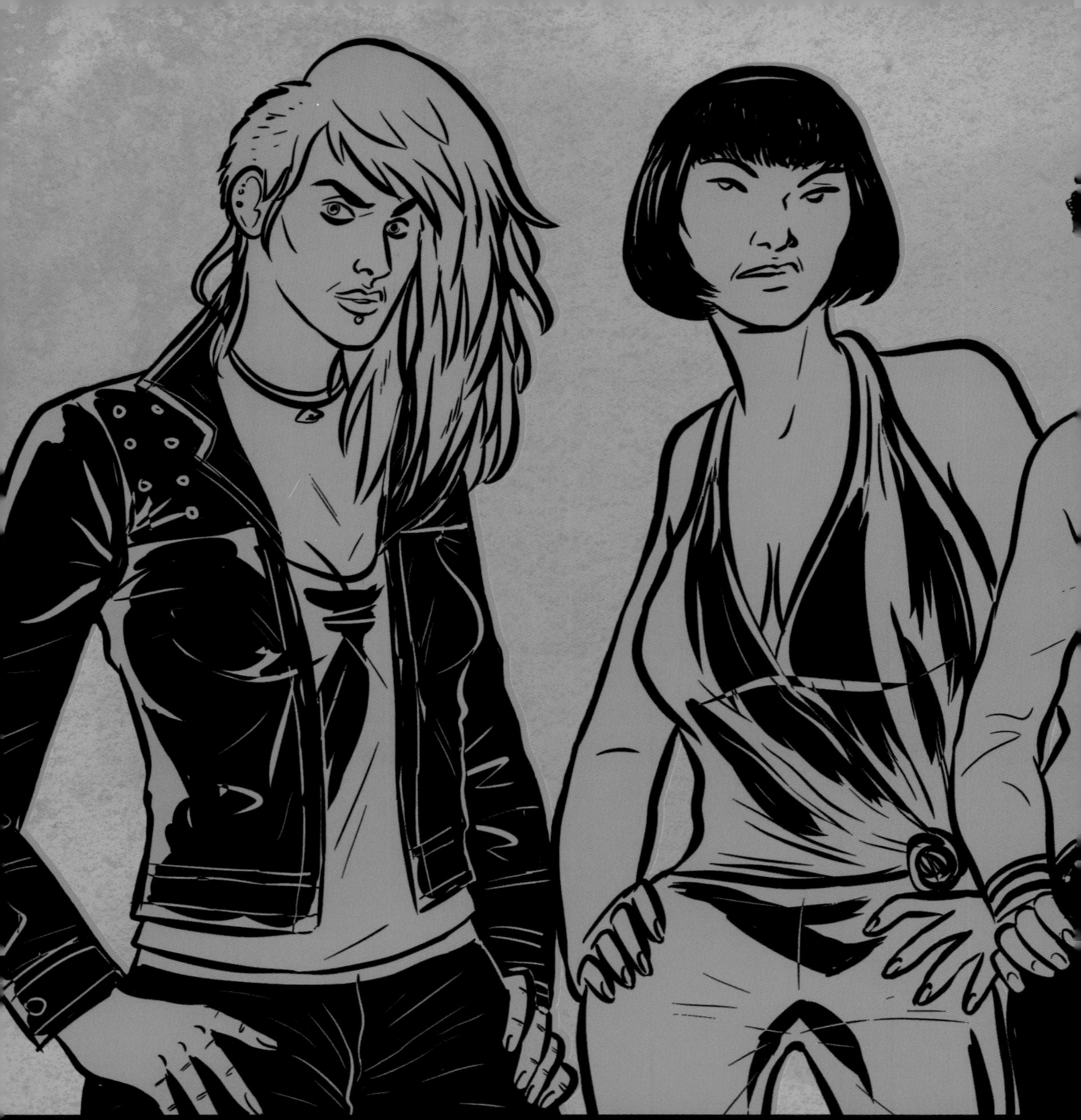

WRITTEN BY

RYAN FERRIER

COLORS BY
JEREMY LAWSON
WITH NEIL LALONDE

LETTERS BY
COLIN BELL

COVER BY
TULA LOTAY

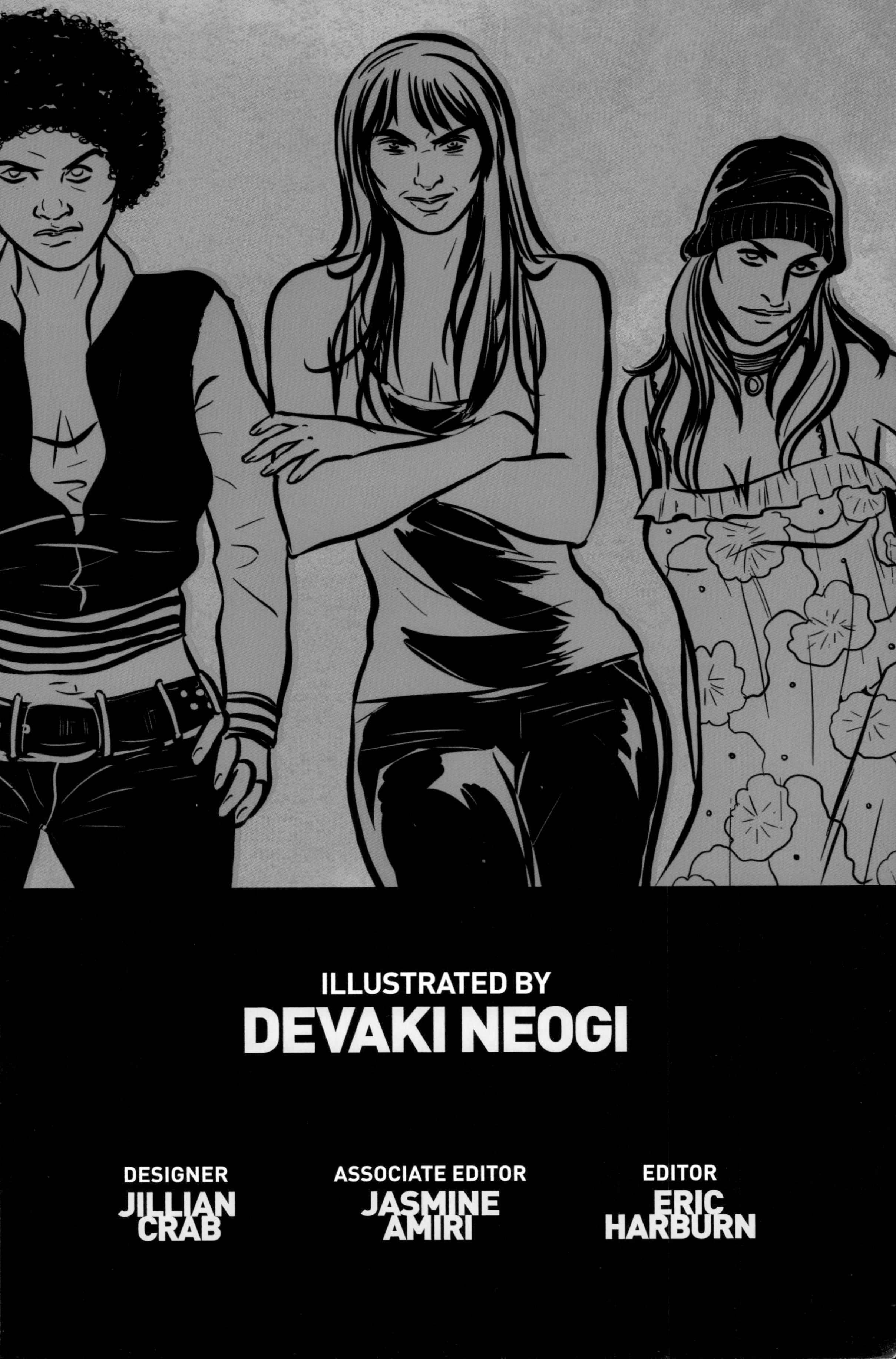

ILLUSTRATED BY

DEVAKI NEOGI

DESIGNER
JILLIAN CRAB

ASSOCIATE EDITOR
JASMINE AMIRI

EDITOR
ERIC HARBURN

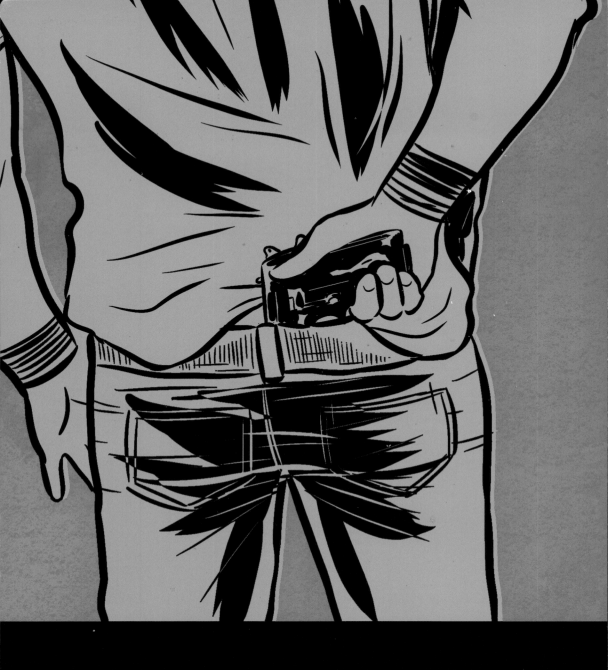

CHAPTER ONE

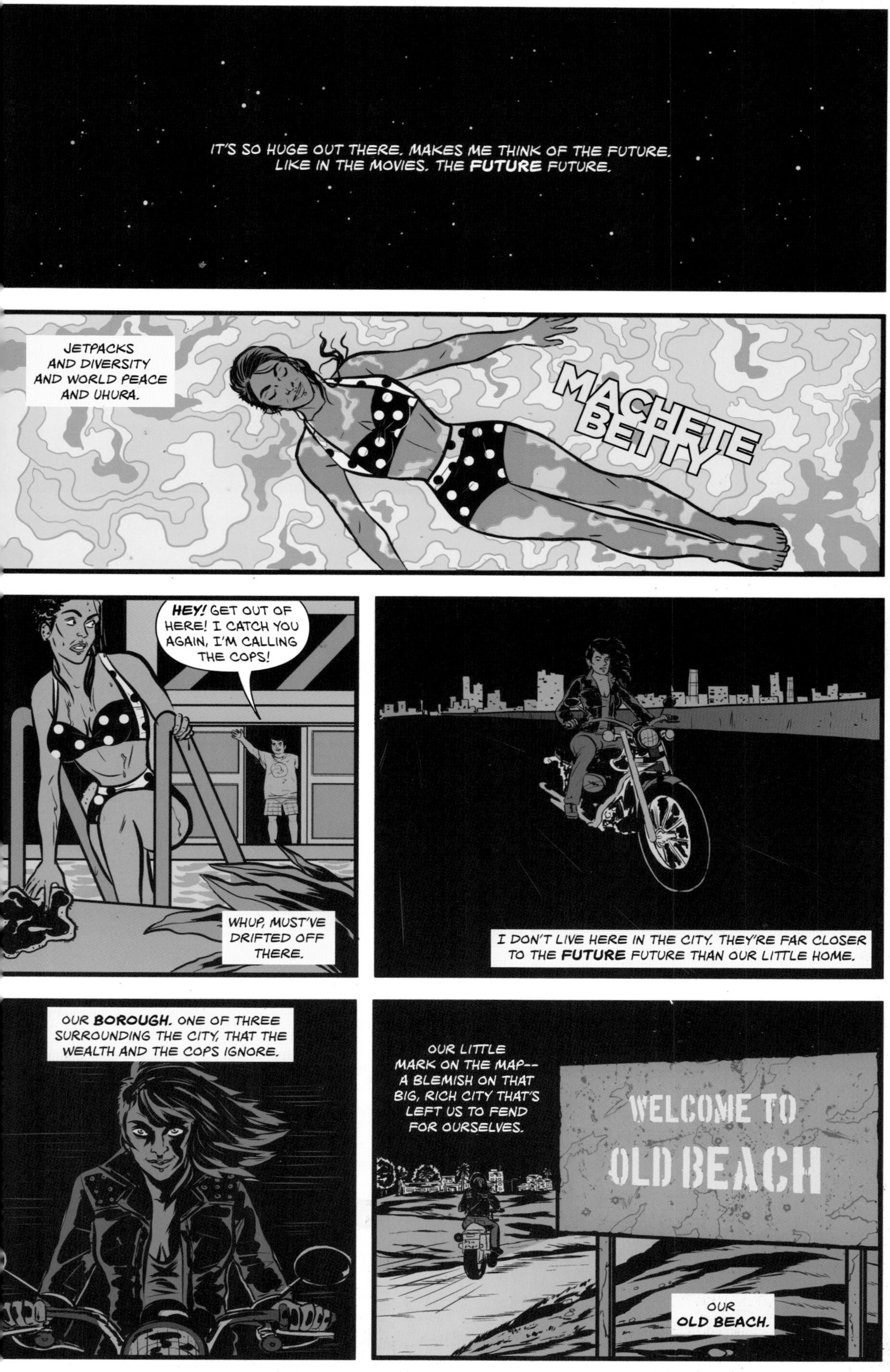
IT'S SO HUGE OUT THERE. MAKES ME THINK OF THE FUTURE. LIKE IN THE MOVIES. THE FUTURE FUTURE.
JETPACKS AND DIVERSITY AND WORLD PEACE AND UHURA.
MACHETE BETTY
HEY! GET OUT OF HERE! I CATCH YOU AGAIN, I'M CALLING THE COPS!
WHUP, MUST'VE DRIFTED OFF THERE.
I DON'T LIVE HERE IN THE CITY. THEY'RE FAR CLOSER TO THE FUTURE FUTURE THAN OUR LITTLE HOME.
OUR BOROUGH. ONE OF THREE SURROUNDING THE CITY, THAT THE WEALTH AND THE COPS IGNORE.
OUR LITTLE MARK ON THE MAP-- A BLEMISH ON THAT BIG, RICH CITY THAT'S LEFT US TO FEND FOR OURSELVES.
WELCOME TO OLD BEACH
OUR OLD BEACH.

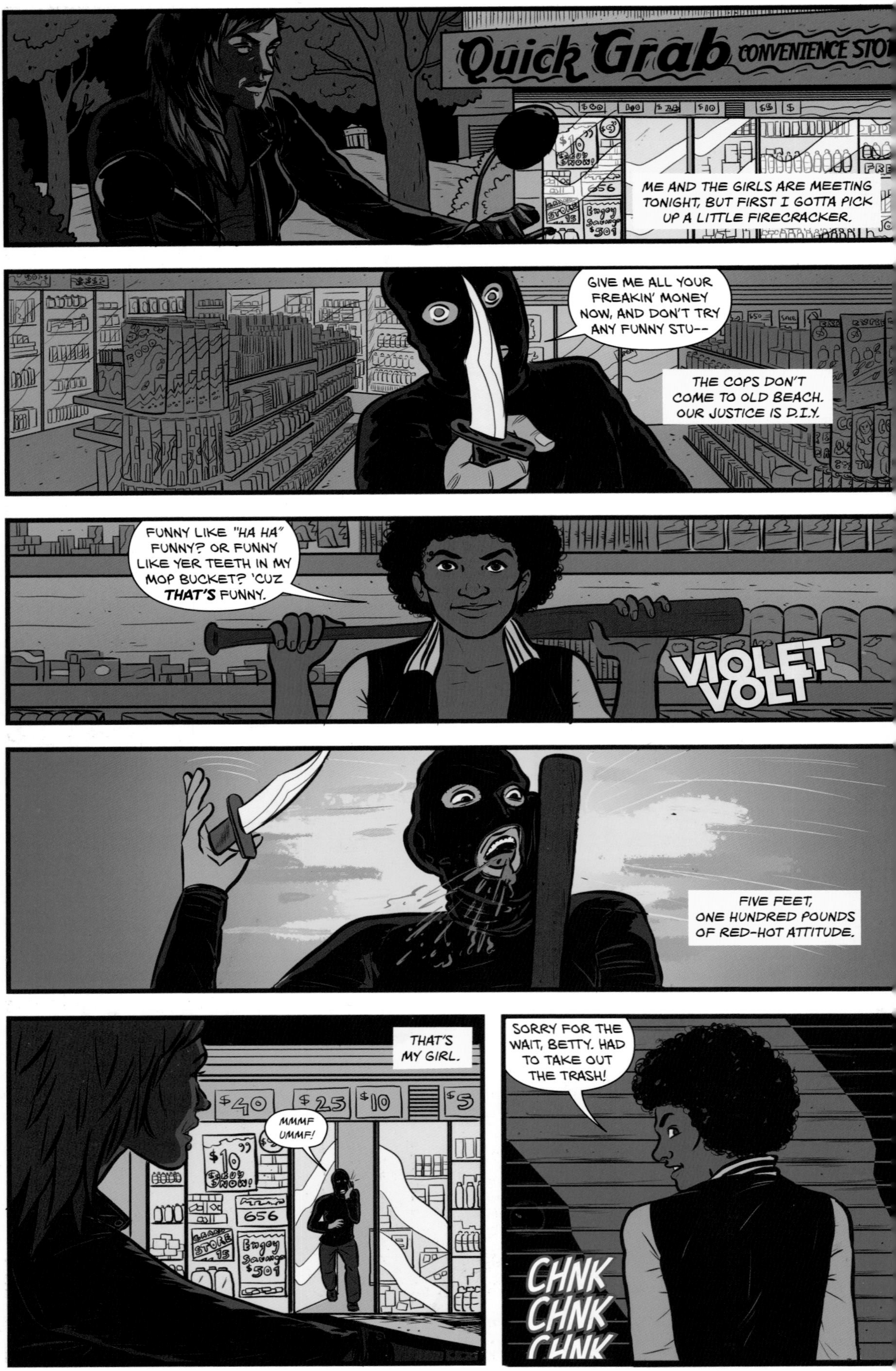
Quick Grab CONVENIENCE STO
ME AND THE GIRLS ARE MEETING TONIGHT, BUT FIRST I GOTTA PICK UP A LITTLE FIRECRACKER.
GIVE ME ALL YOUR FREAKIN' MONEY NOW, AND DON'T TRY ANY FUNNY STU--
THE COPS DON'T COME TO OLD BEACH. OUR JUSTICE IS D.I.Y.
FUNNY LIKE "HA HA" FUNNY? OR FUNNY LIKE YER TEETH IN MY MOP BUCKET? 'CUZ THAT'S FUNNY.
VIOLET VOLT
FIVE FEET, ONE HUNDRED POUNDS OF RED-HOT ATTITUDE.
THAT'S MY GIRL.
MMMF UMMF!
SORRY FOR THE WAIT, BETTY. HAD TO TAKE OUT THE TRASH!
CHNK
CHNK
CHNK

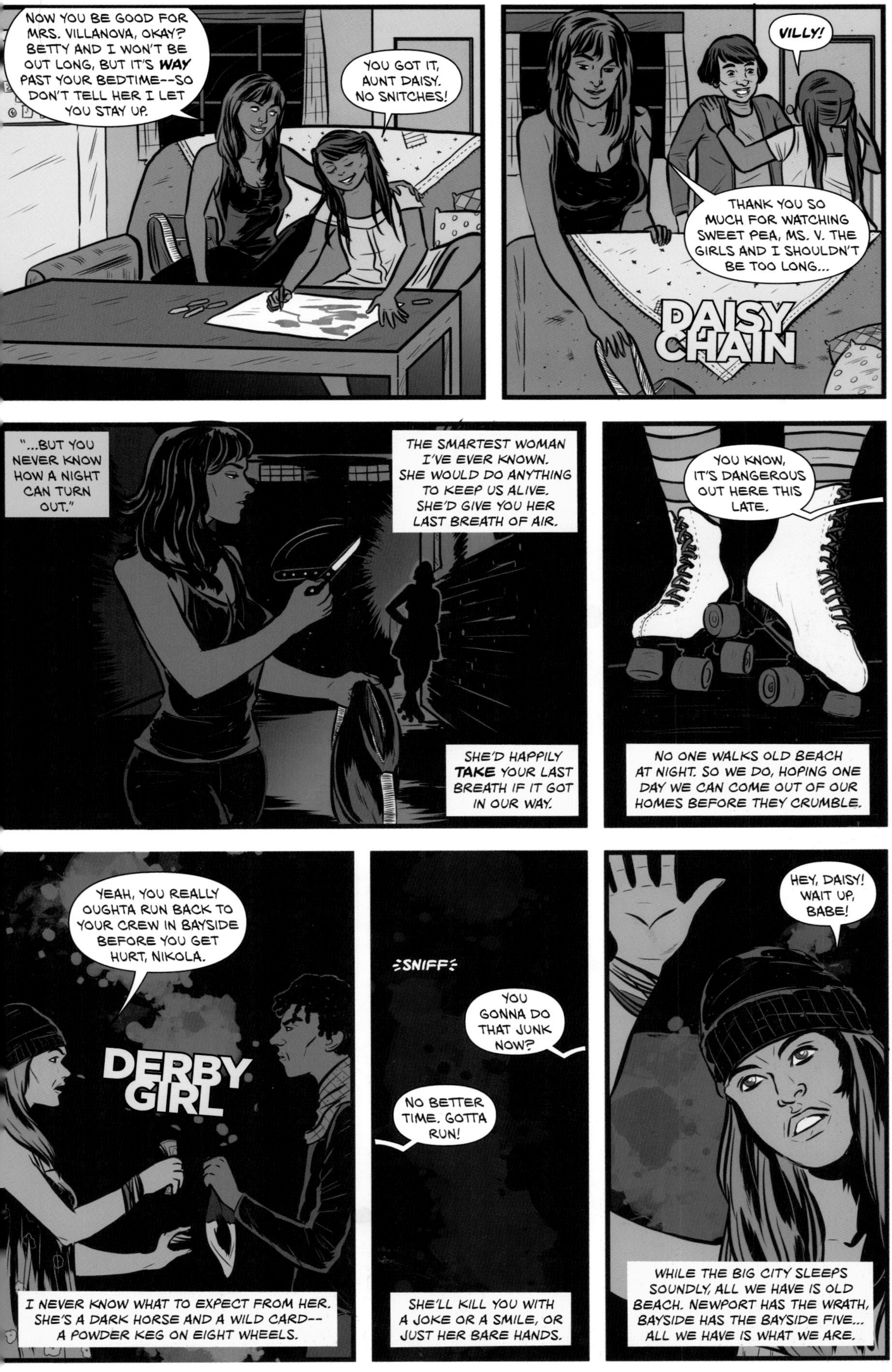
NOW YOU BE GOOD FOR MRS. VILLANOVA, OKAY? BETTY AND I WON'T BE OUT LONG, BUT IT'S **WAY** PAST YOUR BEDTIME--SO DON'T TELL HER I LET YOU STAY UP.
YOU GOT IT, AUNT DAISY. NO SNITCHES!
VILLY!
THANK YOU SO MUCH FOR WATCHING SWEET PEA, MS. V. THE GIRLS AND I SHOULDN'T BE TOO LONG...
DAISY CHAIN
"...BUT YOU NEVER KNOW HOW A NIGHT CAN TURN OUT."
THE SMARTEST WOMAN I'VE EVER KNOWN. SHE WOULD DO ANYTHING TO KEEP US ALIVE. SHE'D GIVE YOU HER LAST BREATH OF AIR.
SHE'D HAPPILY **TAKE** YOUR LAST BREATH IF IT GOT IN OUR WAY.
YOU KNOW, IT'S DANGEROUS OUT HERE THIS LATE.
NO ONE WALKS OLD BEACH AT NIGHT. SO WE DO, HOPING ONE DAY WE CAN COME OUT OF OUR HOMES BEFORE THEY CRUMBLE.
YEAH, YOU REALLY OUGHTA RUN BACK TO YOUR CREW IN BAYSIDE BEFORE YOU GET HURT, NIKOLA.
DERBY GIRL
I NEVER KNOW WHAT TO EXPECT FROM HER. SHE'S A DARK HORSE AND A WILD CARD-- A POWDER KEG ON EIGHT WHEELS.
SNIFF
YOU GONNA DO THAT JUNK NOW?
NO BETTER TIME. GOTTA RUN!
SHE'LL KILL YOU WITH A JOKE OR A SMILE, OR JUST HER BARE HANDS.
HEY, DAISY! WAIT UP, BABE!
WHILE THE BIG CITY SLEEPS SOUNDLY, ALL WE HAVE IS OLD BEACH. NEWPORT HAS THE WRATH, BAYSIDE HAS THE BAYSIDE FIVE... ALL WE HAVE IS WHAT WE ARE.

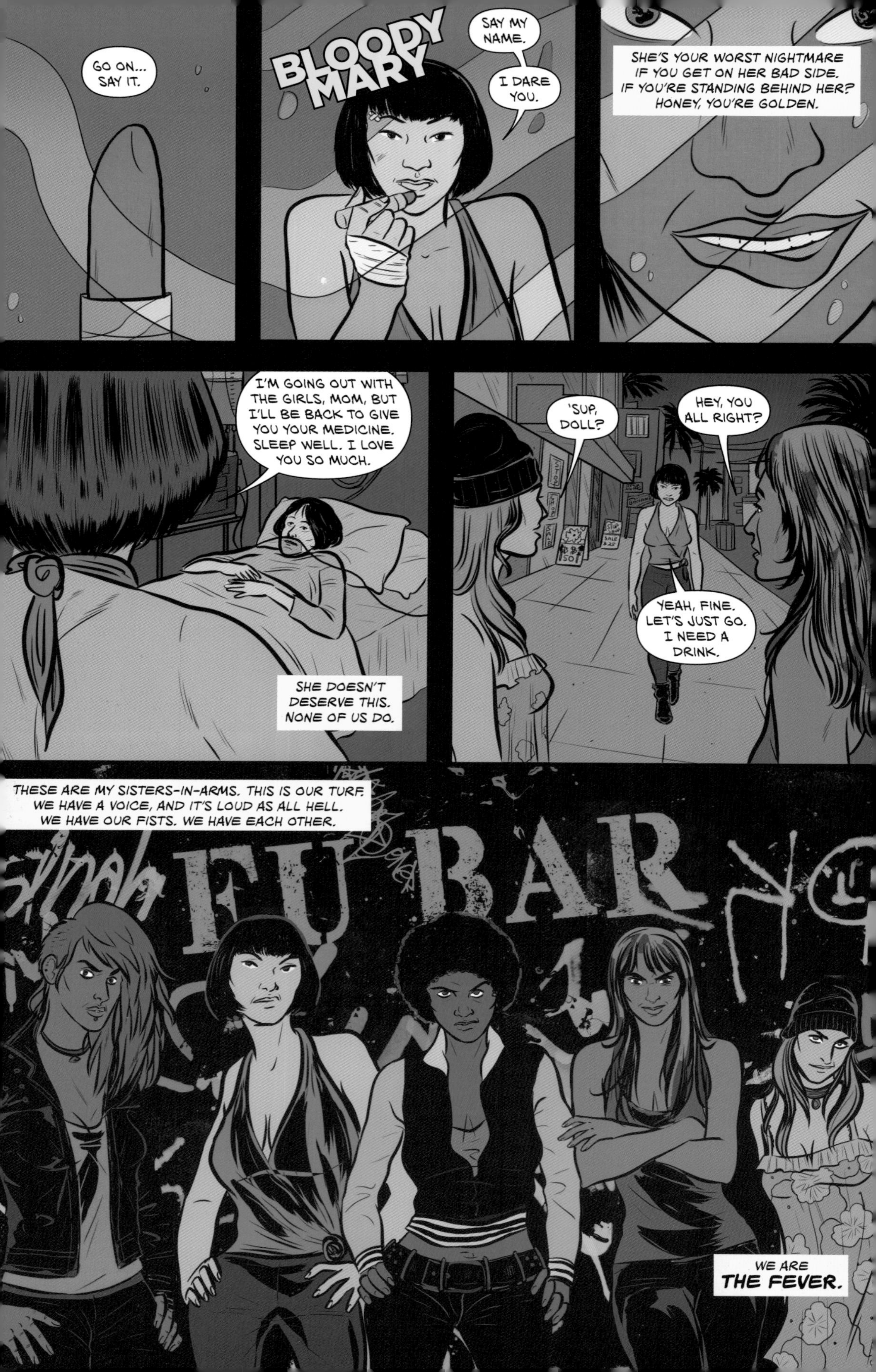
GO ON... SAY IT.
BLOODY MARY
SAY MY NAME.
I DARE YOU.
SHE'S YOUR WORST NIGHTMARE IF YOU GET ON HER BAD SIDE. IF YOU'RE STANDING BEHIND HER? HONEY, YOU'RE GOLDEN.
I'M GOING OUT WITH THE GIRLS, MOM, BUT I'LL BE BACK TO GIVE YOU YOUR MEDICINE. SLEEP WELL. I LOVE YOU SO MUCH.
SHE DOESN'T DESERVE THIS. NONE OF US DO.
'SUP, DOLL?
HEY, YOU ALL RIGHT?
YEAH, FINE. LET'S JUST GO. I NEED A DRINK.
THESE ARE MY SISTERS-IN-ARMS. THIS IS OUR TURF. WE HAVE A VOICE, AND IT'S LOUD AS ALL HELL. WE HAVE OUR FISTS. WE HAVE EACH OTHER.
FUBAR
WE ARE THE FEVER.

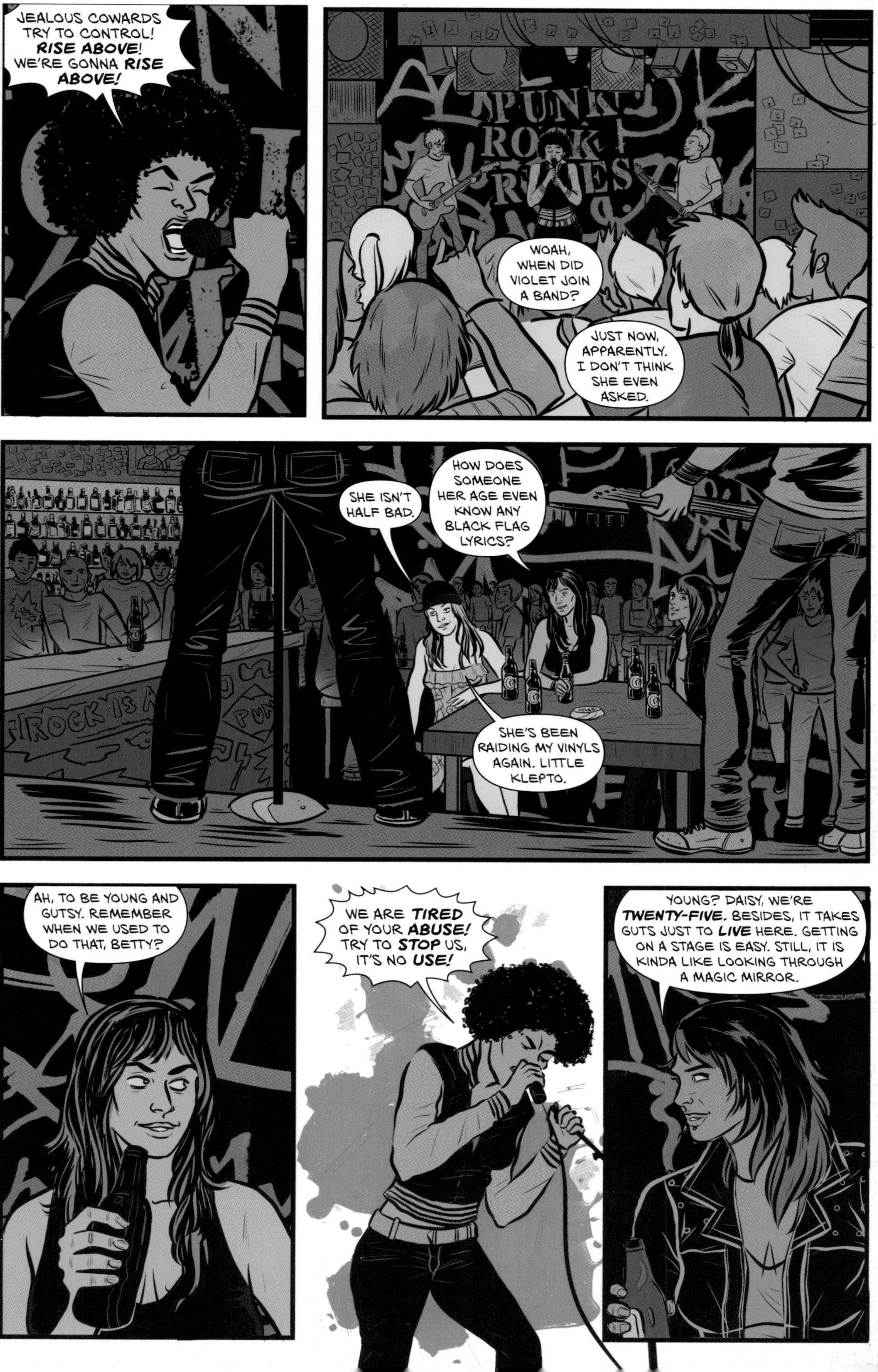
JEALOUS COWARDS TRY TO CONTROL! **RISE ABOVE**! WE'RE GONNA **RISE ABOVE**!
PUNK ROCK RULES
WOAH, WHEN DID VIOLET JOIN A BAND?
JUST NOW, APPARENTLY. I DON'T THINK SHE EVEN ASKED.
SHE ISN'T HALF BAD.
HOW DOES SOMEONE HER AGE EVEN KNOW ANY BLACK FLAG LYRICS?
SHE'S BEEN RAIDING MY VINYLS AGAIN. LITTLE KLEPTO.
ROCK IS
AH, TO BE YOUNG AND GUTSY. REMEMBER WHEN WE USED TO DO THAT, BETTY?
WE ARE **TIRED** OF YOUR **ABUSE!** TRY TO **STOP** US, IT'S NO **USE!**
YOUNG? DAISY, WE'RE **TWENTY-FIVE.** BESIDES, IT TAKES GUTS JUST TO **LIVE** HERE. GETTING ON A STAGE IS EASY. STILL, IT IS KINDA LIKE LOOKING THROUGH A MAGIC MIRROR.

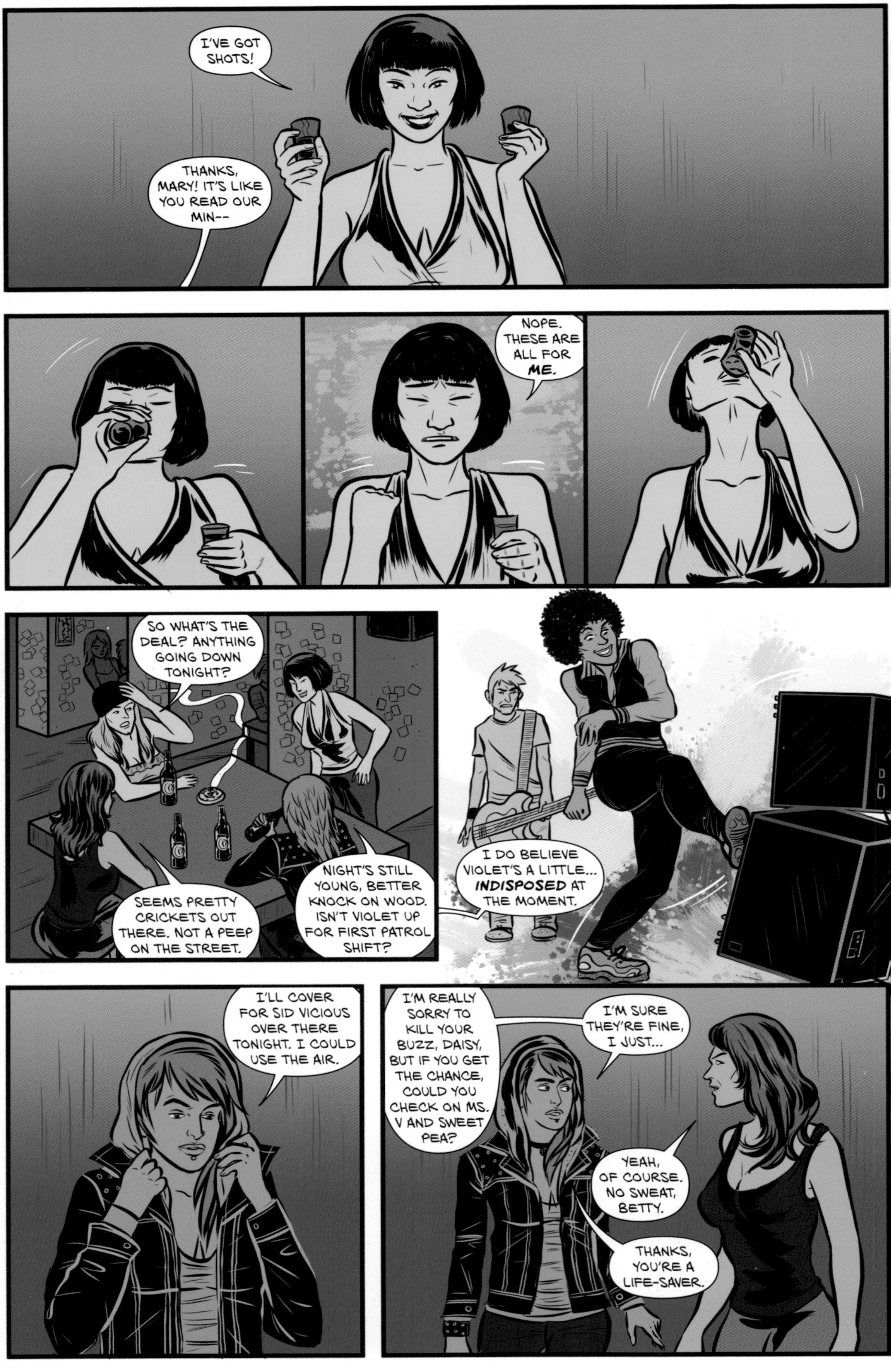

I'VE GOT SHOTS!
THANKS, MARY! IT'S LIKE YOU READ OUR MIN--
NOPE. THESE ARE ALL FOR **ME**.
SO WHAT'S THE DEAL? ANYTHING GOING DOWN TONIGHT?
SEEMS PRETTY CRICKETS OUT THERE. NOT A PEEP ON THE STREET.
NIGHT'S STILL YOUNG, BETTER KNOCK ON WOOD. ISN'T VIOLET UP FOR FIRST PATROL SHIFT?
I DO BELIEVE VIOLET'S A LITTLE... ***INDISPOSED*** AT THE MOMENT.
I'LL COVER FOR SID VICIOUS OVER THERE TONIGHT. I COULD USE THE AIR.
I'M REALLY SORRY TO KILL YOUR BUZZ, DAISY, BUT IF YOU GET THE CHANCE, COULD YOU CHECK ON MS. V AND SWEET PEA?
I'M SURE THEY'RE FINE, I JUST...
YEAH, OF COURSE. NO SWEAT, BETTY.
THANKS, YOU'RE A LIFE-SAVER.

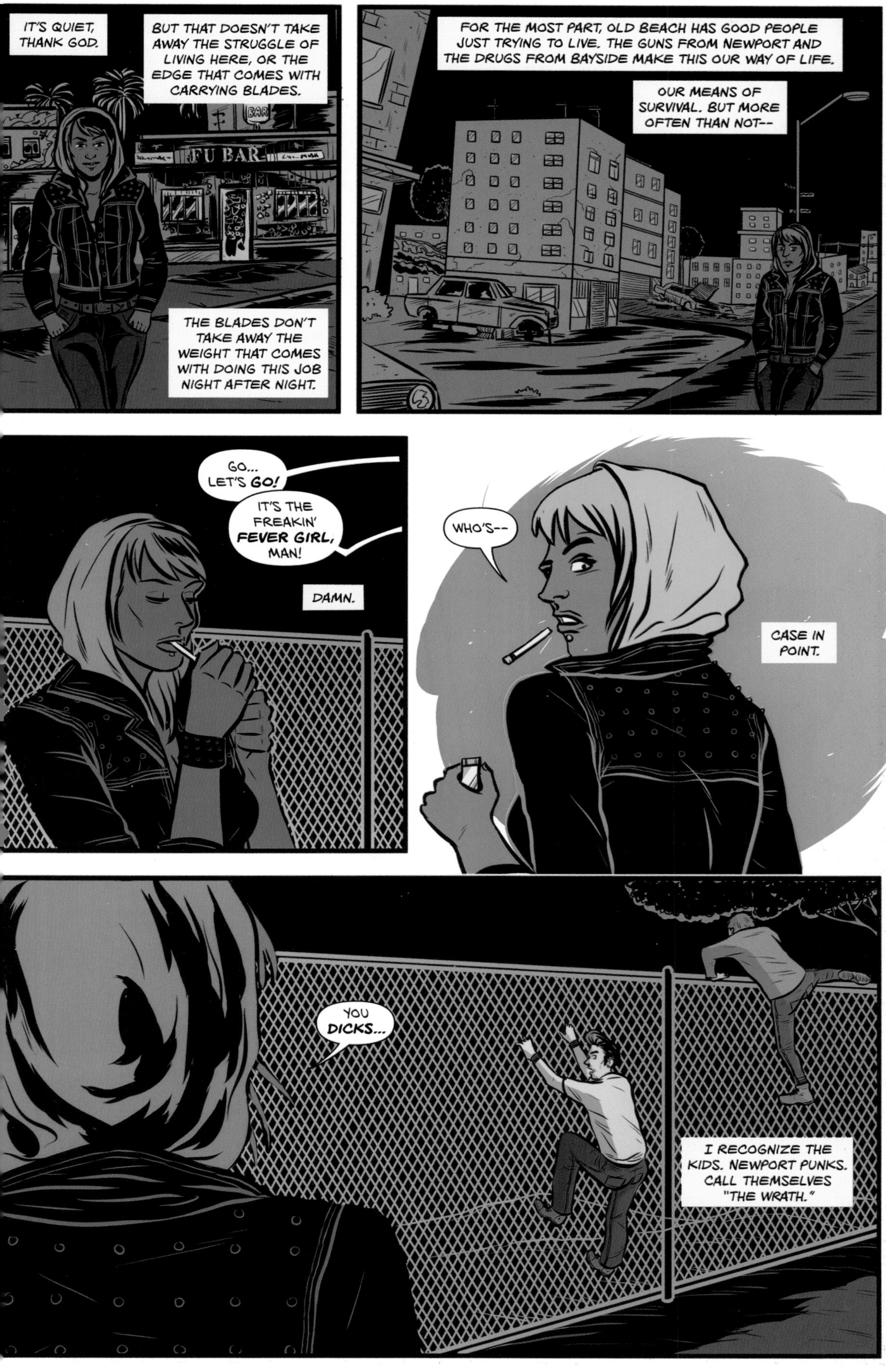

IT'S QUIET, THANK GOD.
BUT THAT DOESN'T TAKE AWAY THE STRUGGLE OF LIVING HERE, OR THE EDGE THAT COMES WITH CARRYING BLADES.
FU BAR
THE BLADES DON'T TAKE AWAY THE WEIGHT THAT COMES WITH DOING THIS JOB NIGHT AFTER NIGHT.
FOR THE MOST PART, OLD BEACH HAS GOOD PEOPLE JUST TRYING TO LIVE. THE GUNS FROM NEWPORT AND THE DRUGS FROM BAYSIDE MAKE THIS OUR WAY OF LIFE.
OUR MEANS OF SURVIVAL. BUT MORE OFTEN THAN NOT--
GO... LET'S GO!
IT'S THE FREAKIN' FEVER GIRL, MAN!
DAMN.
WHO'S--
CASE IN POINT.
YOU DICKS...
I RECOGNIZE THE KIDS. NEWPORT PUNKS. CALL THEMSELVES "THE WRATH."

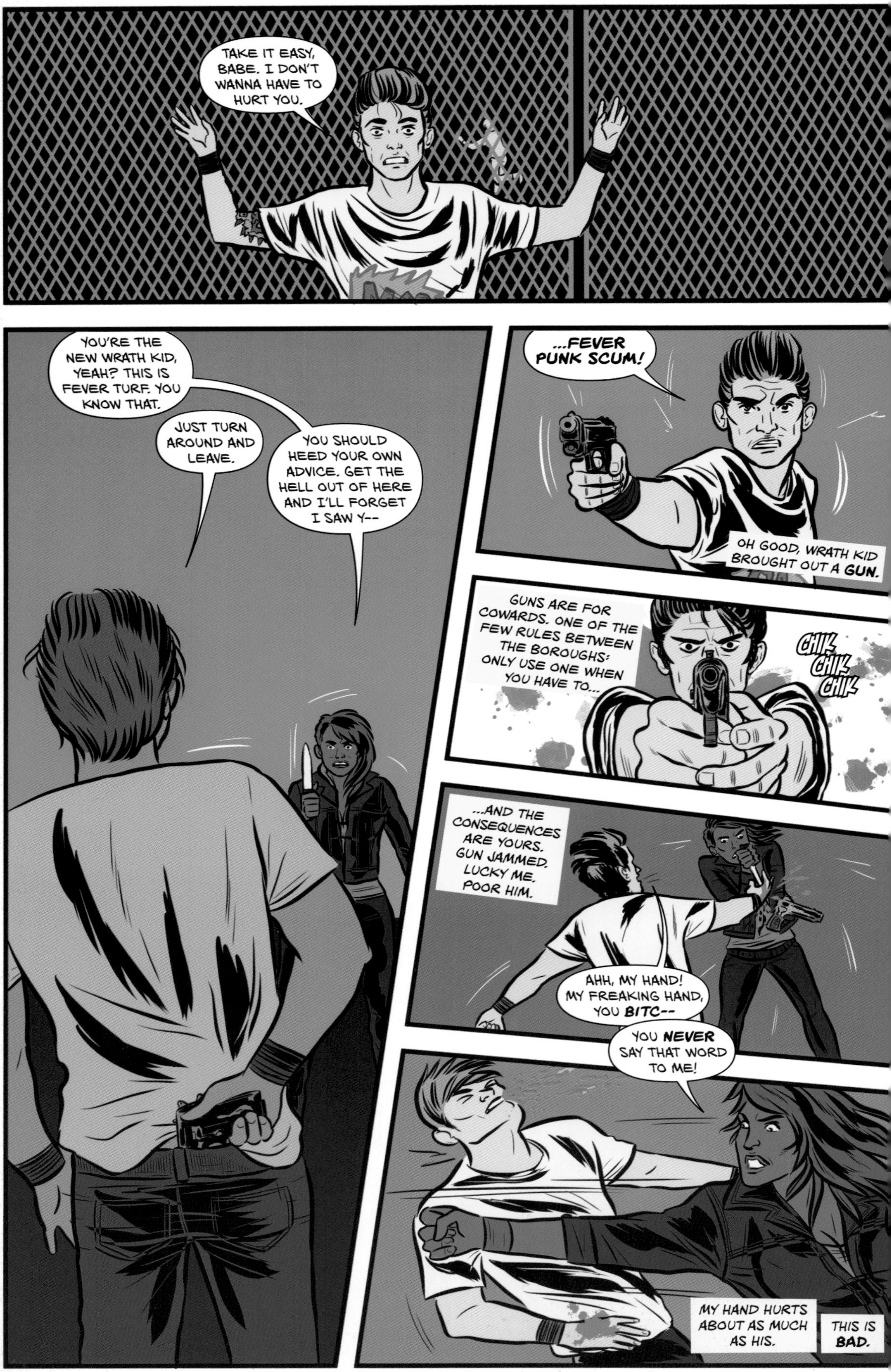
TAKE IT EASY, BABE. I DON'T WANNA HAVE TO HURT YOU.
YOU'RE THE NEW WRATH KID, YEAH? THIS IS FEVER TURF. YOU KNOW THAT.
JUST TURN AROUND AND LEAVE.
YOU SHOULD HEED YOUR OWN ADVICE. GET THE HELL OUT OF HERE AND I'LL FORGET I SAW Y--
...FEVER PUNK SCUM!
OH GOOD, WRATH KID BROUGHT OUT A GUN.
GUNS ARE FOR COWARDS. ONE OF THE FEW RULES BETWEEN THE BOROUGHS: ONLY USE ONE WHEN YOU HAVE TO...
CHIK CHIK CHIK
...AND THE CONSEQUENCES ARE YOURS. GUN JAMMED. LUCKY ME. POOR HIM.
AHH, MY HAND! MY FREAKING HAND, YOU BITC--
YOU NEVER SAY THAT WORD TO ME!
MY HAND HURTS ABOUT AS MUCH AS HIS.
THIS IS BAD.

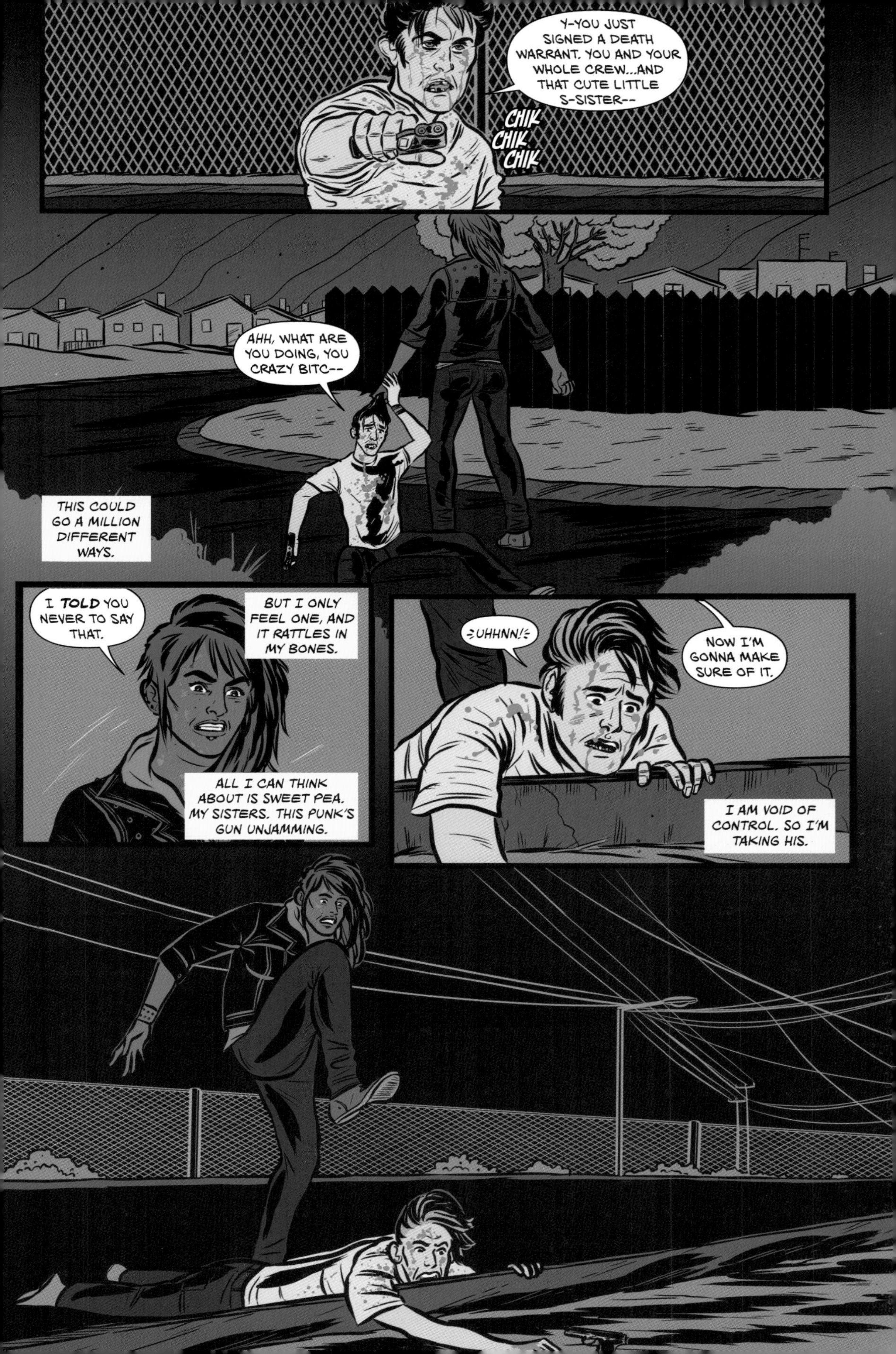
Y-YOU JUST SIGNED A DEATH WARRANT. YOU AND YOUR WHOLE CREW...AND THAT CUTE LITTLE S-SISTER--
CHIK CHIK CHIK
AHH, WHAT ARE YOU DOING, YOU CRAZY BITC--
THIS COULD GO A MILLION DIFFERENT WAYS.
I TOLD YOU NEVER TO SAY THAT.
BUT I ONLY FEEL ONE, AND IT RATTLES IN MY BONES.
ALL I CAN THINK ABOUT IS SWEET PEA. MY SISTERS. THIS PUNK'S GUN UNJAMMING.
UHHNN!
NOW I'M GONNA MAKE SURE OF IT.
I AM VOID OF CONTROL. SO I'M TAKING HIS.

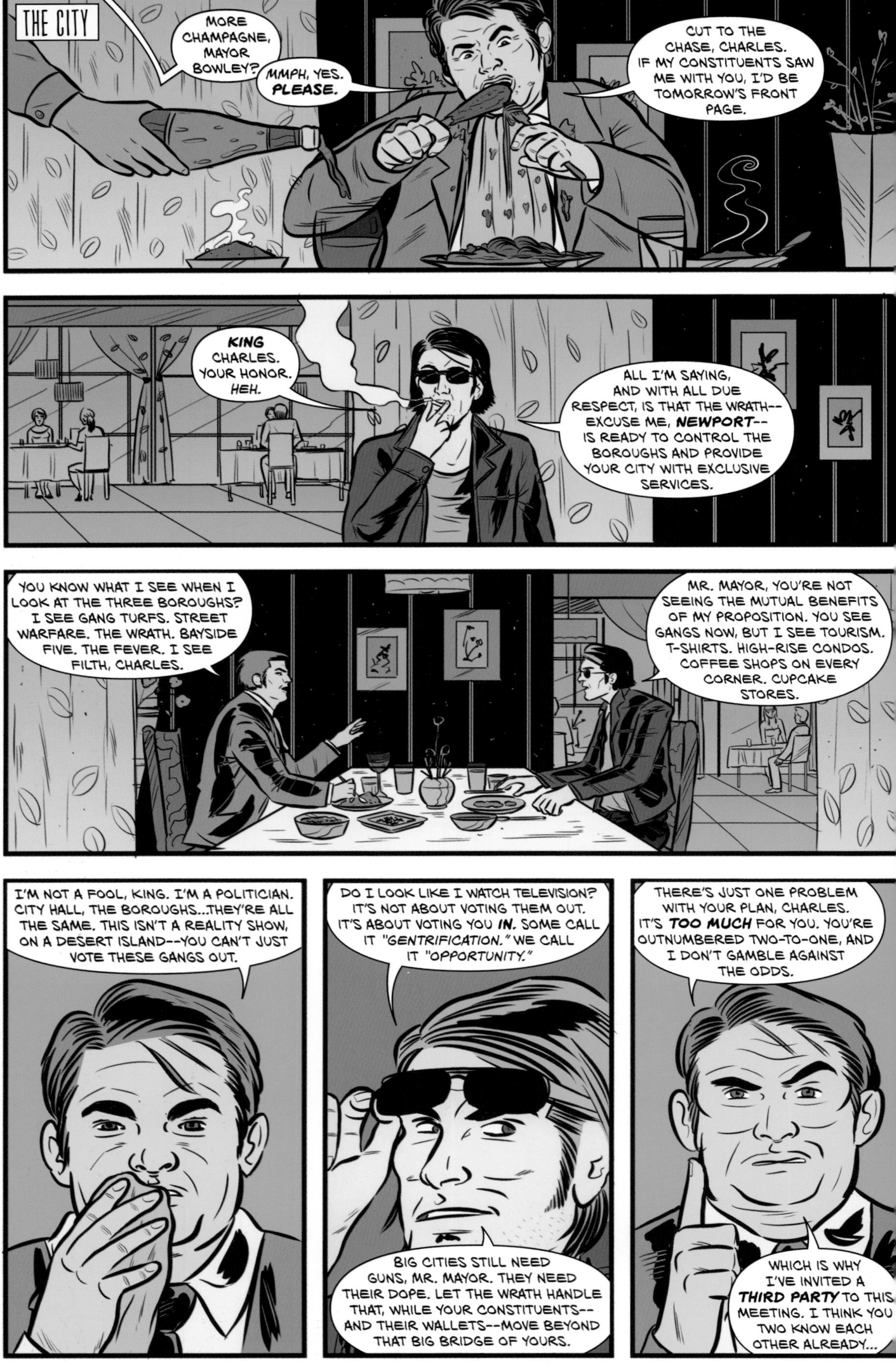
THE CITY
MORE CHAMPAGNE, MAYOR BOWLEY?
MMPH, YES. PLEASE.
CUT TO THE CHASE, CHARLES. IF MY CONSTITUENTS SAW ME WITH YOU, I'D BE TOMORROW'S FRONT PAGE.
KING CHARLES. YOUR HONOR. HEH.
ALL I'M SAYING, AND WITH ALL DUE RESPECT, IS THAT THE WRATH-- EXCUSE ME, NEWPORT-- IS READY TO CONTROL THE BOROUGHS AND PROVIDE YOUR CITY WITH EXCLUSIVE SERVICES.
YOU KNOW WHAT I SEE WHEN I LOOK AT THE THREE BOROUGHS? I SEE GANG TURFS. STREET WARFARE. THE WRATH. BAYSIDE FIVE. THE FEVER. I SEE FILTH, CHARLES.
MR. MAYOR, YOU'RE NOT SEEING THE MUTUAL BENEFITS OF MY PROPOSITION. YOU SEE GANGS NOW, BUT I SEE TOURISM. T-SHIRTS. HIGH-RISE CONDOS. COFFEE SHOPS ON EVERY CORNER. CUPCAKE STORES.
I'M NOT A FOOL, KING. I'M A POLITICIAN. CITY HALL, THE BOROUGHS...THEY'RE ALL THE SAME. THIS ISN'T A REALITY SHOW, ON A DESERT ISLAND--YOU CAN'T JUST VOTE THESE GANGS OUT.
DO I LOOK LIKE I WATCH TELEVISION? IT'S NOT ABOUT VOTING THEM OUT. IT'S ABOUT VOTING YOU IN. SOME CALL IT "GENTRIFICATION." WE CALL IT "OPPORTUNITY."
BIG CITIES STILL NEED GUNS, MR. MAYOR. THEY NEED THEIR DOPE. LET THE WRATH HANDLE THAT, WHILE YOUR CONSTITUENTS-- AND THEIR WALLETS--MOVE BEYOND THAT BIG BRIDGE OF YOURS.
THERE'S JUST ONE PROBLEM WITH YOUR PLAN, CHARLES. IT'S TOO MUCH FOR YOU. YOU'RE OUTNUMBERED TWO-TO-ONE, AND I DON'T GAMBLE AGAINST THE ODDS.
WHICH IS WHY I'VE INVITED A THIRD PARTY TO THIS MEETING. I THINK YOU TWO KNOW EACH OTHER ALREADY...

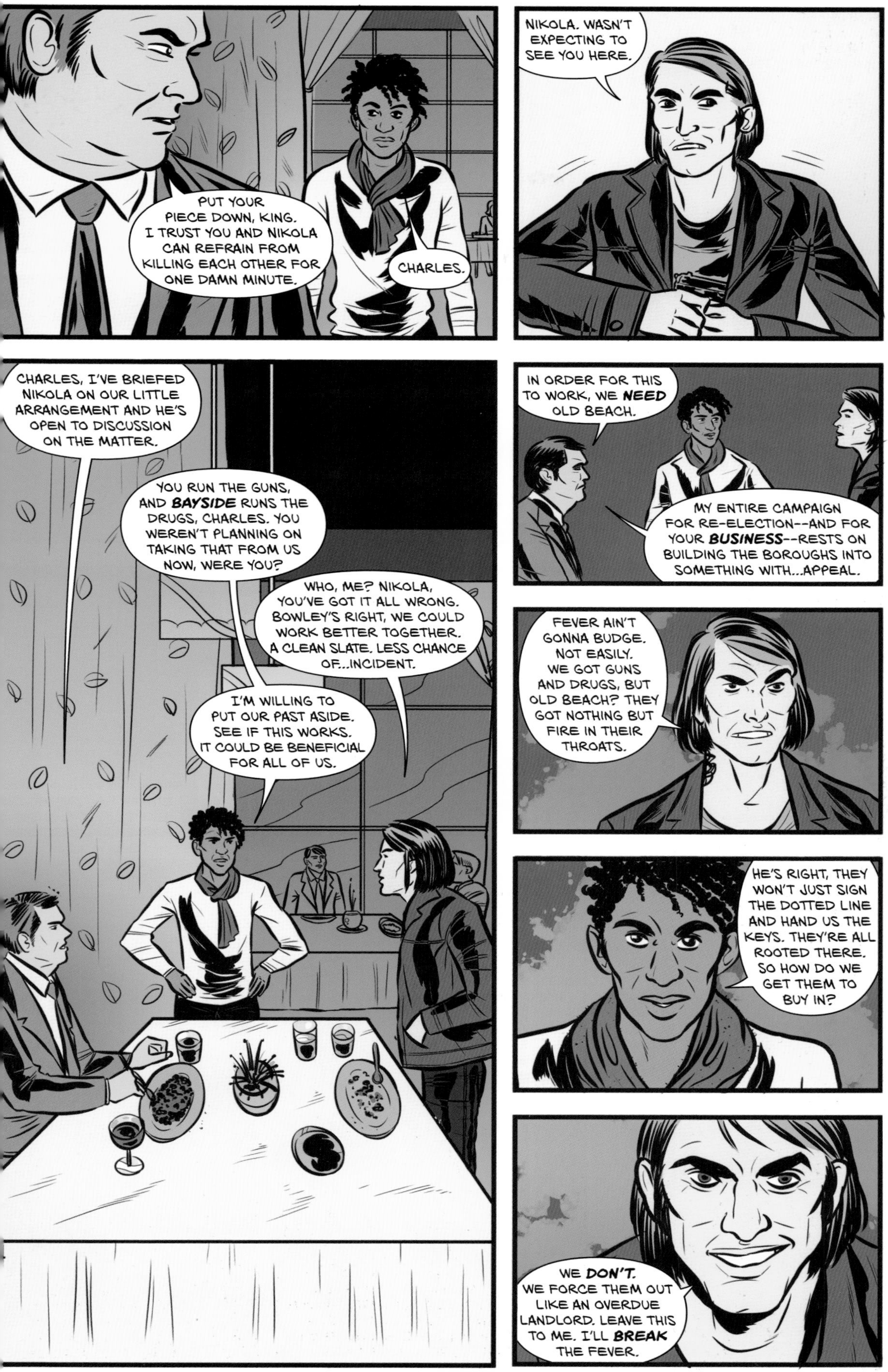
PUT YOUR PIECE DOWN, KING. I TRUST YOU AND NIKOLA CAN REFRAIN FROM KILLING EACH OTHER FOR ONE DAMN MINUTE.
CHARLES.
NIKOLA. WASN'T EXPECTING TO SEE YOU HERE.
CHARLES, I'VE BRIEFED NIKOLA ON OUR LITTLE ARRANGEMENT AND HE'S OPEN TO DISCUSSION ON THE MATTER.
YOU RUN THE GUNS, AND BAYSIDE RUNS THE DRUGS, CHARLES. YOU WEREN'T PLANNING ON TAKING THAT FROM US NOW, WERE YOU?
WHO, ME? NIKOLA, YOU'VE GOT IT ALL WRONG. BOWLEY'S RIGHT, WE COULD WORK BETTER TOGETHER. A CLEAN SLATE. LESS CHANCE OF...INCIDENT.
I'M WILLING TO PUT OUR PAST ASIDE. SEE IF THIS WORKS. IT COULD BE BENEFICIAL FOR ALL OF US.
IN ORDER FOR THIS TO WORK, WE NEED OLD BEACH.
MY ENTIRE CAMPAIGN FOR RE-ELECTION--AND FOR YOUR BUSINESS--RESTS ON BUILDING THE BOROUGHS INTO SOMETHING WITH...APPEAL.
FEVER AIN'T GONNA BUDGE. NOT EASILY. WE GOT GUNS AND DRUGS, BUT OLD BEACH? THEY GOT NOTHING BUT FIRE IN THEIR THROATS.
HE'S RIGHT, THEY WON'T JUST SIGN THE DOTTED LINE AND HAND US THE KEYS. THEY'RE ALL ROOTED THERE. SO HOW DO WE GET THEM TO BUY IN?
WE DON'T. WE FORCE THEM OUT LIKE AN OVERDUE LANDLORD. LEAVE THIS TO ME. I'LL BREAK THE FEVER.

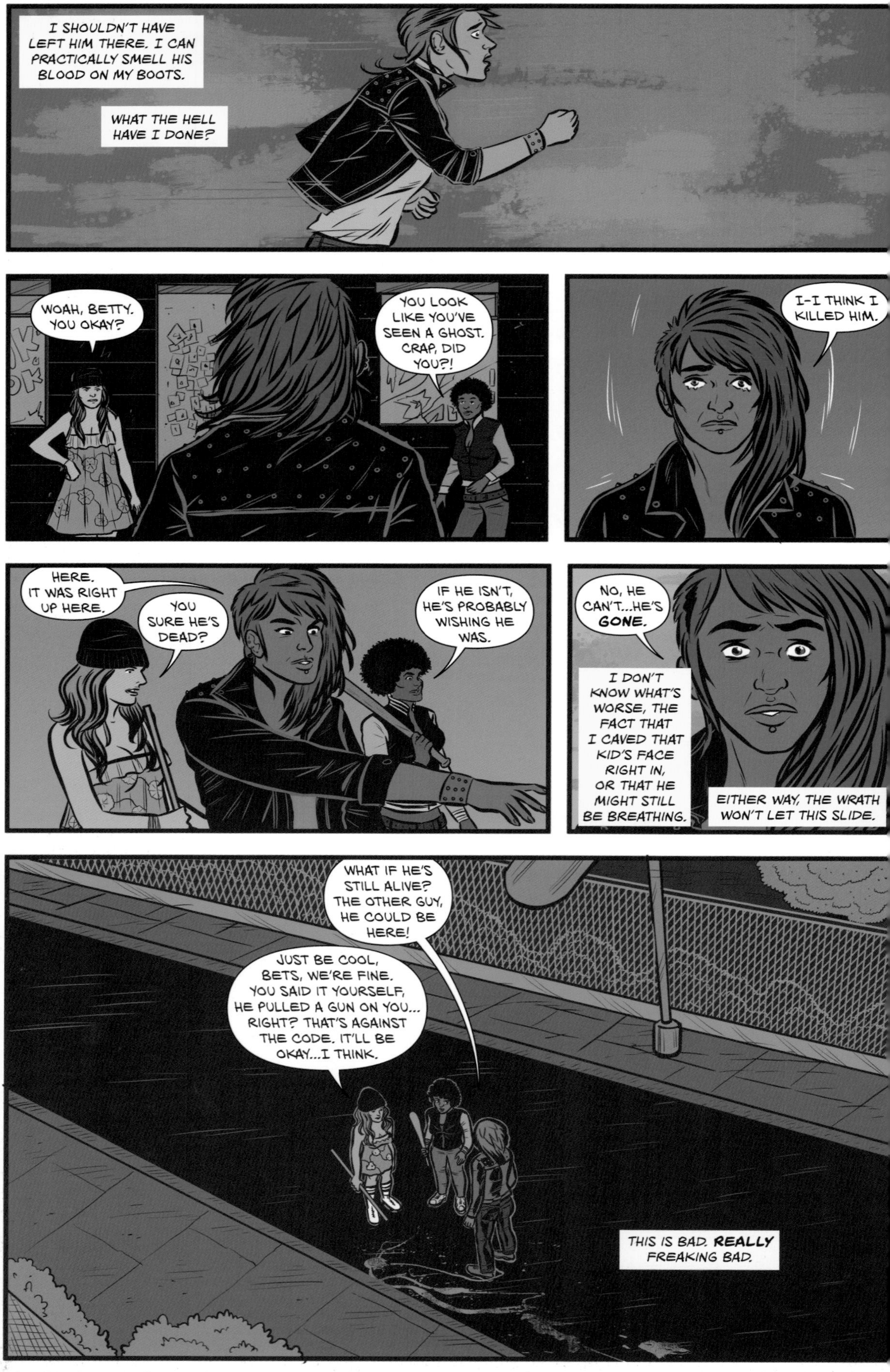
I SHOULDN'T HAVE LEFT HIM THERE. I CAN PRACTICALLY SMELL HIS BLOOD ON MY BOOTS.
WHAT THE HELL HAVE I DONE?
WOAH, BETTY. YOU OKAY?
YOU LOOK LIKE YOU'VE SEEN A GHOST. CRAP, DID YOU?!
I-I THINK I KILLED HIM.
HERE. IT WAS RIGHT UP HERE.
YOU SURE HE'S DEAD?
IF HE ISN'T, HE'S PROBABLY WISHING HE WAS.
NO, HE CAN'T...HE'S **GONE.**
I DON'T KNOW WHAT'S WORSE, THE FACT THAT I CAVED THAT KID'S FACE RIGHT IN, OR THAT HE MIGHT STILL BE BREATHING.
EITHER WAY, THE WRATH WON'T LET THIS SLIDE.
WHAT IF HE'S STILL ALIVE? THE OTHER GUY, HE COULD BE HERE!
JUST BE COOL, BETS, WE'RE FINE. YOU SAID IT YOURSELF, HE PULLED A GUN ON YOU... RIGHT? THAT'S AGAINST THE CODE. IT'LL BE OKAY...I THINK.
THIS IS BAD. **REALLY** FREAKING BAD.

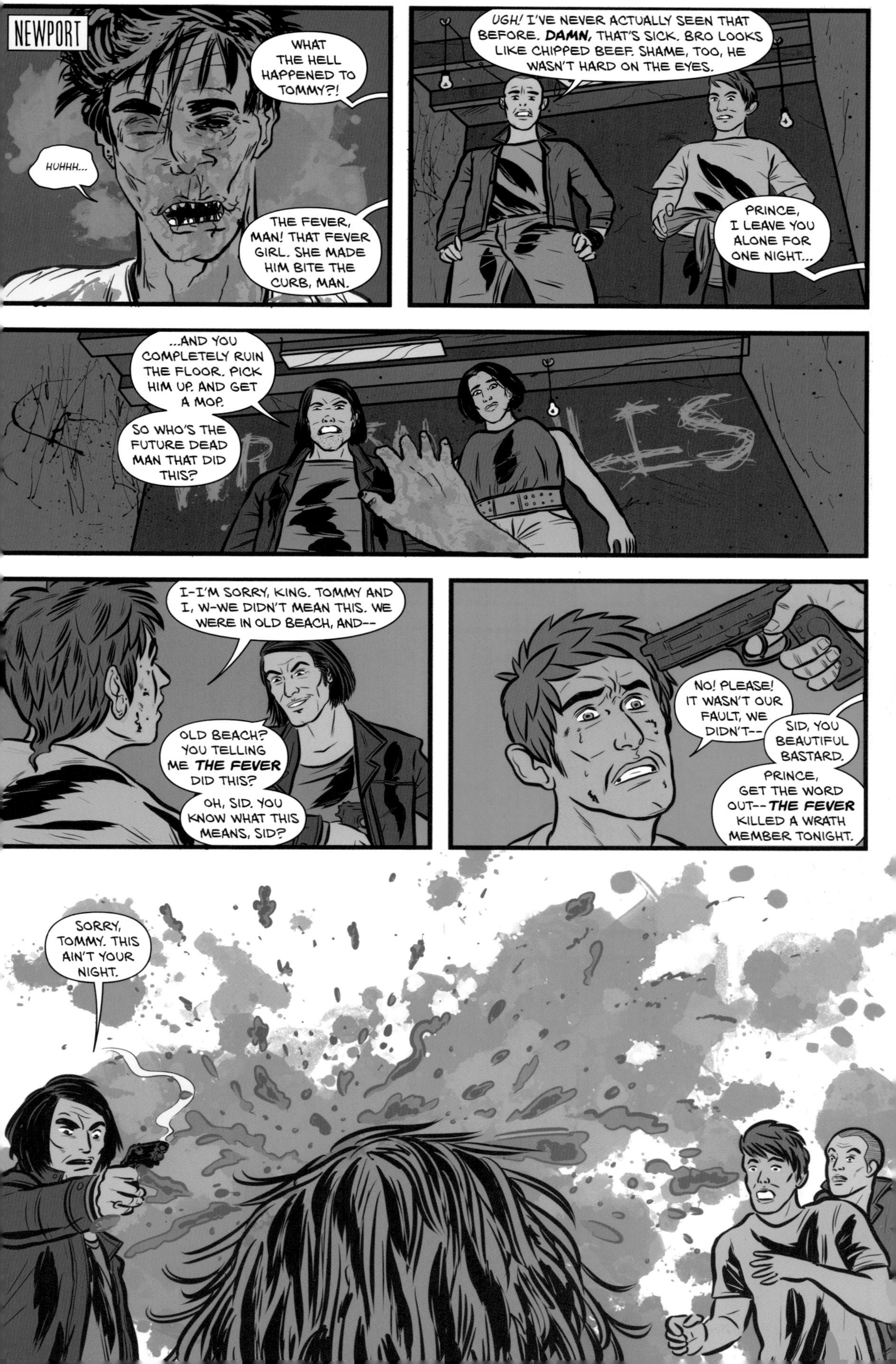
NEWPORT
WHAT THE HELL HAPPENED TO TOMMY?!
HUHHH...
THE FEVER, MAN! THAT FEVER GIRL. SHE MADE HIM BITE THE CURB, MAN.
UGH! I'VE NEVER ACTUALLY SEEN THAT BEFORE. DAMN, THAT'S SICK. BRO LOOKS LIKE CHIPPED BEEF. SHAME, TOO, HE WASN'T HARD ON THE EYES.
PRINCE, I LEAVE YOU ALONE FOR ONE NIGHT...
...AND YOU COMPLETELY RUIN THE FLOOR. PICK HIM UP. AND GET A MOP.
SO WHO'S THE FUTURE DEAD MAN THAT DID THIS?
I-I'M SORRY, KING. TOMMY AND I, W-WE DIDN'T MEAN THIS. WE WERE IN OLD BEACH, AND--
OLD BEACH? YOU TELLING ME THE FEVER DID THIS?
OH, SID. YOU KNOW WHAT THIS MEANS, SID?
NO! PLEASE! IT WASN'T OUR FAULT, WE DIDN'T--
SID, YOU BEAUTIFUL BASTARD.
PRINCE, GET THE WORD OUT--THE FEVER KILLED A WRATH MEMBER TONIGHT.
SORRY, TOMMY. THIS AIN'T YOUR NIGHT.

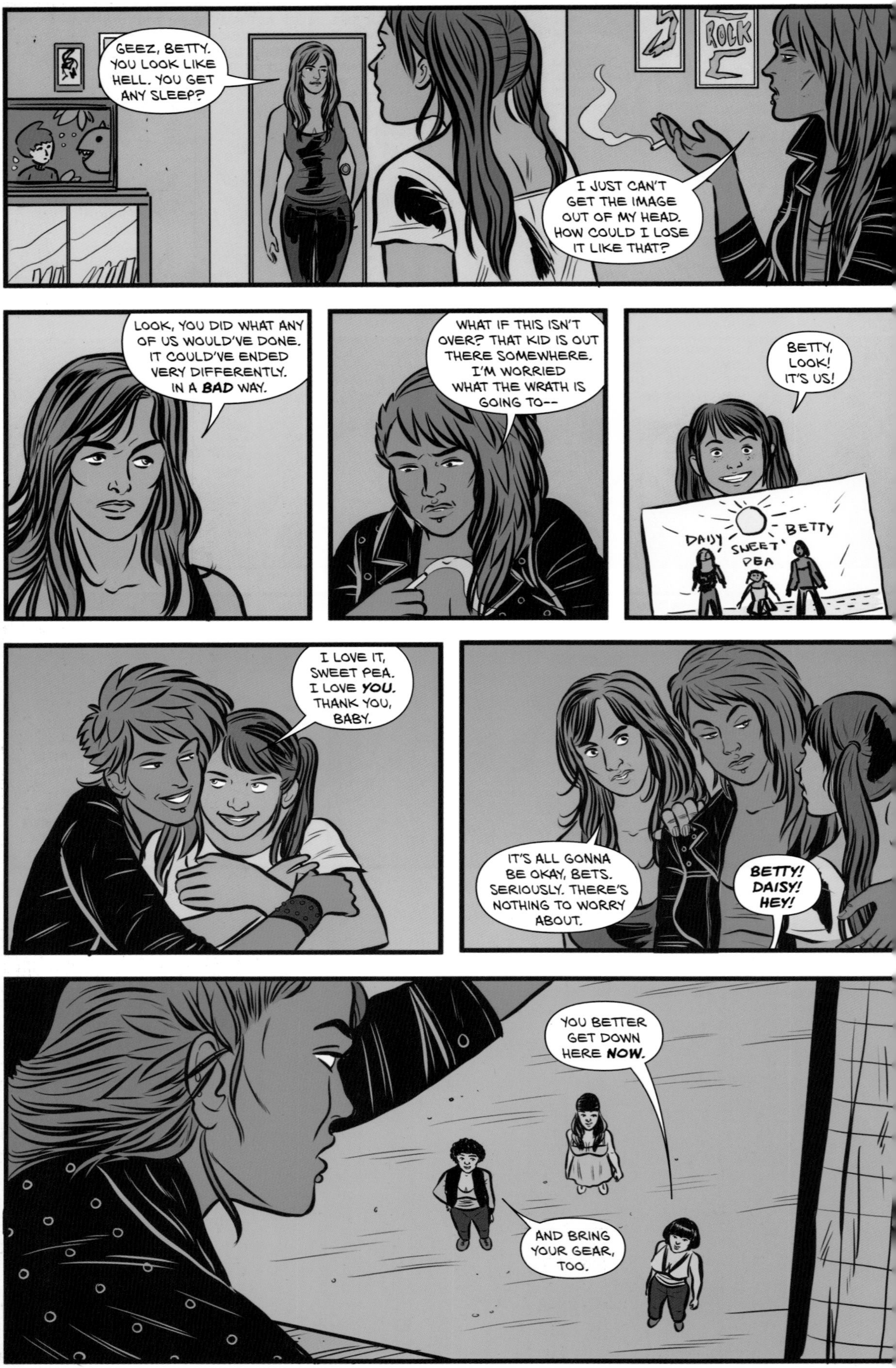

GEEZ, BETTY. YOU LOOK LIKE HELL. YOU GET ANY SLEEP?
ROCK
I JUST CAN'T GET THE IMAGE OUT OF MY HEAD. HOW COULD I LOSE IT LIKE THAT?
LOOK, YOU DID WHAT ANY OF US WOULD'VE DONE. IT COULD'VE ENDED VERY DIFFERENTLY. IN A **BAD** WAY.
WHAT IF THIS ISN'T OVER? THAT KID IS OUT THERE SOMEWHERE. I'M WORRIED WHAT THE WRATH IS GOING TO--
BETTY, LOOK! IT'S US!
DAISY
SWEET PEA
BETTY
I LOVE IT, SWEET PEA. I LOVE ***YOU.*** THANK YOU, BABY.
IT'S ALL GONNA BE OKAY, BETS. SERIOUSLY. THERE'S NOTHING TO WORRY ABOUT.
BETTY! DAISY! HEY!
YOU BETTER GET DOWN HERE **NOW.**
AND BRING YOUR GEAR, TOO.

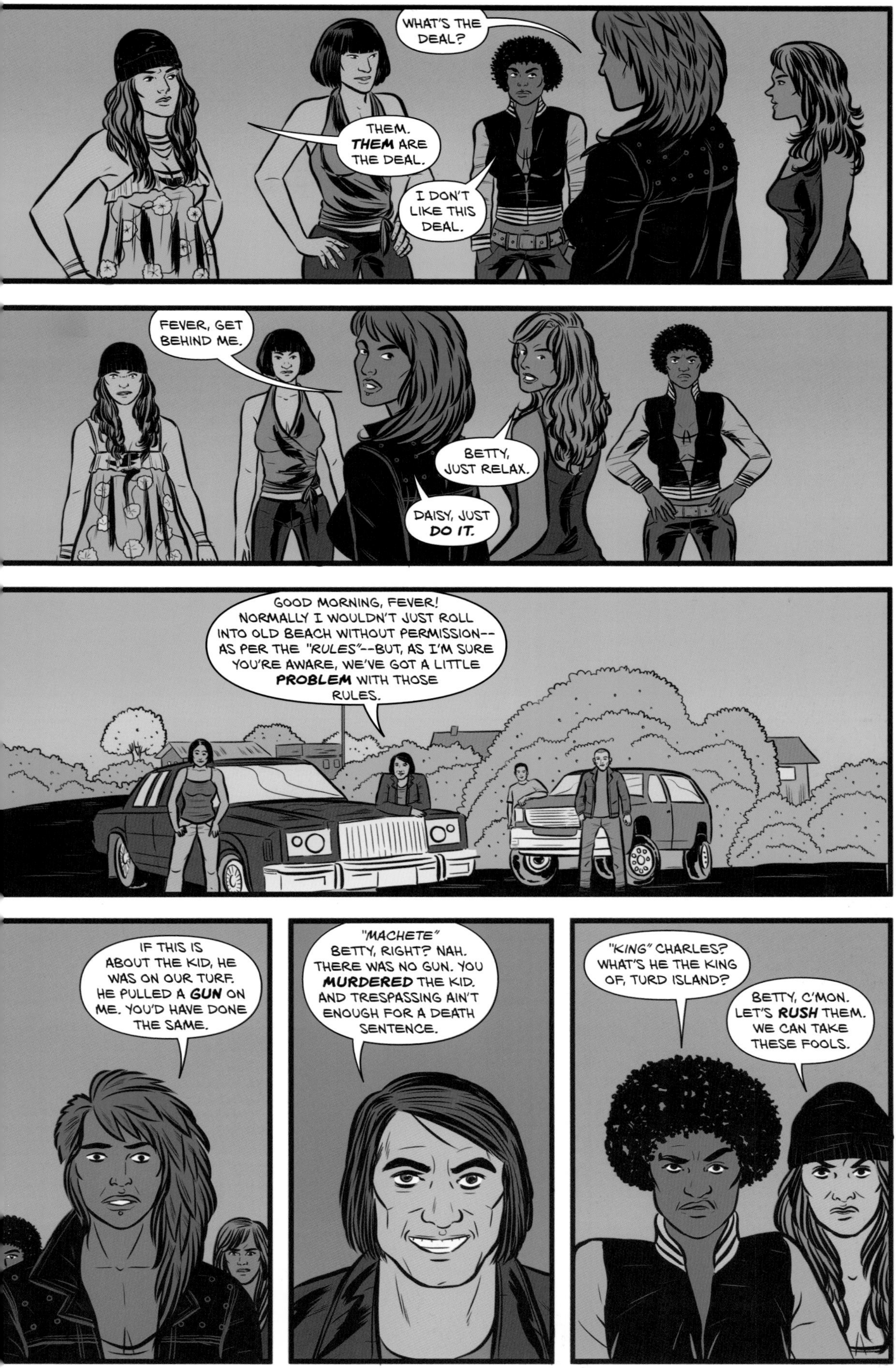
WHAT'S THE DEAL?
THEM. **THEM** ARE THE DEAL.
I DON'T LIKE THIS DEAL.
FEVER, GET BEHIND ME.
BETTY, JUST RELAX.
DAISY, JUST **DO IT.**
GOOD MORNING, FEVER! NORMALLY I WOULDN'T JUST ROLL INTO OLD BEACH WITHOUT PERMISSION--AS PER THE *"RULES"*--BUT, AS I'M SURE YOU'RE AWARE, WE'VE GOT A LITTLE **PROBLEM** WITH THOSE RULES.
IF THIS IS ABOUT THE KID, HE WAS ON OUR TURF. HE PULLED A **GUN** ON ME. YOU'D HAVE DONE THE SAME.
"MACHETE" BETTY, RIGHT? NAH. THERE WAS NO GUN. YOU **MURDERED** THE KID. AND TRESPASSING AIN'T ENOUGH FOR A DEATH SENTENCE.
"KING" CHARLES? WHAT'S HE THE KING OF, TURD ISLAND?
BETTY, C'MON. LET'S **RUSH** THEM. WE CAN TAKE THESE FOOLS.

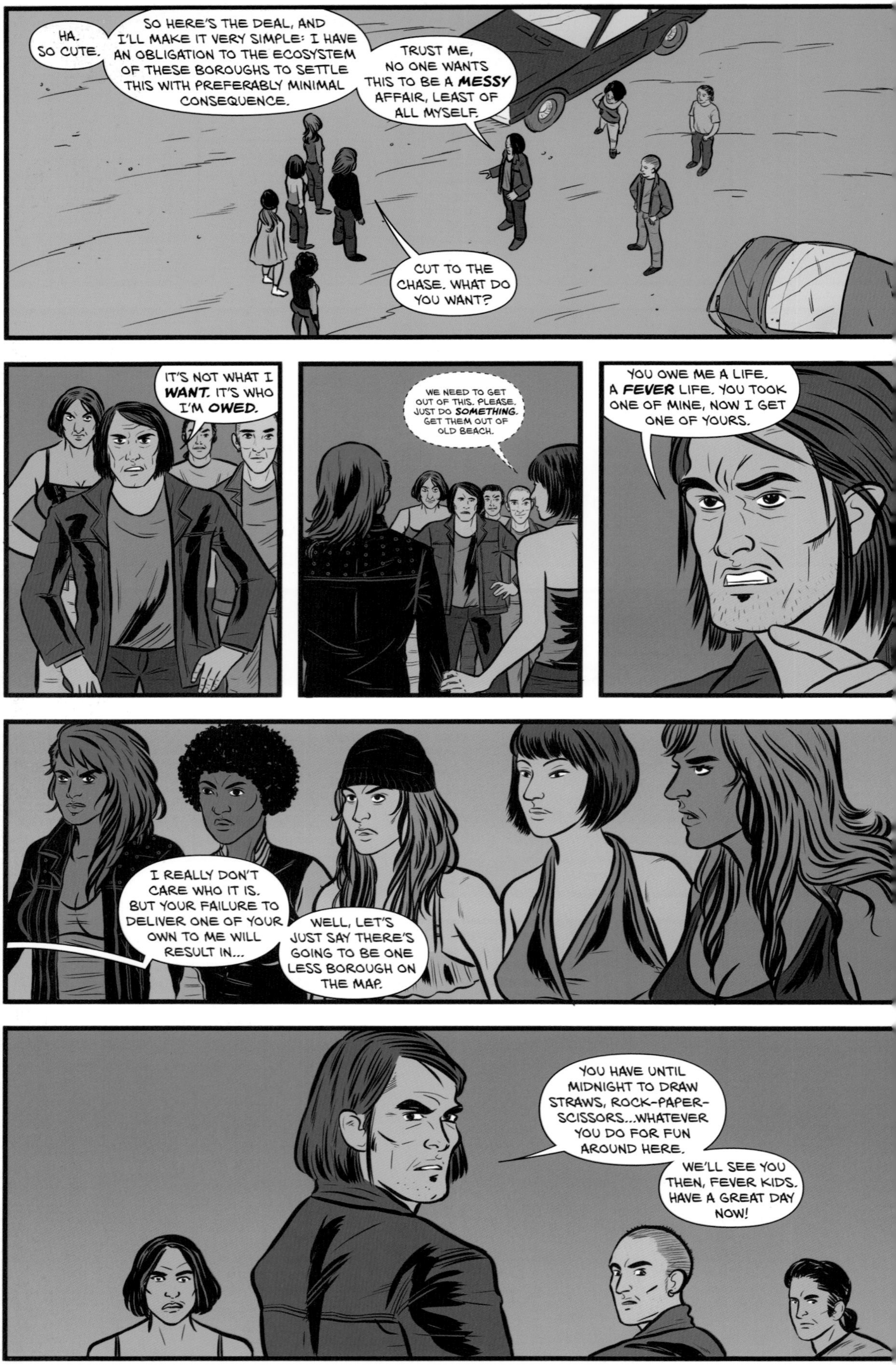
HA. SO CUTE.
SO HERE'S THE DEAL, AND I'LL MAKE IT VERY SIMPLE: I HAVE AN OBLIGATION TO THE ECOSYSTEM OF THESE BOROUGHS TO SETTLE THIS WITH PREFERABLY MINIMAL CONSEQUENCE.
TRUST ME, NO ONE WANTS THIS TO BE A **MESSY** AFFAIR, LEAST OF ALL MYSELF.
CUT TO THE CHASE. WHAT DO YOU WANT?
IT'S NOT WHAT I **WANT.** IT'S WHO I'M **OWED.**
WE NEED TO GET OUT OF THIS. PLEASE. JUST DO **SOMETHING.** GET THEM OUT OF OLD BEACH.
YOU OWE ME A LIFE. A **FEVER** LIFE. YOU TOOK ONE OF MINE, NOW I GET ONE OF YOURS.
I REALLY DON'T CARE WHO IT IS. BUT YOUR FAILURE TO DELIVER ONE OF YOUR OWN TO ME WILL RESULT IN...
WELL, LET'S JUST SAY THERE'S GOING TO BE ONE LESS BOROUGH ON THE MAP.
YOU HAVE UNTIL MIDNIGHT TO DRAW STRAWS, ROCK-PAPER-SCISSORS...WHATEVER YOU DO FOR FUN AROUND HERE.
WE'LL SEE YOU THEN, FEVER KIDS. HAVE A GREAT DAY NOW!

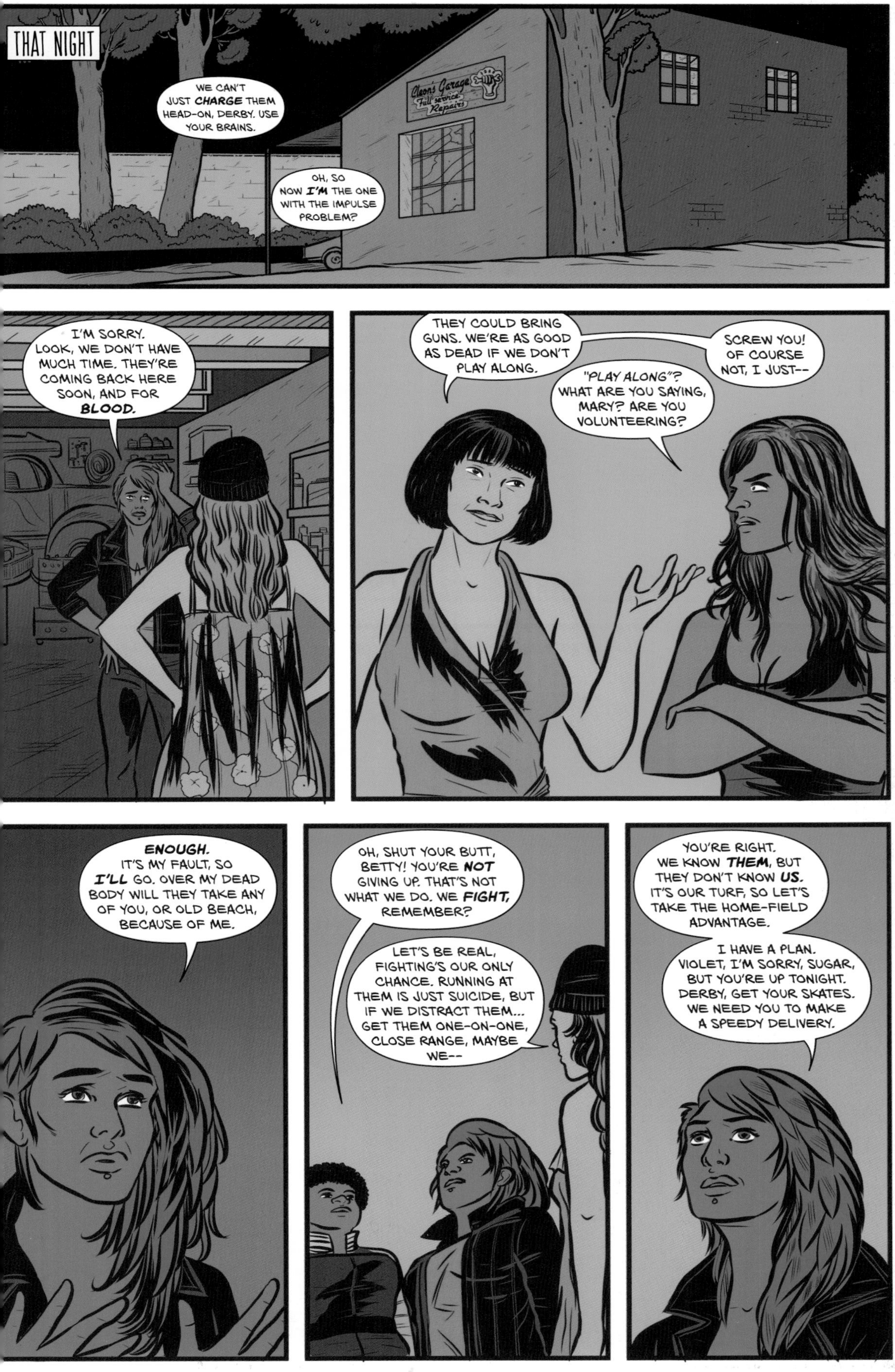
THAT NIGHT
Cleon's Garage Full service Repairs
WE CAN'T JUST CHARGE THEM HEAD-ON, DERBY. USE YOUR BRAINS.
OH, SO NOW I'M THE ONE WITH THE IMPULSE PROBLEM?
I'M SORRY. LOOK, WE DON'T HAVE MUCH TIME. THEY'RE COMING BACK HERE SOON, AND FOR BLOOD.
THEY COULD BRING GUNS. WE'RE AS GOOD AS DEAD IF WE DON'T PLAY ALONG.
"PLAY ALONG"? WHAT ARE YOU SAYING, MARY? ARE YOU VOLUNTEERING?
SCREW YOU! OF COURSE NOT, I JUST--
ENOUGH. IT'S MY FAULT, SO I'LL GO. OVER MY DEAD BODY WILL THEY TAKE ANY OF YOU, OR OLD BEACH, BECAUSE OF ME.
OH, SHUT YOUR BUTT, BETTY! YOU'RE NOT GIVING UP. THAT'S NOT WHAT WE DO. WE FIGHT, REMEMBER?
LET'S BE REAL, FIGHTING'S OUR ONLY CHANCE. RUNNING AT THEM IS JUST SUICIDE, BUT IF WE DISTRACT THEM... GET THEM ONE-ON-ONE, CLOSE RANGE, MAYBE WE--
YOU'RE RIGHT. WE KNOW THEM, BUT THEY DON'T KNOW US. IT'S OUR TURF, SO LET'S TAKE THE HOME-FIELD ADVANTAGE.
I HAVE A PLAN. VIOLET, I'M SORRY, SUGAR, BUT YOU'RE UP TONIGHT. DERBY, GET YOUR SKATES. WE NEED YOU TO MAKE A SPEEDY DELIVERY.

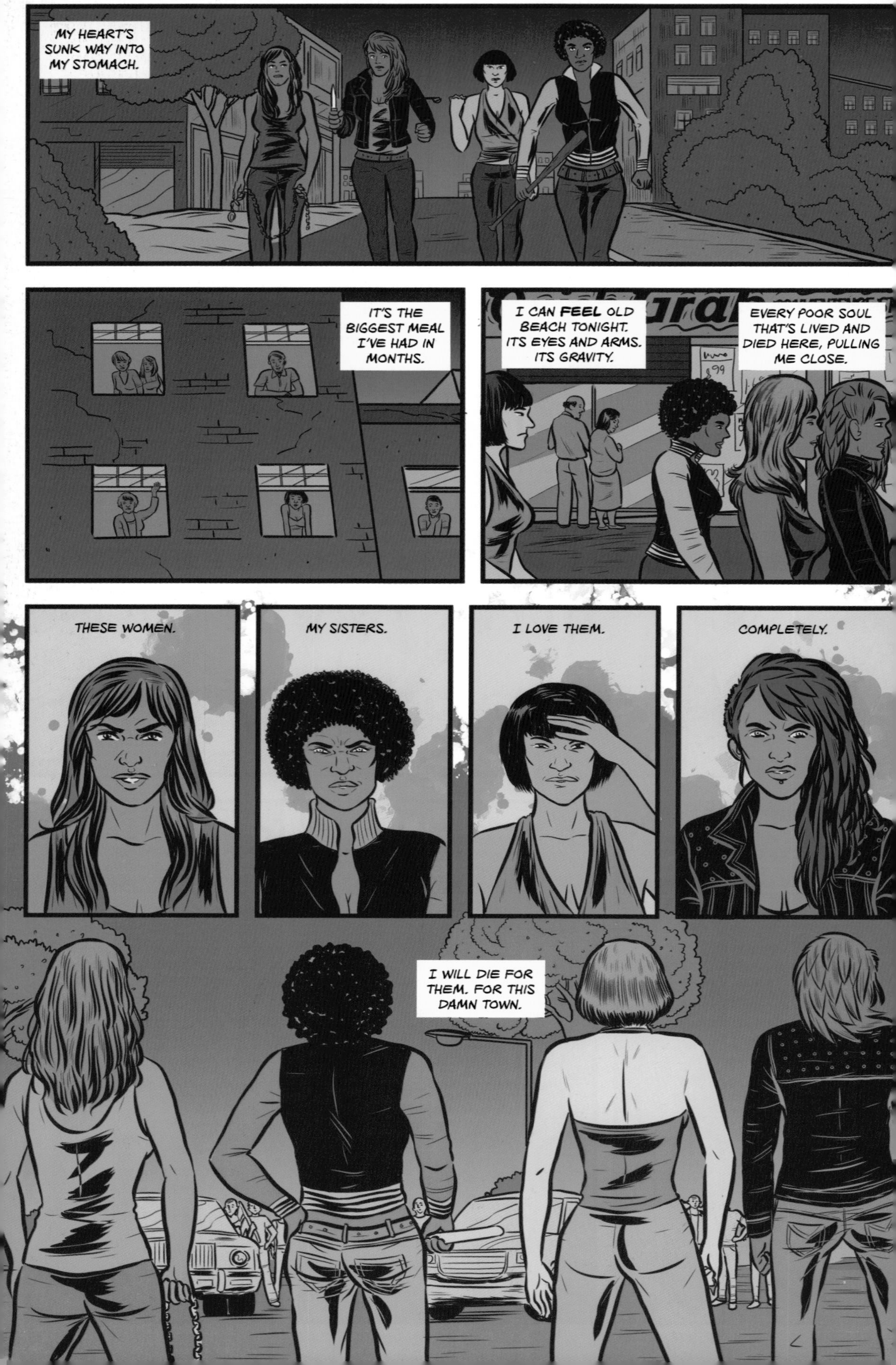
MY HEART'S SUNK WAY INTO MY STOMACH.
IT'S THE BIGGEST MEAL I'VE HAD IN MONTHS.
I CAN **FEEL** OLD BEACH TONIGHT. ITS EYES AND ARMS. ITS GRAVITY.
EVERY POOR SOUL THAT'S LIVED AND DIED HERE, PULLING ME CLOSE.
THESE WOMEN.
MY SISTERS.
I LOVE THEM.
COMPLETELY.
I WILL DIE FOR THEM. FOR THIS DAMN TOWN.

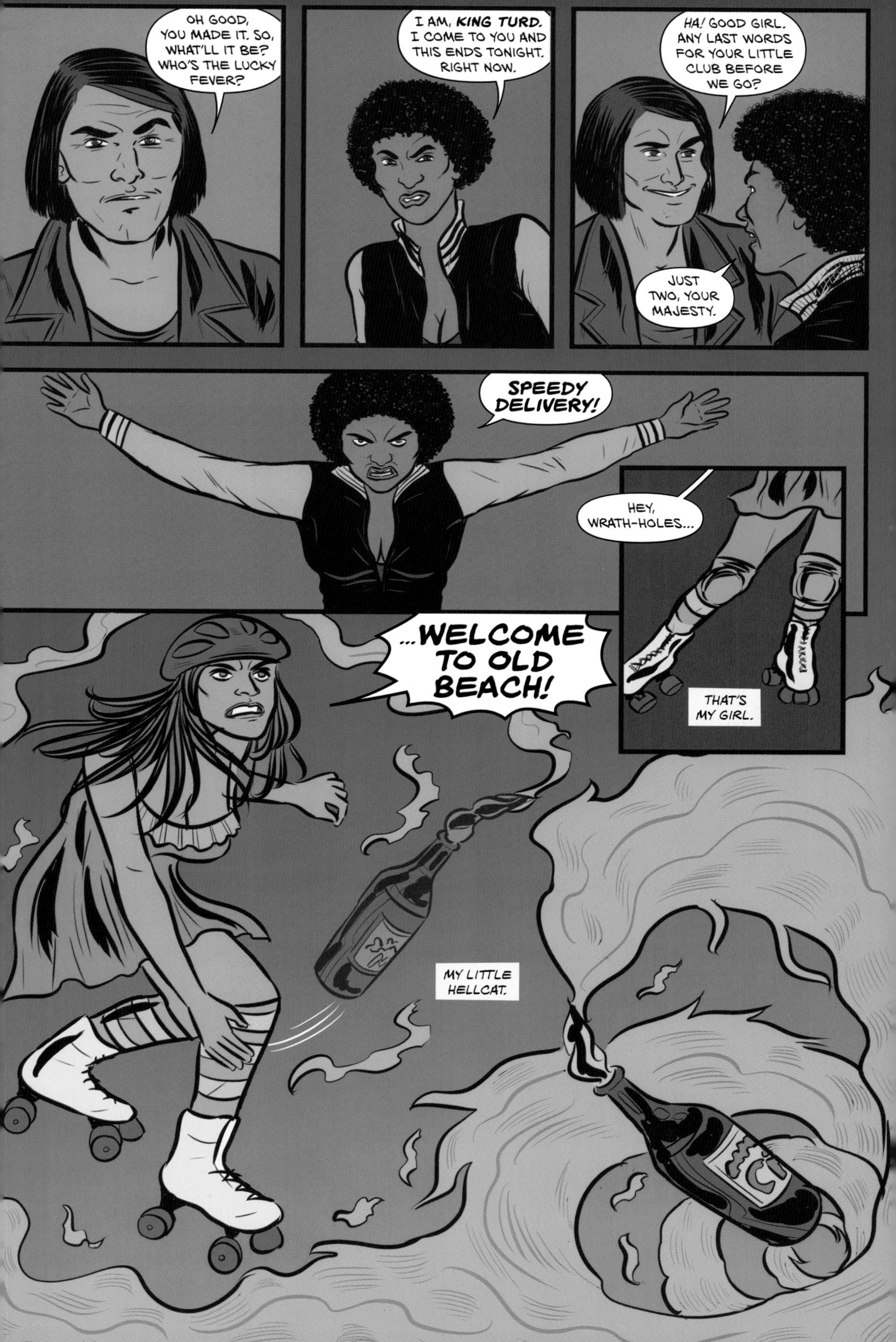

OH GOOD, YOU MADE IT. SO, WHAT'LL IT BE? WHO'S THE LUCKY FEVER?
I AM, KING TURD. I COME TO YOU AND THIS ENDS TONIGHT. RIGHT NOW.
HA! GOOD GIRL. ANY LAST WORDS FOR YOUR LITTLE CLUB BEFORE WE GO?
JUST TWO, YOUR MAJESTY.
SPEEDY DELIVERY!
HEY, WRATH-HOLES...
...WELCOME TO OLD BEACH!
THAT'S MY GIRL.
MY LITTLE HELLCAT.

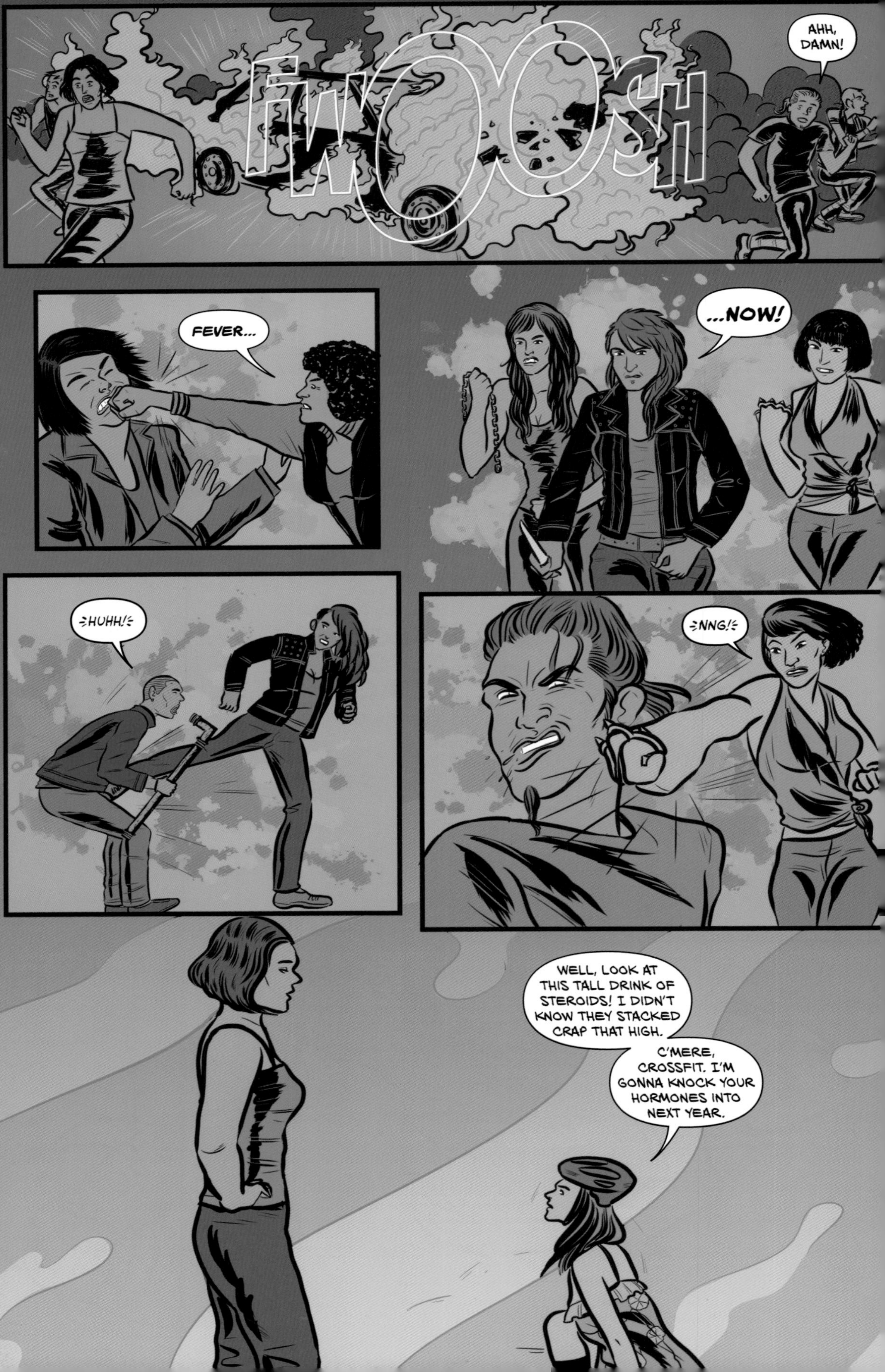
FWOOSH
AHH, DAMN!
FEVER...
...NOW!
HUHH!
NNG!
WELL, LOOK AT THIS TALL DRINK OF STEROIDS! I DIDN'T KNOW THEY STACKED CRAP THAT HIGH.
C'MERE, CROSSFIT. I'M GONNA KNOCK YOUR HORMONES INTO NEXT YEAR.

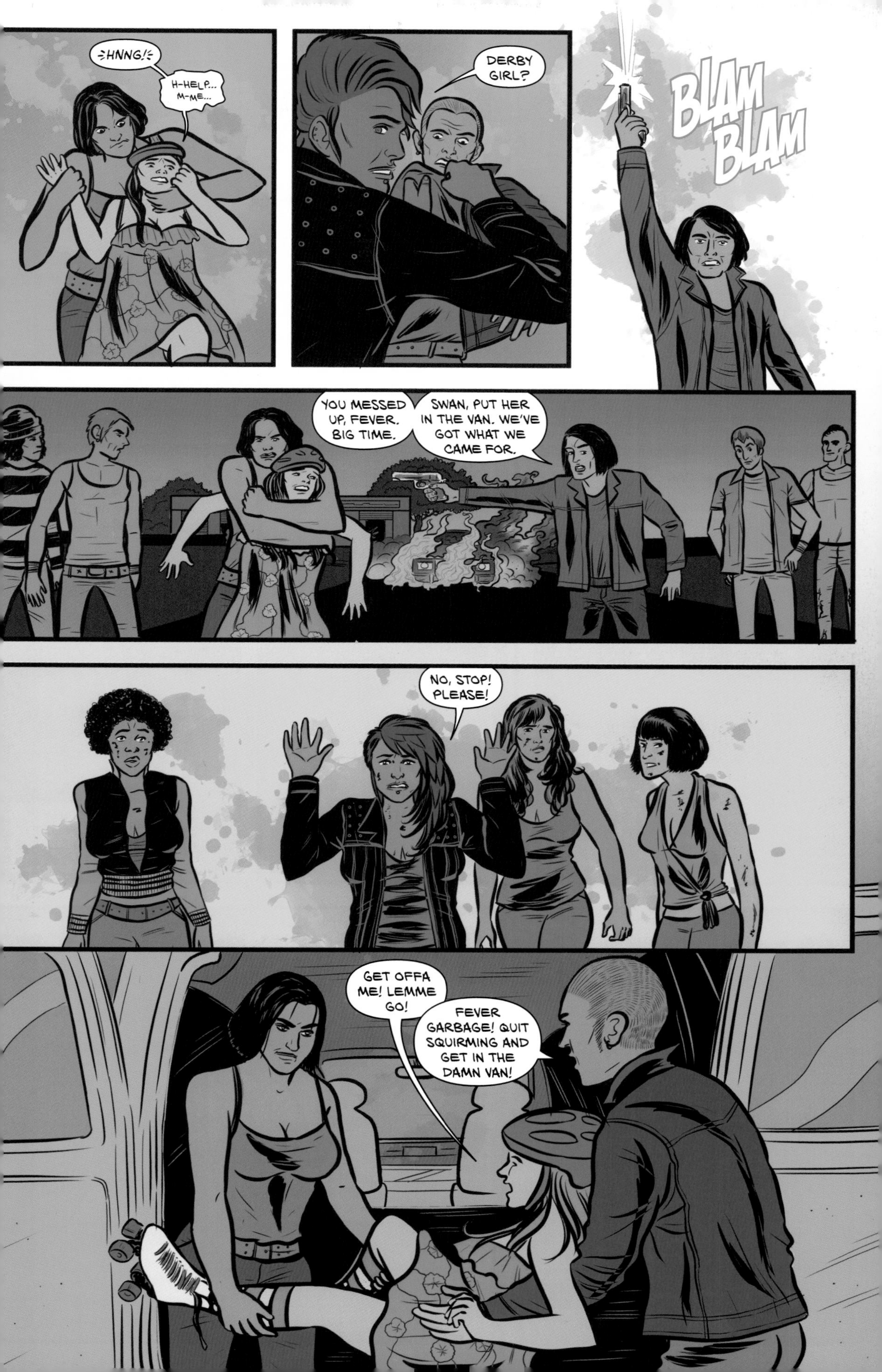
HNNG!
H-HELP... M-ME...
DERBY GIRL?
BLAM BLAM
YOU MESSED UP, FEVER. BIG TIME.
SWAN, PUT HER IN THE VAN. WE'VE GOT WHAT WE CAME FOR.
NO, STOP! PLEASE!
GET OFFA ME! LEMME GO!
FEVER GARBAGE! QUIT SQUIRMING AND GET IN THE DAMN VAN!

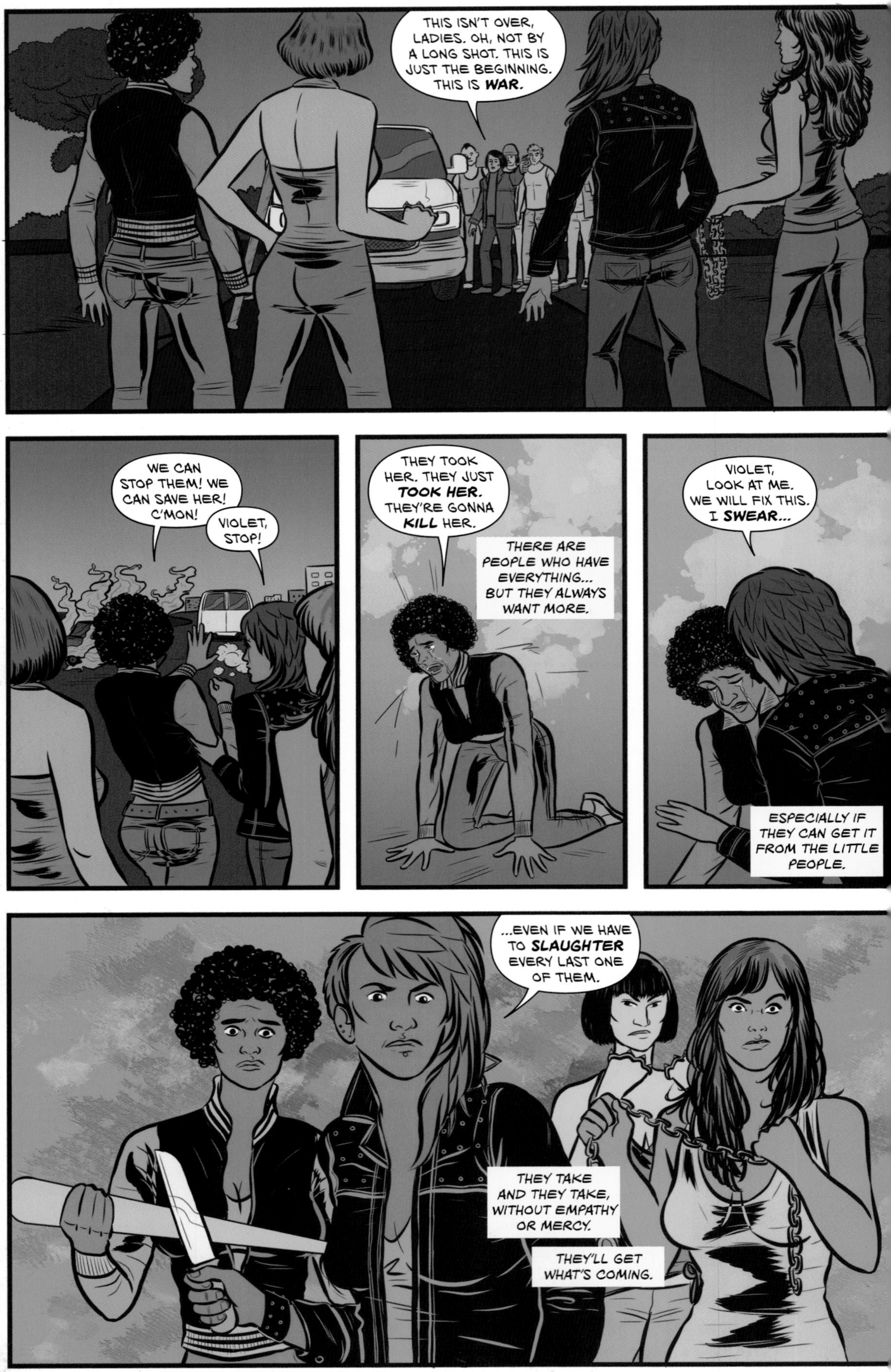
THIS ISN'T OVER, LADIES. OH, NOT BY A LONG SHOT. THIS IS JUST THE BEGINNING. THIS IS WAR.
WE CAN STOP THEM! WE CAN SAVE HER! C'MON!
VIOLET, STOP!
THEY TOOK HER. THEY JUST TOOK HER. THEY'RE GONNA KILL HER.
THERE ARE PEOPLE WHO HAVE EVERYTHING... BUT THEY ALWAYS WANT MORE.
VIOLET, LOOK AT ME. WE WILL FIX THIS. I SWEAR...
ESPECIALLY IF THEY CAN GET IT FROM THE LITTLE PEOPLE.
...EVEN IF WE HAVE TO SLAUGHTER EVERY LAST ONE OF THEM.
THEY TAKE AND THEY TAKE, WITHOUT EMPATHY OR MERCY.
THEY'LL GET WHAT'S COMING.

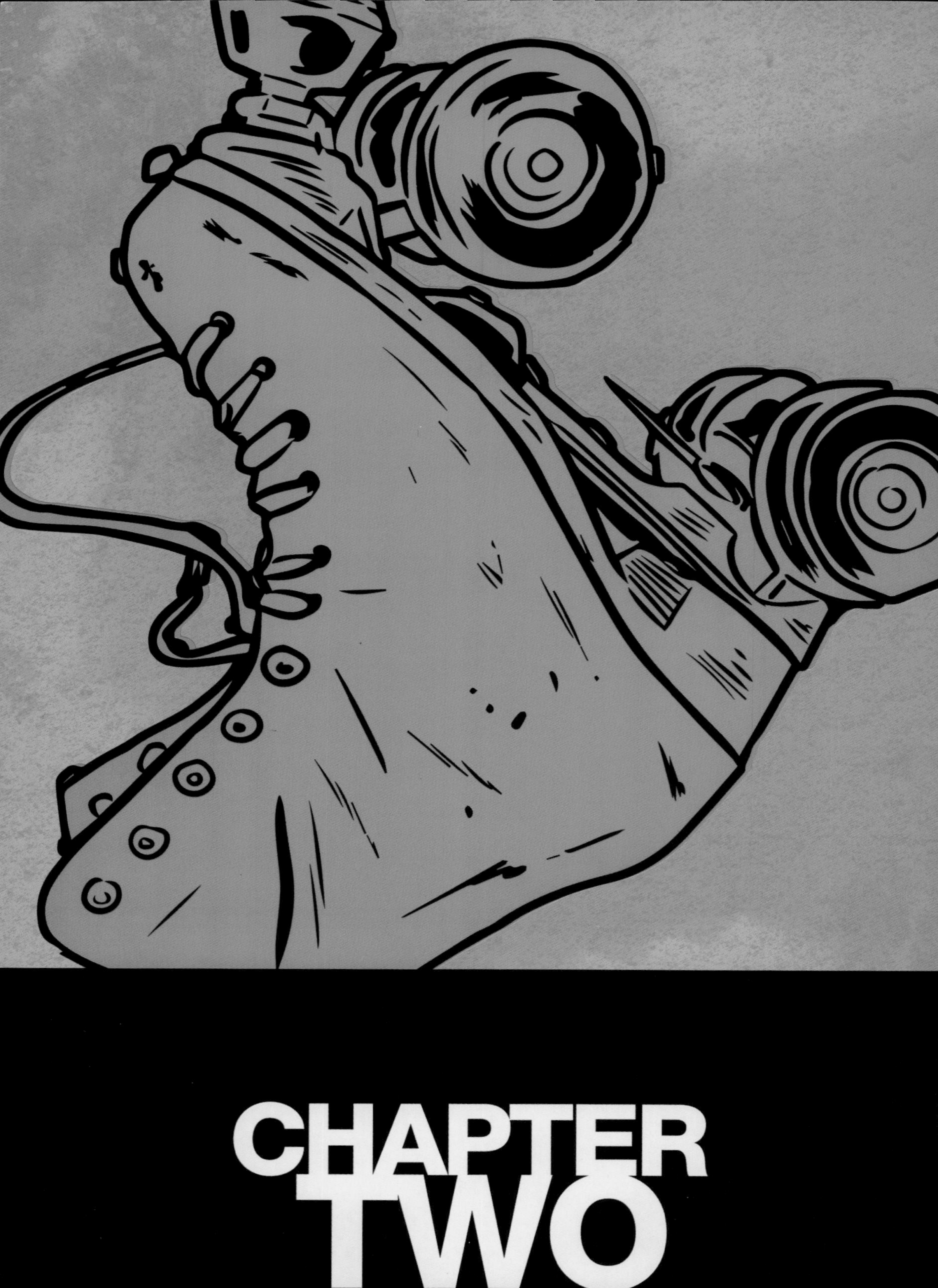

CHAPTER TWO

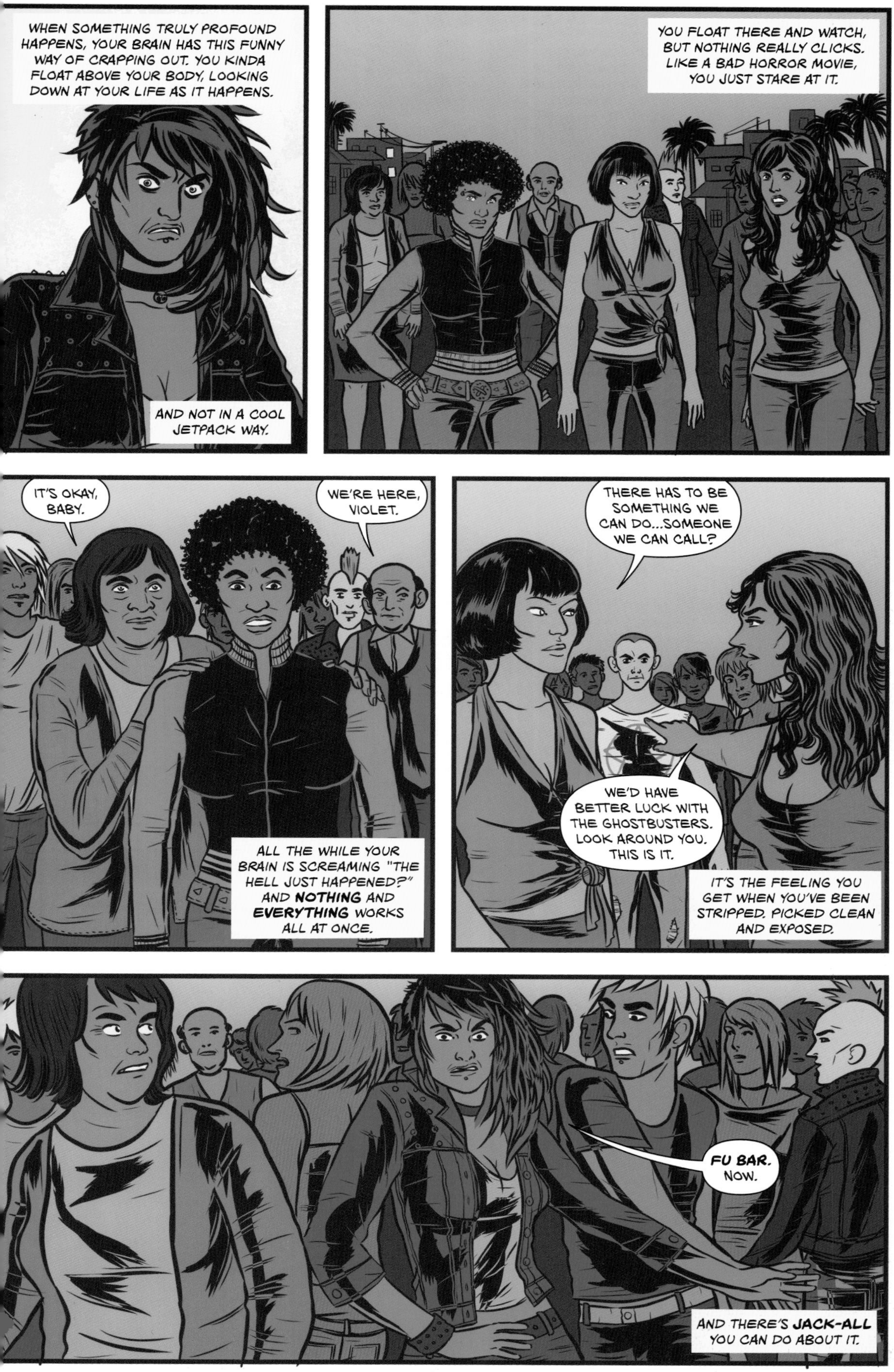
WHEN SOMETHING TRULY PROFOUND HAPPENS, YOUR BRAIN HAS THIS FUNNY WAY OF CRAPPING OUT. YOU KINDA FLOAT ABOVE YOUR BODY, LOOKING DOWN AT YOUR LIFE AS IT HAPPENS.
AND NOT IN A COOL JETPACK WAY.
YOU FLOAT THERE AND WATCH, BUT NOTHING REALLY CLICKS. LIKE A BAD HORROR MOVIE, YOU JUST STARE AT IT.
IT'S OKAY, BABY.
WE'RE HERE, VIOLET.
ALL THE WHILE YOUR BRAIN IS SCREAMING "THE HELL JUST HAPPENED?" AND NOTHING AND EVERYTHING WORKS ALL AT ONCE.
THERE HAS TO BE SOMETHING WE CAN DO...SOMEONE WE CAN CALL?
WE'D HAVE BETTER LUCK WITH THE GHOSTBUSTERS. LOOK AROUND YOU. THIS IS IT.
IT'S THE FEELING YOU GET WHEN YOU'VE BEEN STRIPPED. PICKED CLEAN AND EXPOSED.
FU BAR. NOW.
AND THERE'S JACK-ALL YOU CAN DO ABOUT IT.

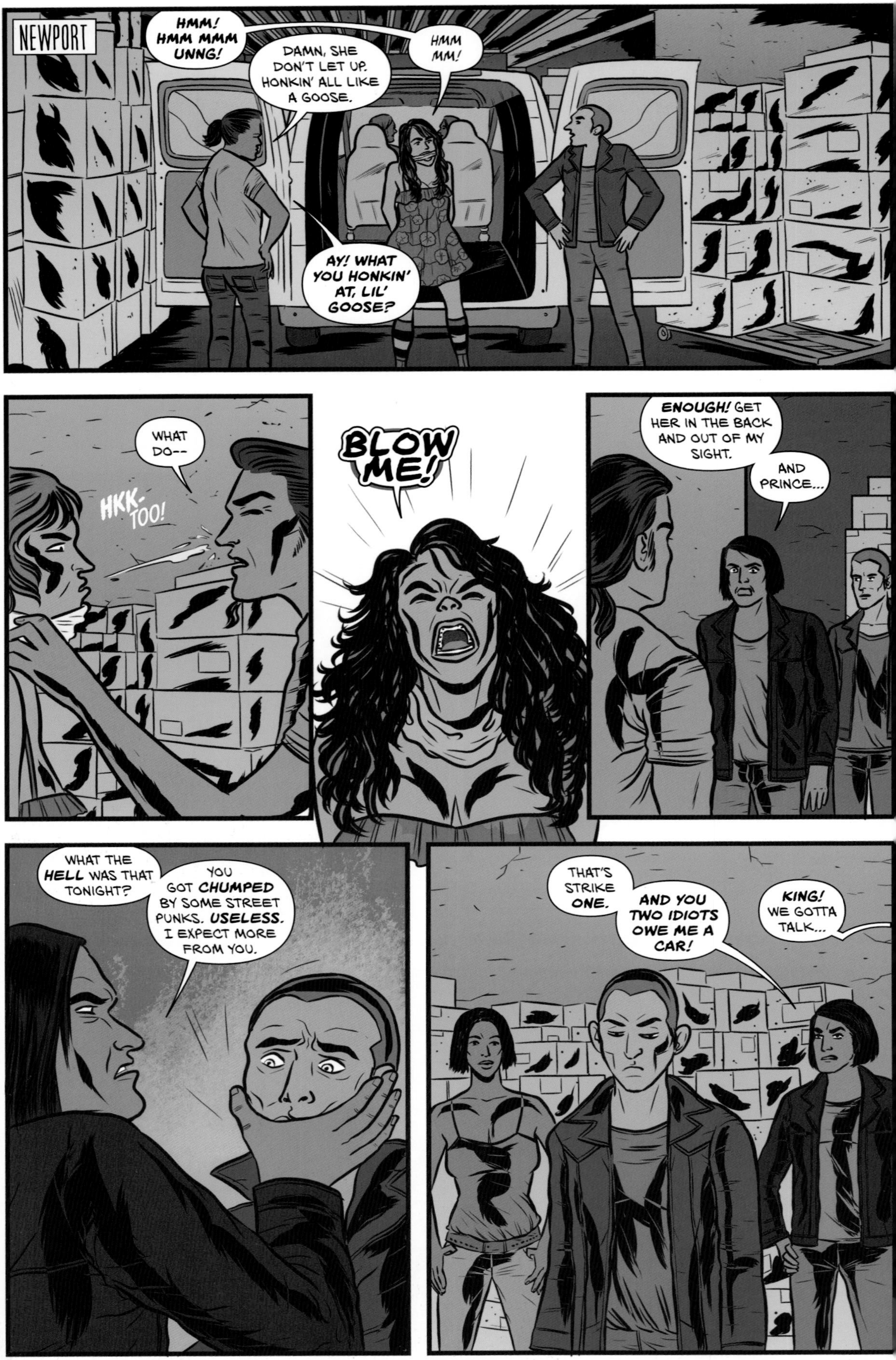
NEWPORT
HMM! HMM MMM UNNG!
DAMN, SHE DON'T LET UP. HONKIN' ALL LIKE A GOOSE.
HMM MM!
AY! WHAT YOU HONKIN' AT, LIL' GOOSE?
WHAT DO--
HKK-TOO!
BLOW ME!
ENOUGH! GET HER IN THE BACK AND OUT OF MY SIGHT.
AND PRINCE...
WHAT THE HELL WAS THAT TONIGHT?
YOU GOT CHUMPED BY SOME STREET PUNKS. USELESS. I EXPECT MORE FROM YOU.
THAT'S STRIKE ONE.
AND YOU TWO IDIOTS OWE ME A CAR!
KING! WE GOTTA TALK...

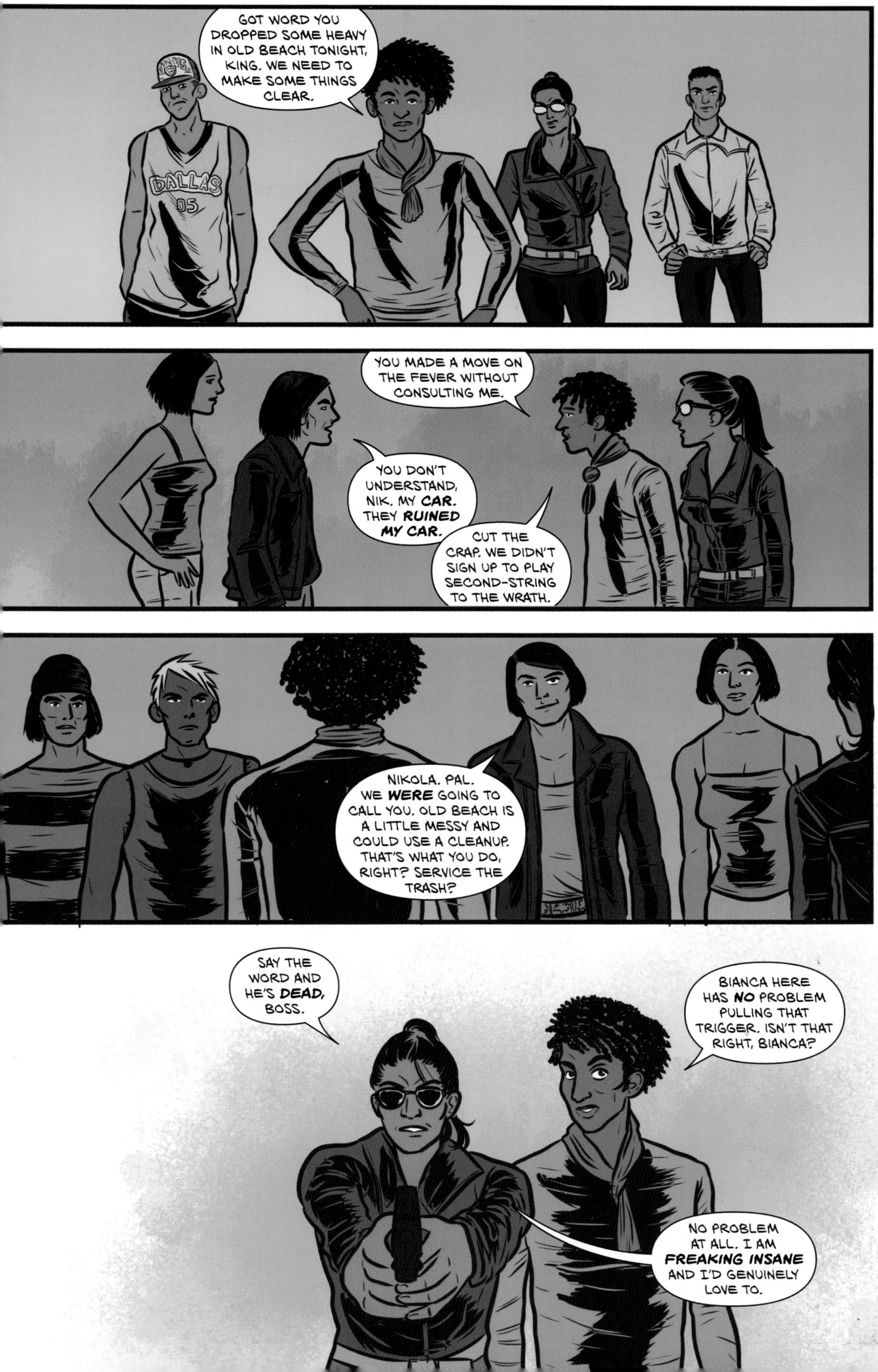
GOT WORD YOU DROPPED SOME HEAVY IN OLD BEACH TONIGHT, KING. WE NEED TO MAKE SOME THINGS CLEAR.
YOU MADE A MOVE ON THE FEVER WITHOUT CONSULTING ME.
YOU DON'T UNDERSTAND, NIK. MY **CAR.** THEY **RUINED MY CAR.**
CUT THE CRAP. WE DIDN'T SIGN UP TO PLAY SECOND-STRING TO THE WRATH.
NIKOLA. PAL. WE **WERE** GOING TO CALL YOU. OLD BEACH IS A LITTLE MESSY AND COULD USE A CLEANUP. THAT'S WHAT YOU DO, RIGHT? SERVICE THE TRASH?
SAY THE WORD AND HE'S ***DEAD,*** BOSS.
BIANCA HERE HAS **NO** PROBLEM PULLING THAT TRIGGER. ISN'T THAT RIGHT, BIANCA?
NO PROBLEM AT ALL. I AM ***FREAKING INSANE*** AND I'D GENUINELY LOVE TO.

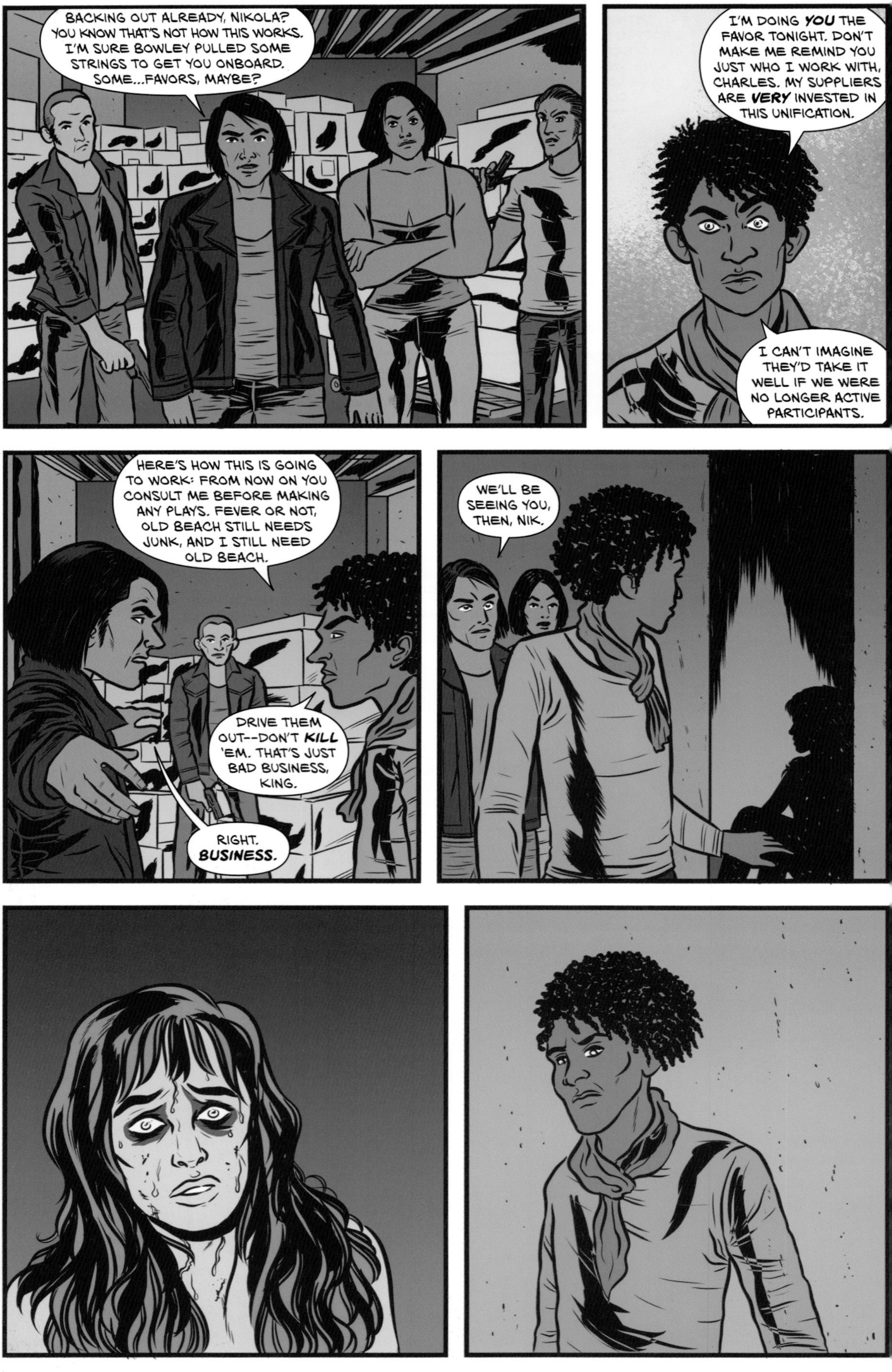
BACKING OUT ALREADY, NIKOLA? YOU KNOW THAT'S NOT HOW THIS WORKS. I'M SURE BOWLEY PULLED SOME STRINGS TO GET YOU ONBOARD. SOME...FAVORS, MAYBE?
I'M DOING YOU THE FAVOR TONIGHT. DON'T MAKE ME REMIND YOU JUST WHO I WORK WITH, CHARLES. MY SUPPLIERS ARE VERY INVESTED IN THIS UNIFICATION.
I CAN'T IMAGINE THEY'D TAKE IT WELL IF WE WERE NO LONGER ACTIVE PARTICIPANTS.
HERE'S HOW THIS IS GOING TO WORK: FROM NOW ON YOU CONSULT ME BEFORE MAKING ANY PLAYS. FEVER OR NOT, OLD BEACH STILL NEEDS JUNK, AND I STILL NEED OLD BEACH.
DRIVE THEM OUT--DON'T KILL 'EM. THAT'S JUST BAD BUSINESS, KING.
RIGHT. BUSINESS.
WE'LL BE SEEING YOU, THEN, NIK.

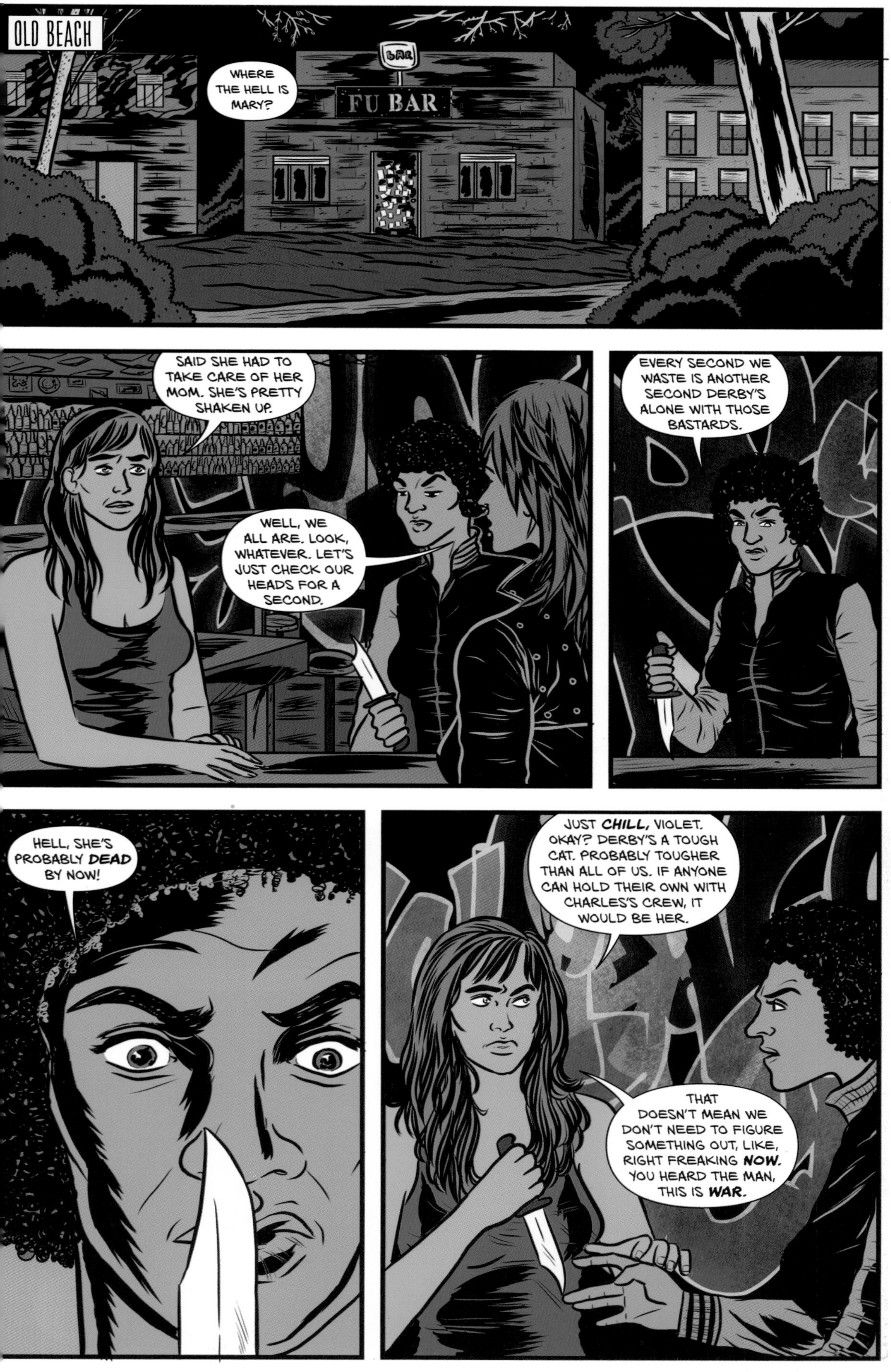
OLD BEACH
WHERE THE HELL IS MARY?
bAR
FU BAR
SAID SHE HAD TO TAKE CARE OF HER MOM. SHE'S PRETTY SHAKEN UP.
WELL, WE ALL ARE. LOOK, WHATEVER. LET'S JUST CHECK OUR HEADS FOR A SECOND.
EVERY SECOND WE WASTE IS ANOTHER SECOND DERBY'S ALONE WITH THOSE BASTARDS.
HELL, SHE'S PROBABLY **DEAD** BY NOW!
JUST **CHILL,** VIOLET. OKAY? DERBY'S A TOUGH CAT. PROBABLY TOUGHER THAN ALL OF US. IF ANYONE CAN HOLD THEIR OWN WITH CHARLES'S CREW, IT WOULD BE HER.
THAT DOESN'T MEAN WE DON'T NEED TO FIGURE SOMETHING OUT, LIKE, RIGHT FREAKING **NOW.** YOU HEARD THE MAN, THIS IS **WAR.**

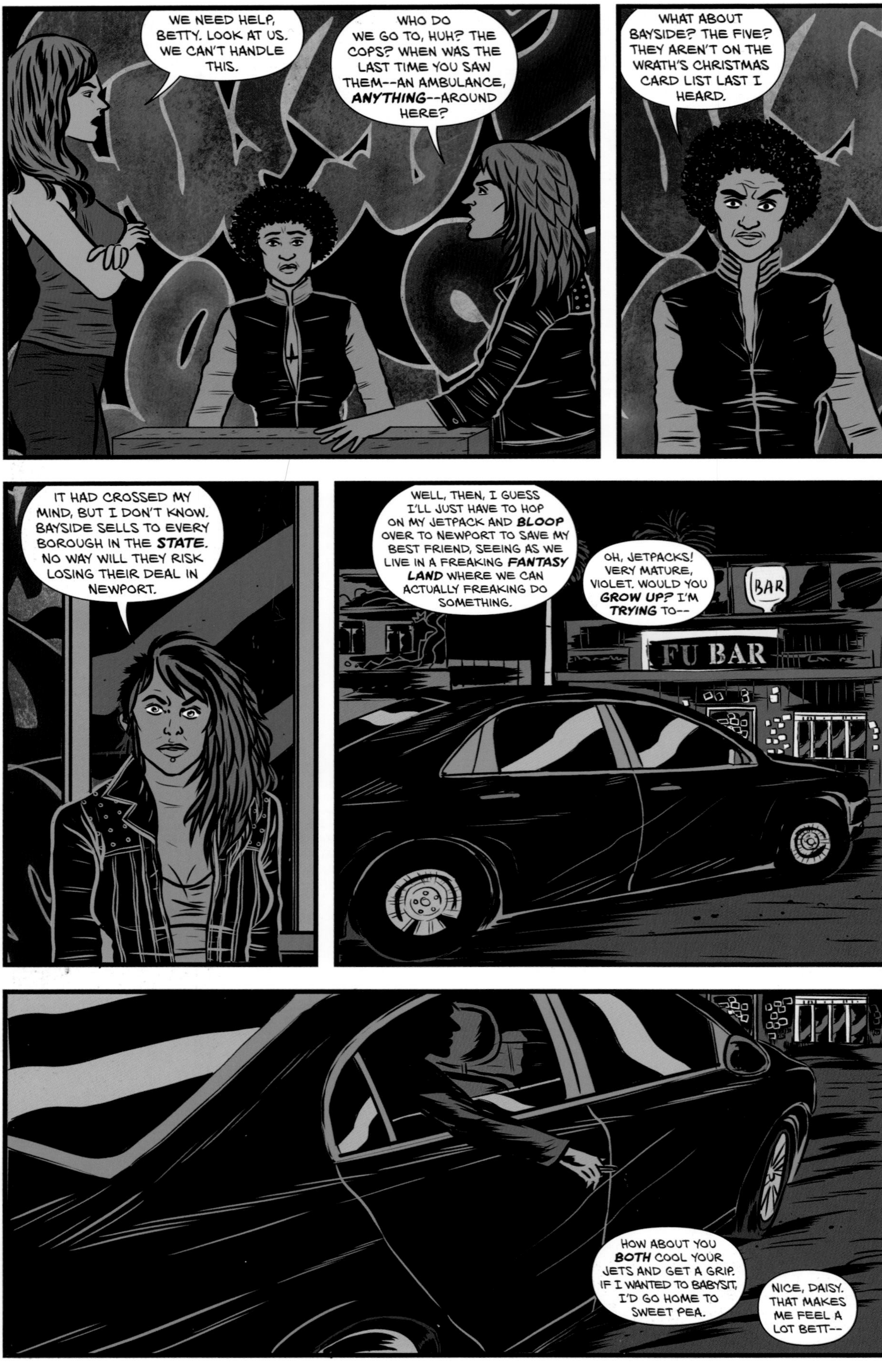
WE NEED HELP, BETTY. LOOK AT US. WE CAN'T HANDLE THIS.
WHO DO WE GO TO, HUH? THE COPS? WHEN WAS THE LAST TIME YOU SAW THEM--AN AMBULANCE, ANYTHING--AROUND HERE?
WHAT ABOUT BAYSIDE? THE FIVE? THEY AREN'T ON THE WRATH'S CHRISTMAS CARD LIST LAST I HEARD.
IT HAD CROSSED MY MIND, BUT I DON'T KNOW. BAYSIDE SELLS TO EVERY BOROUGH IN THE STATE. NO WAY WILL THEY RISK LOSING THEIR DEAL IN NEWPORT.
WELL, THEN, I GUESS I'LL JUST HAVE TO HOP ON MY JETPACK AND BLOOP OVER TO NEWPORT TO SAVE MY BEST FRIEND, SEEING AS WE LIVE IN A FREAKING FANTASY LAND WHERE WE CAN ACTUALLY FREAKING DO SOMETHING.
OH, JETPACKS! VERY MATURE, VIOLET. WOULD YOU GROW UP? I'M TRYING TO--
BAR
FU BAR
HOW ABOUT YOU BOTH COOL YOUR JETS AND GET A GRIP. IF I WANTED TO BABYSIT, I'D GO HOME TO SWEET PEA.
NICE, DAISY. THAT MAKES ME FEEL A LOT BETT--

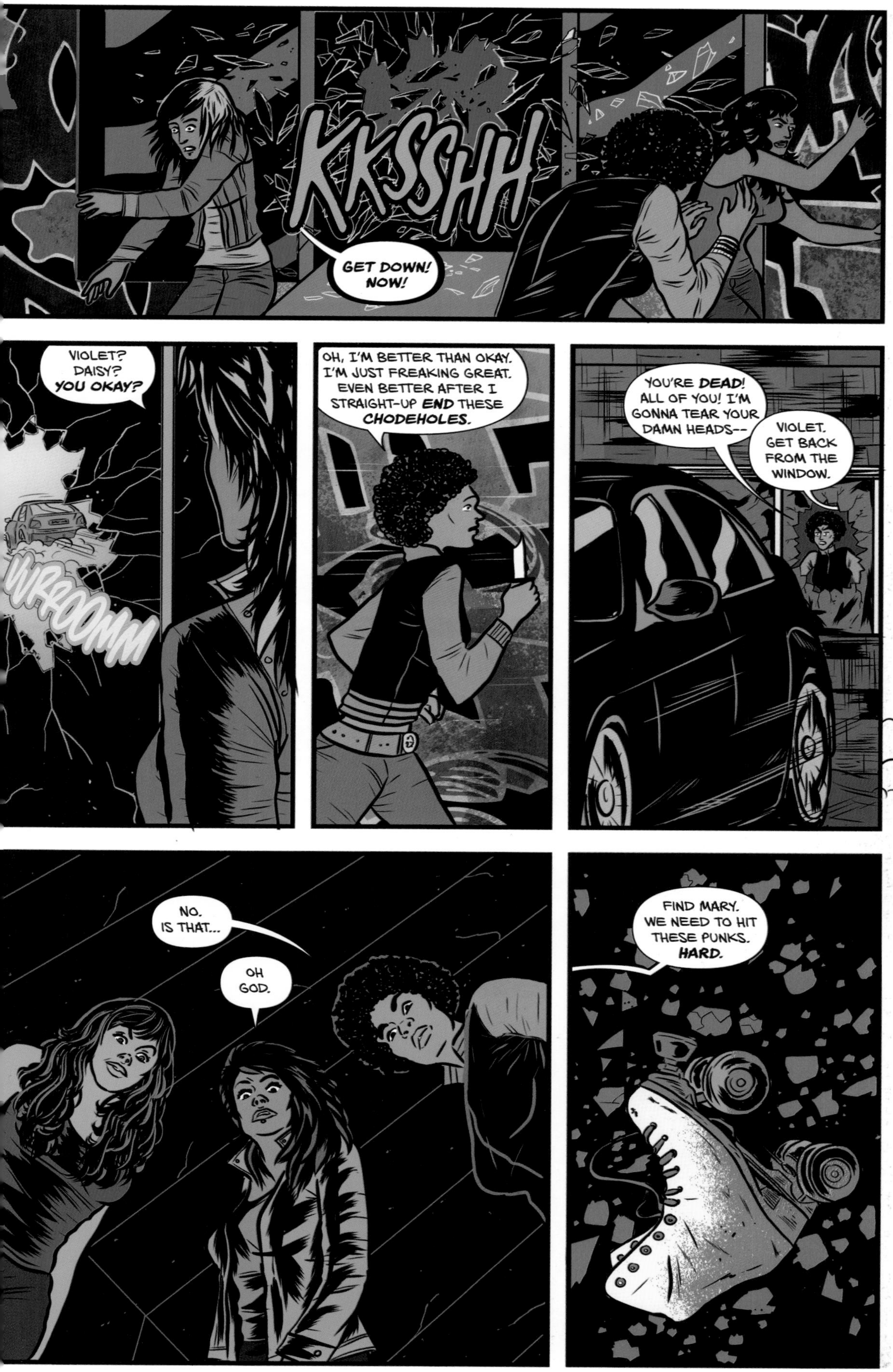
KKSSHH
GET DOWN! NOW!
VIOLET? DAISY? YOU OKAY?
VVRROOMM
OH, I'M BETTER THAN OKAY. I'M JUST FREAKING GREAT. EVEN BETTER AFTER I STRAIGHT-UP END THESE CHODEHOLES.
YOU'RE DEAD! ALL OF YOU! I'M GONNA TEAR YOUR DAMN HEADS--
VIOLET. GET BACK FROM THE WINDOW.
NO. IS THAT...
OH GOD.
FIND MARY. WE NEED TO HIT THESE PUNKS. HARD.

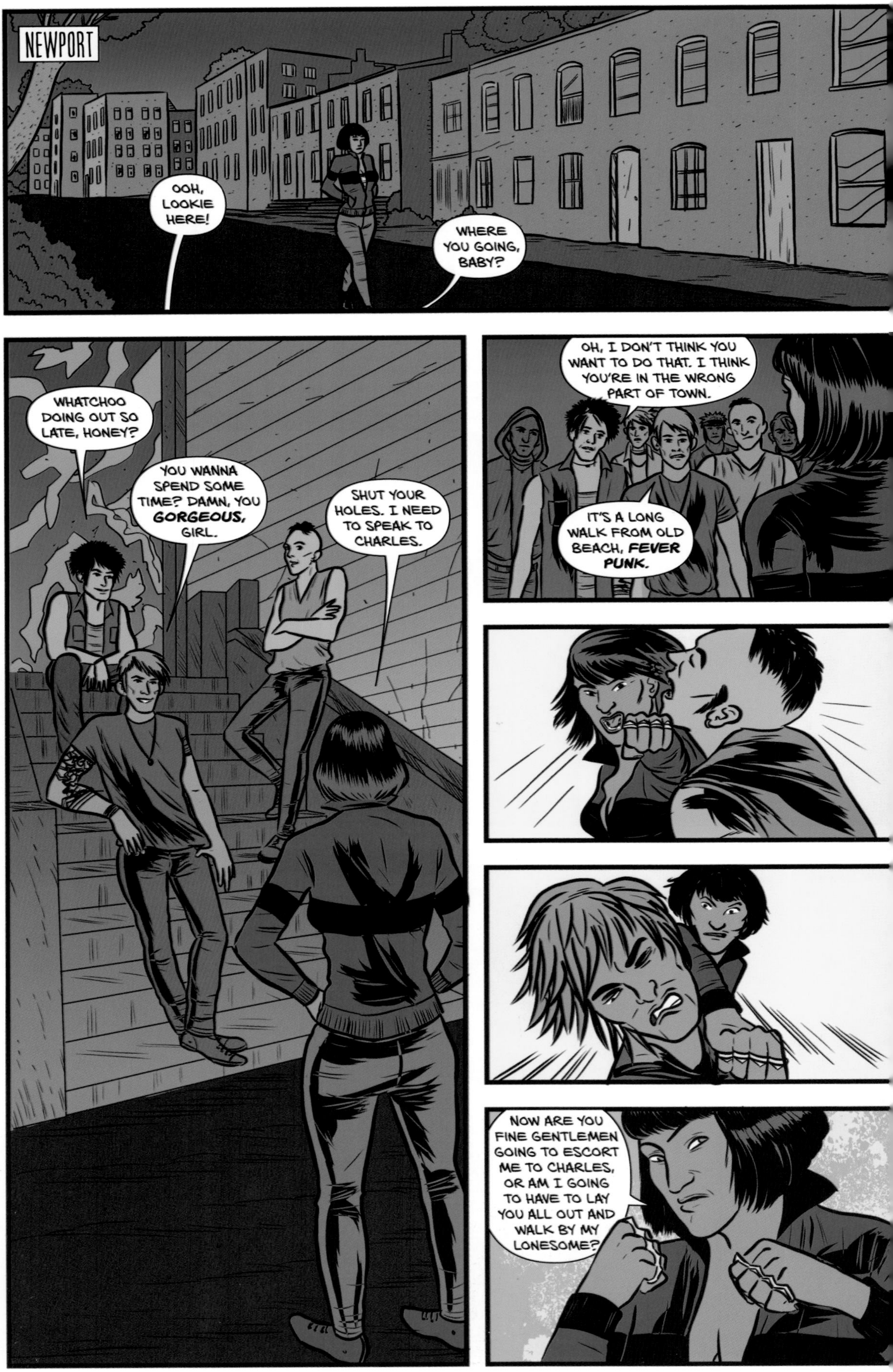
NEWPORT
OOH, LOOKIE HERE!
WHERE YOU GOING, BABY?
WHATCHOO DOING OUT SO LATE, HONEY?
YOU WANNA SPEND SOME TIME? DAMN, YOU **GORGEOUS,** GIRL.
SHUT YOUR HOLES. I NEED TO SPEAK TO CHARLES.
OH, I DON'T THINK YOU WANT TO DO THAT. I THINK YOU'RE IN THE WRONG PART OF TOWN.
IT'S A LONG WALK FROM OLD BEACH, **FEVER PUNK.**
NOW ARE YOU FINE GENTLEMEN GOING TO ESCORT ME TO CHARLES, OR AM I GOING TO HAVE TO LAY YOU ALL OUT AND WALK BY MY LONESOME?

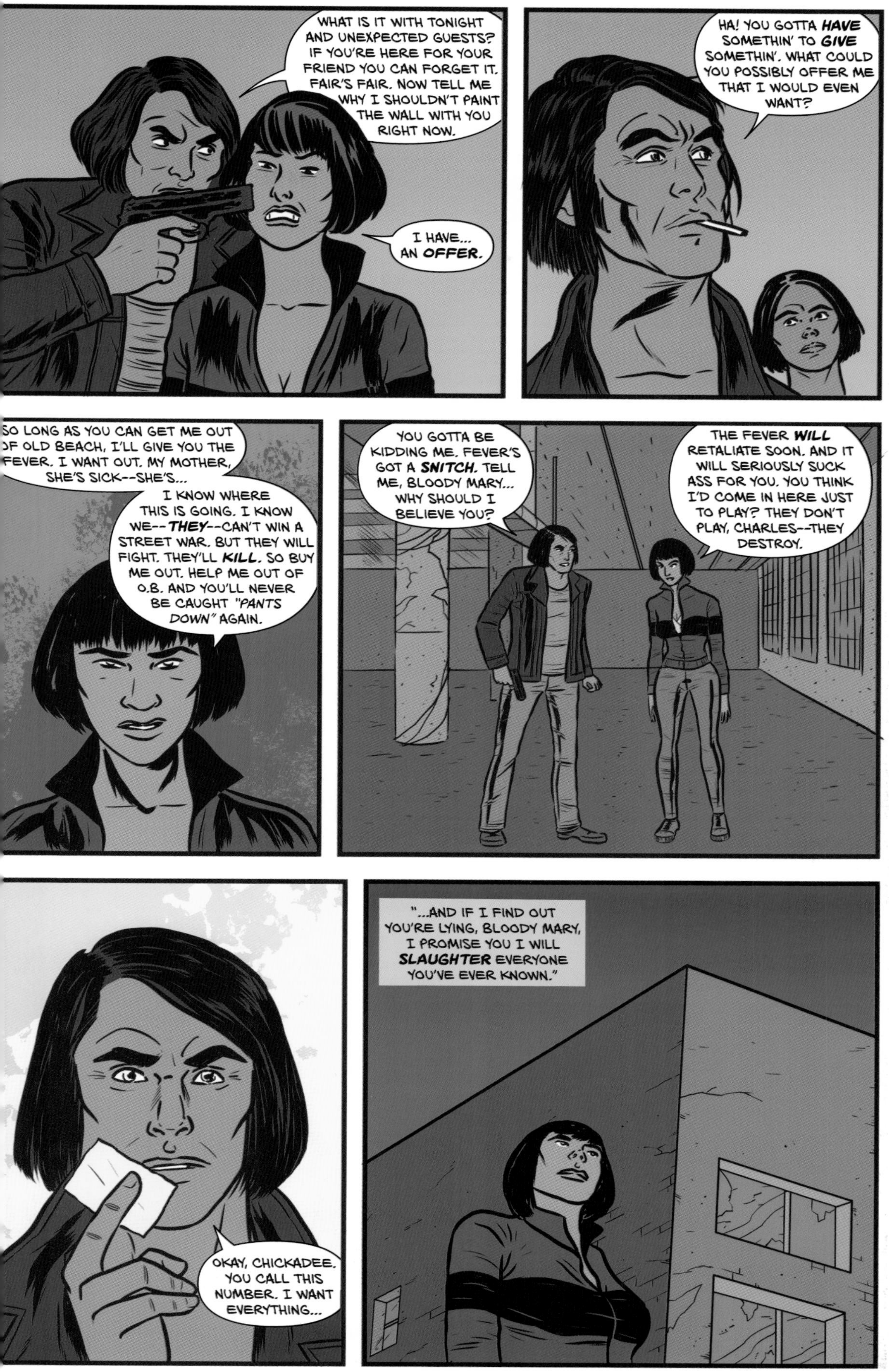
WHAT IS IT WITH TONIGHT AND UNEXPECTED GUESTS? IF YOU'RE HERE FOR YOUR FRIEND YOU CAN FORGET IT. FAIR'S FAIR. NOW TELL ME WHY I SHOULDN'T PAINT THE WALL WITH YOU RIGHT NOW.
I HAVE... AN OFFER.
HA! YOU GOTTA HAVE SOMETHIN' TO GIVE SOMETHIN'. WHAT COULD YOU POSSIBLY OFFER ME THAT I WOULD EVEN WANT?
SO LONG AS YOU CAN GET ME OUT OF OLD BEACH, I'LL GIVE YOU THE FEVER. I WANT OUT. MY MOTHER, SHE'S SICK--SHE'S...
I KNOW WHERE THIS IS GOING. I KNOW WE--THEY--CAN'T WIN A STREET WAR. BUT THEY WILL FIGHT. THEY'LL KILL. SO BUY ME OUT. HELP ME OUT OF O.B. AND YOU'LL NEVER BE CAUGHT "PANTS DOWN" AGAIN.
YOU GOTTA BE KIDDING ME. FEVER'S GOT A SNITCH. TELL ME, BLOODY MARY... WHY SHOULD I BELIEVE YOU?
THE FEVER WILL RETALIATE SOON. AND IT WILL SERIOUSLY SUCK ASS FOR YOU. YOU THINK I'D COME IN HERE JUST TO PLAY? THEY DON'T PLAY, CHARLES--THEY DESTROY.
OKAY, CHICKADEE. YOU CALL THIS NUMBER. I WANT EVERYTHING...
"...AND IF I FIND OUT YOU'RE LYING, BLOODY MARY, I PROMISE YOU I WILL SLAUGHTER EVERYONE YOU'VE EVER KNOWN."

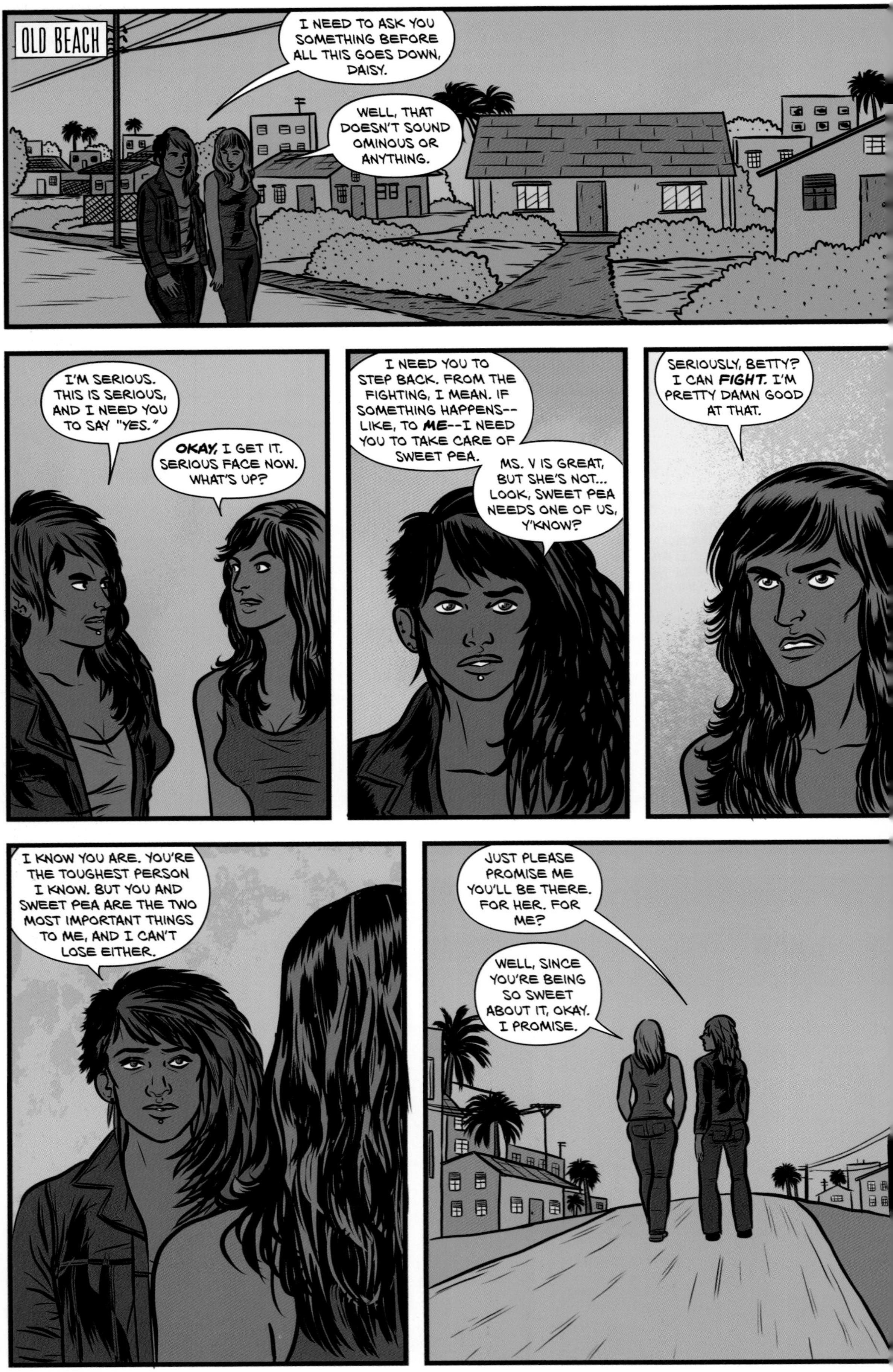
OLD BEACH
I NEED TO ASK YOU SOMETHING BEFORE ALL THIS GOES DOWN, DAISY.
WELL, THAT DOESN'T SOUND OMINOUS OR ANYTHING.
I'M SERIOUS. THIS IS SERIOUS, AND I NEED YOU TO SAY "YES."
OKAY, I GET IT. SERIOUS FACE NOW. WHAT'S UP?
I NEED YOU TO STEP BACK. FROM THE FIGHTING, I MEAN. IF SOMETHING HAPPENS-- LIKE, TO ME--I NEED YOU TO TAKE CARE OF SWEET PEA.
MS. V IS GREAT, BUT SHE'S NOT... LOOK, SWEET PEA NEEDS ONE OF US, Y'KNOW?
SERIOUSLY, BETTY? I CAN FIGHT. I'M PRETTY DAMN GOOD AT THAT.
I KNOW YOU ARE. YOU'RE THE TOUGHEST PERSON I KNOW. BUT YOU AND SWEET PEA ARE THE TWO MOST IMPORTANT THINGS TO ME, AND I CAN'T LOSE EITHER.
JUST PLEASE PROMISE ME YOU'LL BE THERE. FOR HER. FOR ME?
WELL, SINCE YOU'RE BEING SO SWEET ABOUT IT, OKAY. I PROMISE.

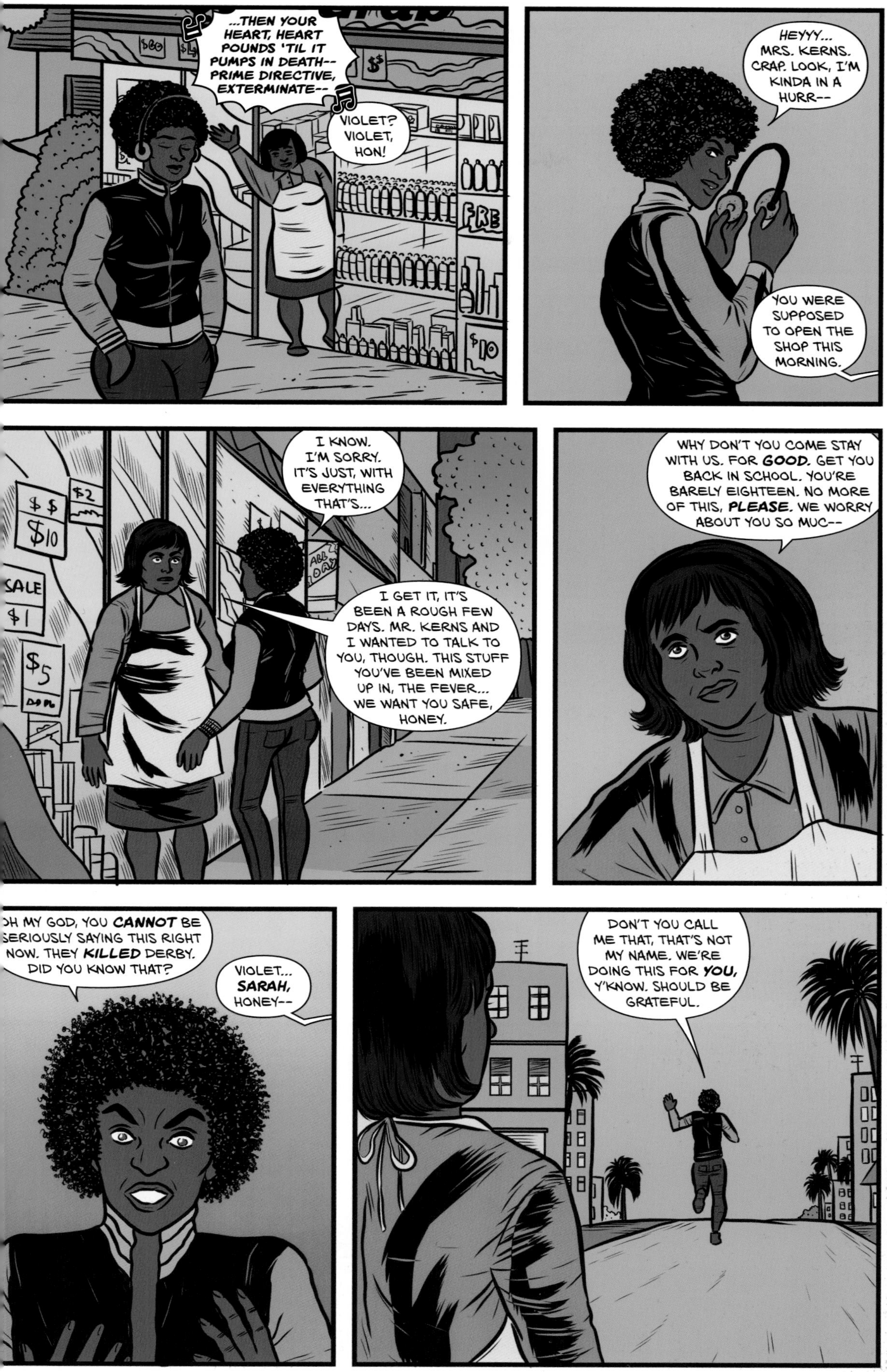

...THEN YOUR HEART, HEART POUNDS 'TIL IT PUMPS IN DEATH-- PRIME DIRECTIVE, EXTERMINATE--
VIOLET? VIOLET, HON!
HEYYY... MRS. KERNS. CRAP. LOOK, I'M KINDA IN A HURR--
YOU WERE SUPPOSED TO OPEN THE SHOP THIS MORNING.
I KNOW. I'M SORRY. IT'S JUST, WITH EVERYTHING THAT'S...
I GET IT, IT'S BEEN A ROUGH FEW DAYS. MR. KERNS AND I WANTED TO TALK TO YOU, THOUGH. THIS STUFF YOU'VE BEEN MIXED UP IN, THE FEVER... WE WANT YOU SAFE, HONEY.
WHY DON'T YOU COME STAY WITH US. FOR **GOOD.** GET YOU BACK IN SCHOOL. YOU'RE BARELY EIGHTEEN. NO MORE OF THIS, **PLEASE.** WE WORRY ABOUT YOU SO MUC--
OH MY GOD, YOU **CANNOT** BE SERIOUSLY SAYING THIS RIGHT NOW. THEY **KILLED** DERBY. DID YOU KNOW THAT?
VIOLET... **SARAH,** HONEY--
DON'T YOU CALL ME THAT, THAT'S NOT MY NAME. WE'RE DOING THIS FOR **YOU,** Y'KNOW. SHOULD BE GRATEFUL.

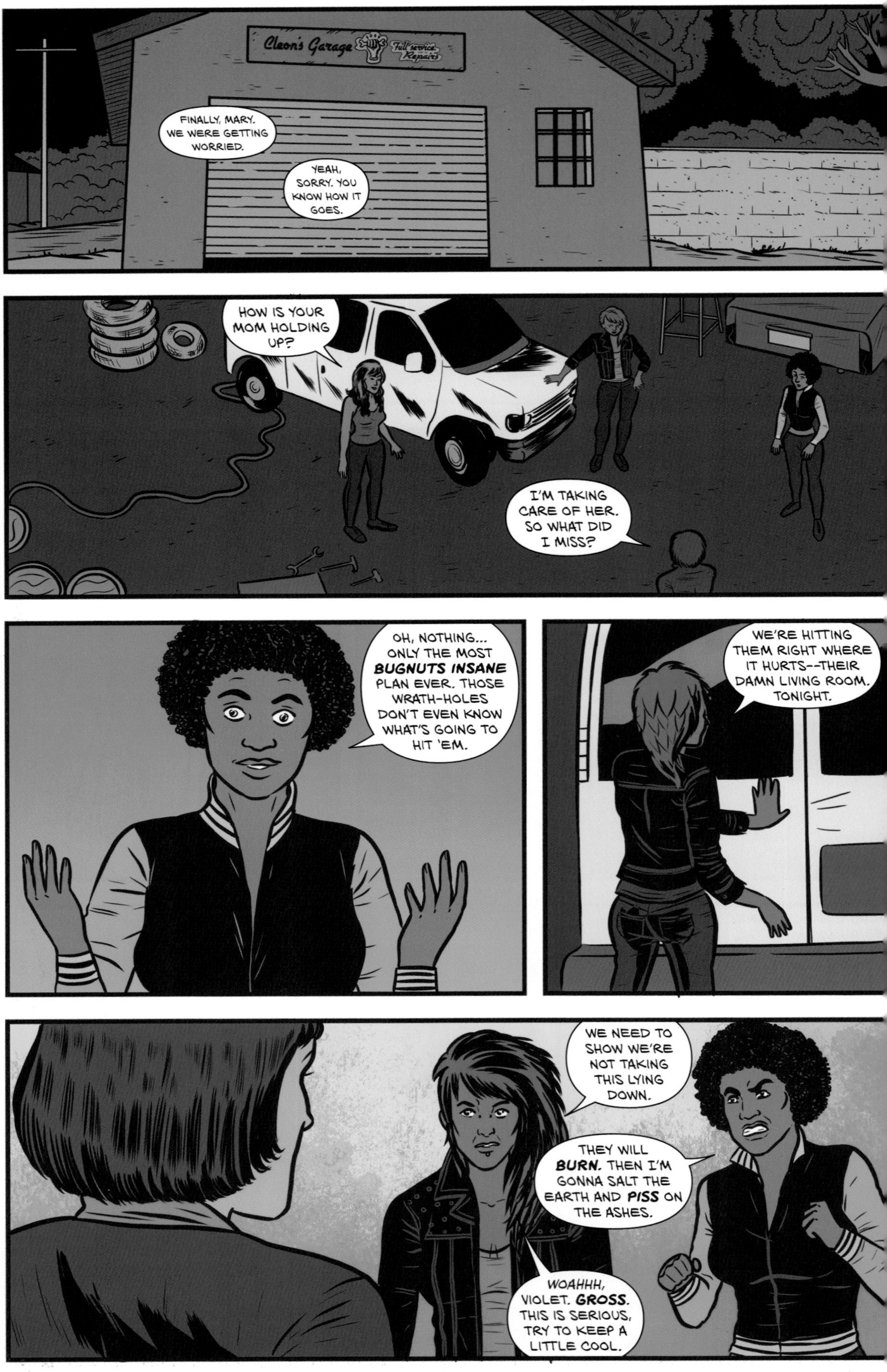

Cleon's Garage
Full service Repairs
FINALLY, MARY. WE WERE GETTING WORRIED.
YEAH, SORRY. YOU KNOW HOW IT GOES.
HOW IS YOUR MOM HOLDING UP?
I'M TAKING CARE OF HER. SO WHAT DID I MISS?
OH, NOTHING... ONLY THE MOST BUGNUTS INSANE PLAN EVER. THOSE WRATH-HOLES DON'T EVEN KNOW WHAT'S GOING TO HIT 'EM.
WE'RE HITTING THEM RIGHT WHERE IT HURTS--THEIR DAMN LIVING ROOM. TONIGHT.
WE NEED TO SHOW WE'RE NOT TAKING THIS LYING DOWN.
THEY WILL BURN. THEN I'M GONNA SALT THE EARTH AND PISS ON THE ASHES.
WOAHHH, VIOLET. GROSS. THIS IS SERIOUS, TRY TO KEEP A LITTLE COOL.

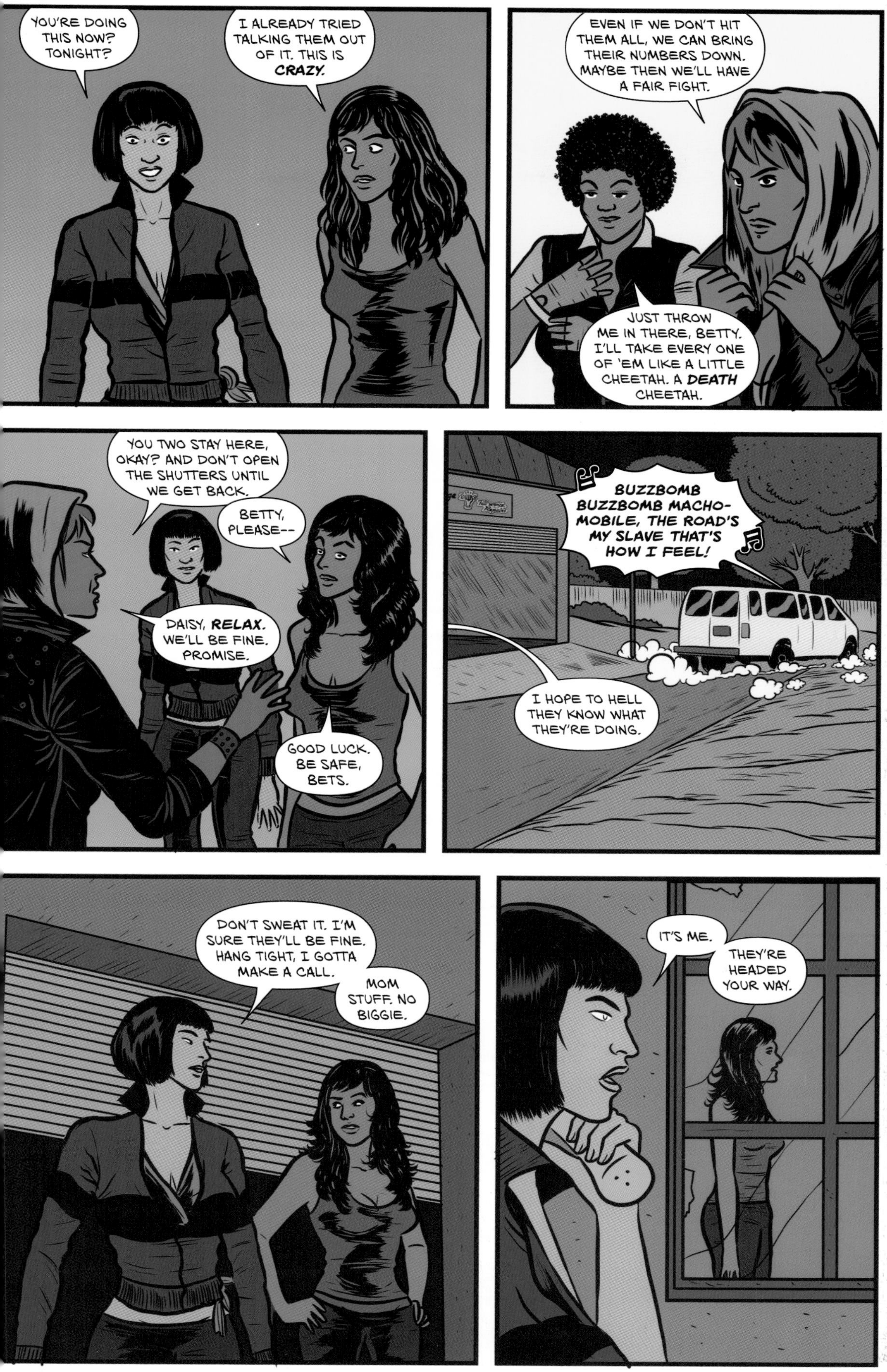
YOU'RE DOING THIS NOW? TONIGHT?
I ALREADY TRIED TALKING THEM OUT OF IT. THIS IS CRAZY.
EVEN IF WE DON'T HIT THEM ALL, WE CAN BRING THEIR NUMBERS DOWN. MAYBE THEN WE'LL HAVE A FAIR FIGHT.
JUST THROW ME IN THERE, BETTY. I'LL TAKE EVERY ONE OF 'EM LIKE A LITTLE CHEETAH. A DEATH CHEETAH.
YOU TWO STAY HERE, OKAY? AND DON'T OPEN THE SHUTTERS UNTIL WE GET BACK.
BETTY, PLEASE--
DAISY, RELAX. WE'LL BE FINE. PROMISE.
GOOD LUCK. BE SAFE, BETS.
BUZZBOMB BUZZBOMB MACHO-MOBILE, THE ROAD'S MY SLAVE THAT'S HOW I FEEL!
I HOPE TO HELL THEY KNOW WHAT THEY'RE DOING.
DON'T SWEAT IT. I'M SURE THEY'LL BE FINE. HANG TIGHT, I GOTTA MAKE A CALL.
MOM STUFF. NO BIGGIE.
IT'S ME.
THEY'RE HEADED YOUR WAY.

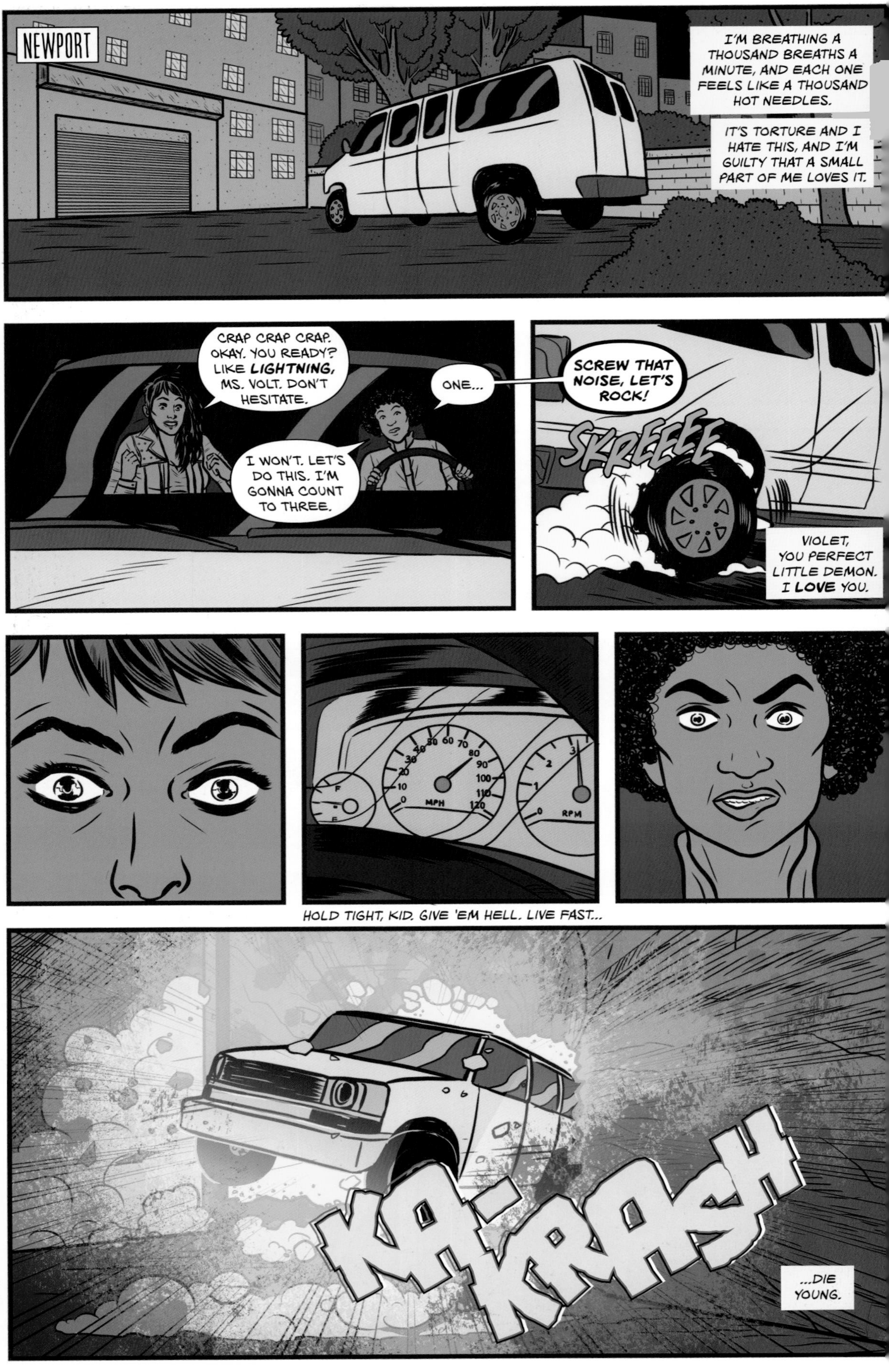
NEWPORT
I'M BREATHING A THOUSAND BREATHS A MINUTE, AND EACH ONE FEELS LIKE A THOUSAND HOT NEEDLES.
IT'S TORTURE AND I HATE THIS, AND I'M GUILTY THAT A SMALL PART OF ME LOVES IT.
CRAP CRAP CRAP. OKAY. YOU READY? LIKE **LIGHTNING,** MS. VOLT. DON'T HESITATE.
I WON'T. LET'S DO THIS. I'M GONNA COUNT TO THREE.
ONE...
SCREW THAT NOISE, LET'S ROCK!
SKREEEE
VIOLET, YOU PERFECT LITTLE DEMON. I **LOVE** YOU.
HOLD TIGHT, KID. GIVE 'EM HELL. LIVE FAST...
KA-KRASH
...DIE YOUNG.

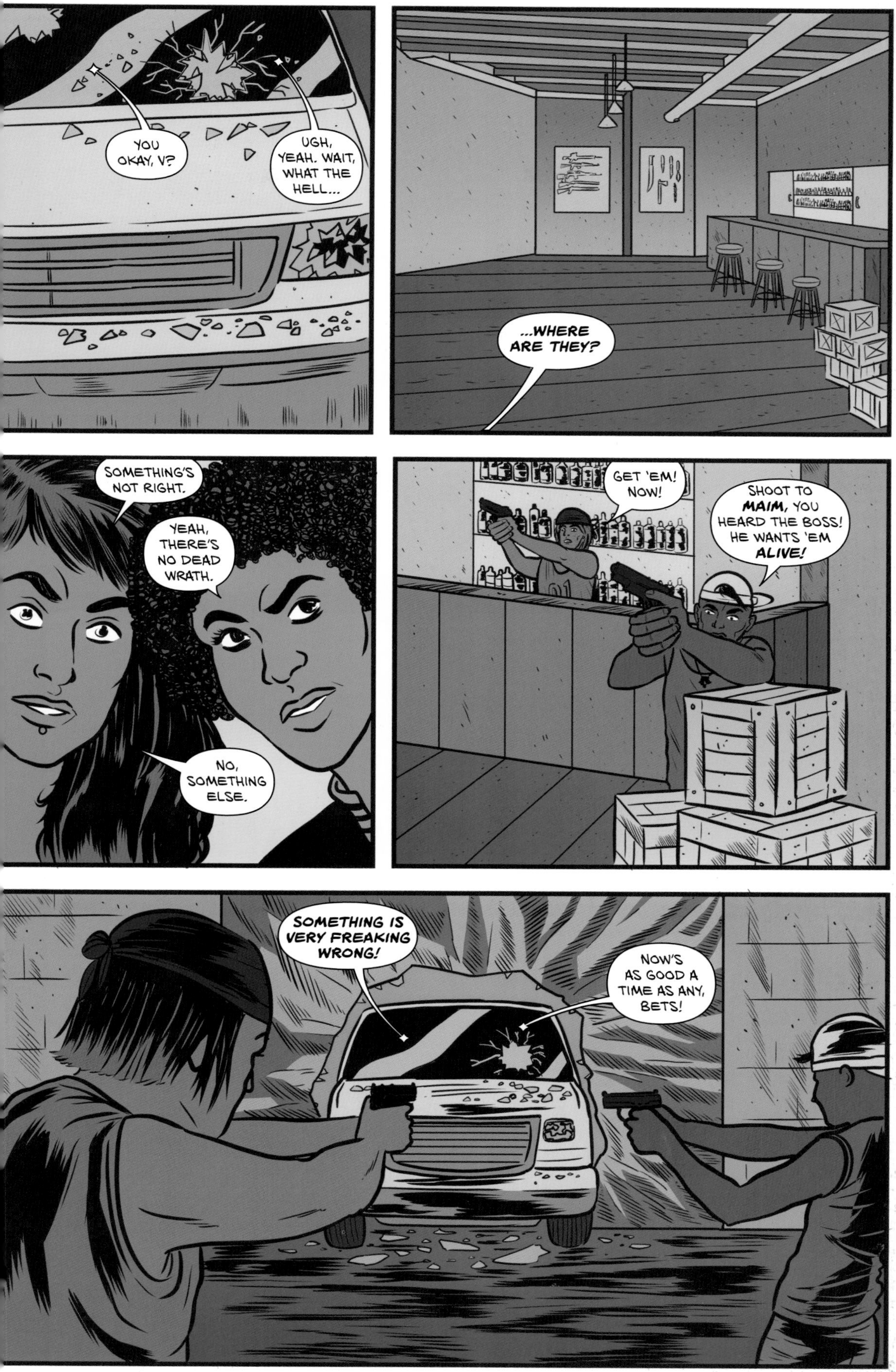
YOU OKAY, V?
UGH, YEAH. WAIT, WHAT THE HELL...
...WHERE ARE THEY?
SOMETHING'S NOT RIGHT.
YEAH, THERE'S NO DEAD WRATH.
NO, SOMETHING ELSE.
GET 'EM! NOW!
SHOOT TO **MAIM,** YOU HEARD THE BOSS! HE WANTS 'EM **ALIVE!**
SOMETHING IS VERY FREAKING WRONG!
NOW'S AS GOOD A TIME AS ANY, BETS!

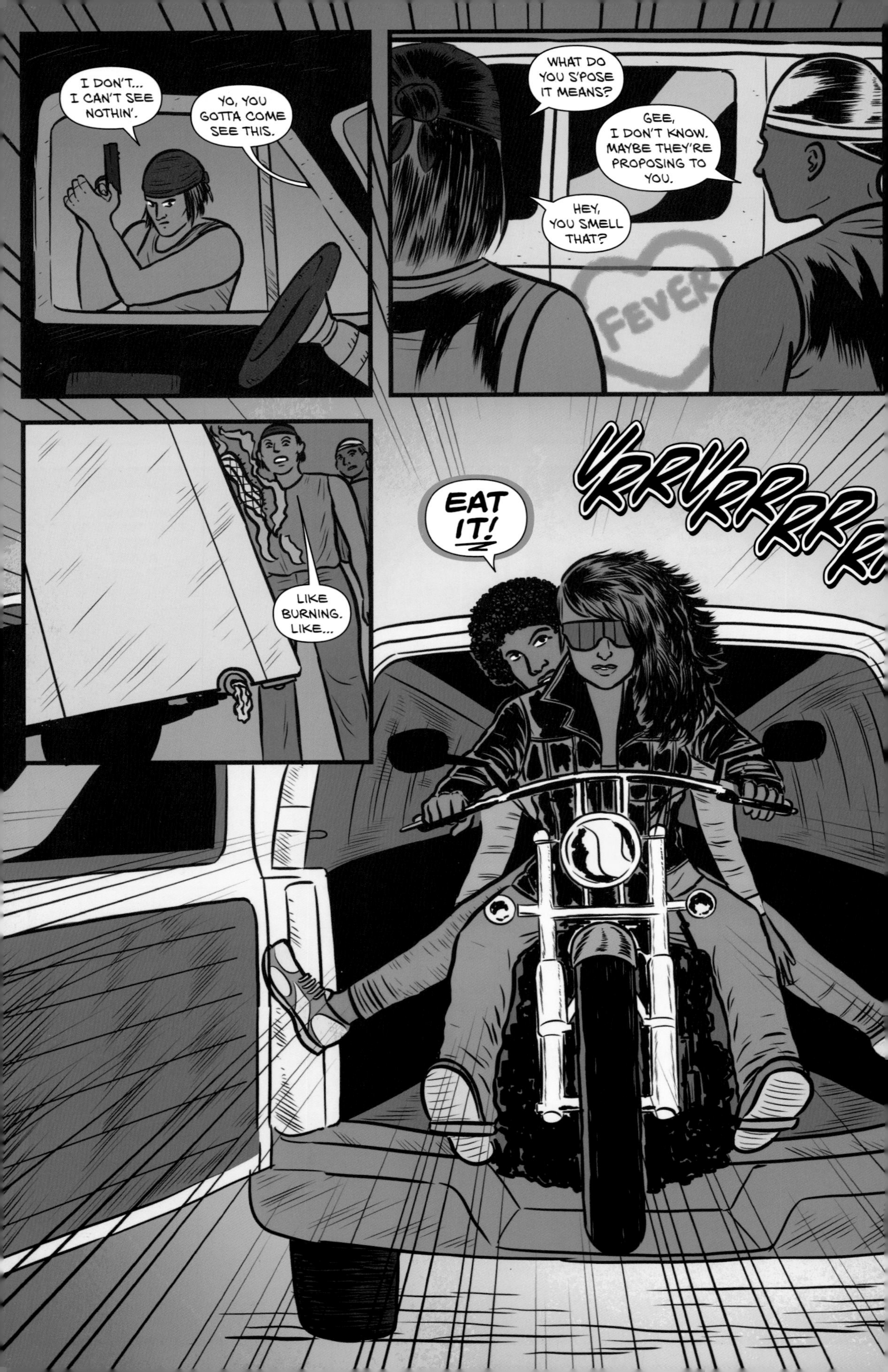
I DON'T... I CAN'T SEE NOTHIN'.
YO, YOU GOTTA COME SEE THIS.
WHAT DO YOU S'POSE IT MEANS?
GEE, I DON'T KNOW. MAYBE THEY'RE PROPOSING TO YOU.
HEY, YOU SMELL THAT?
FEVER
LIKE BURNING. LIKE...
EAT IT!
VRRVRRRRRR

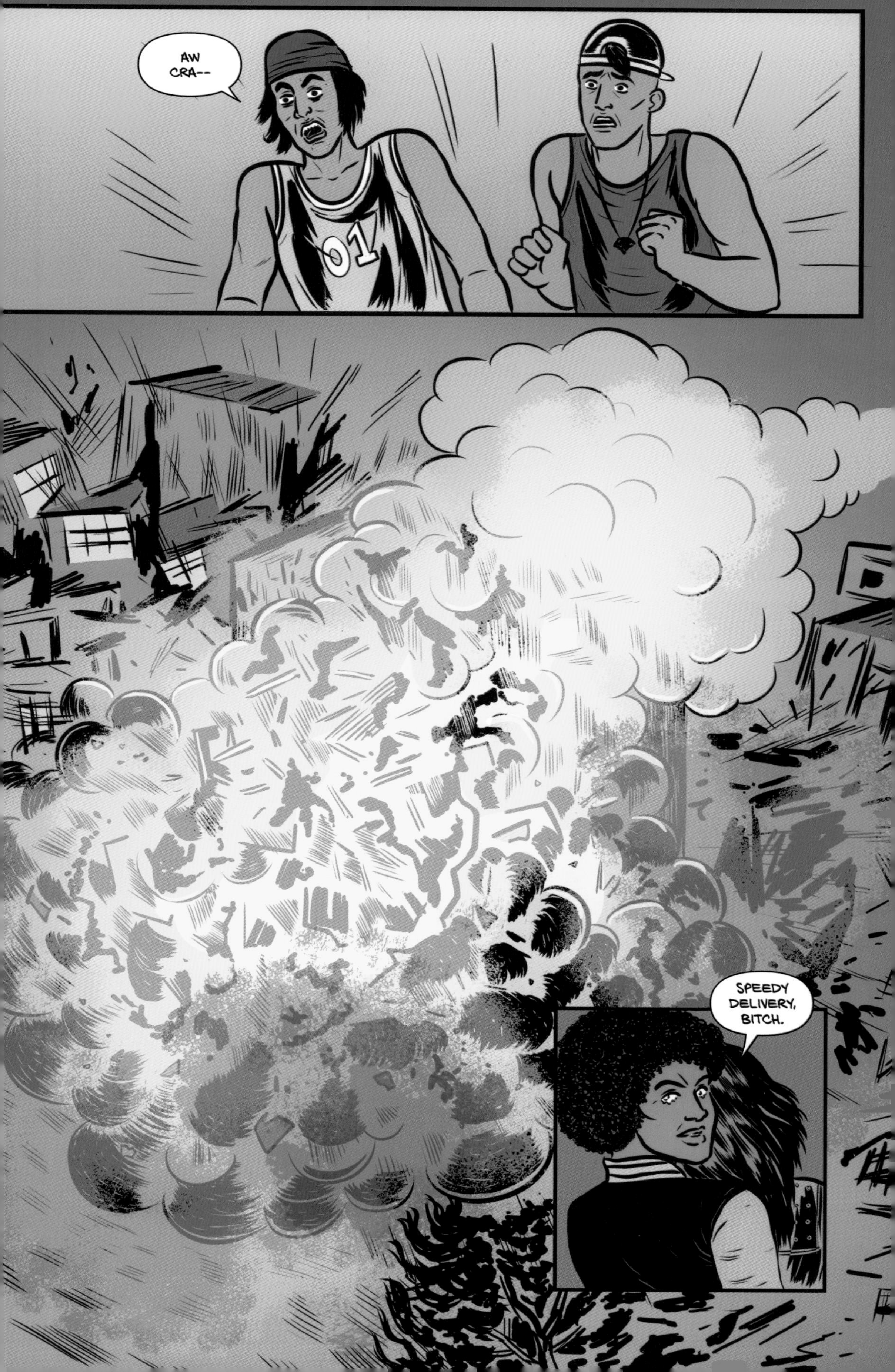
AW CRA--
SPEEDY DELIVERY, BITCH.

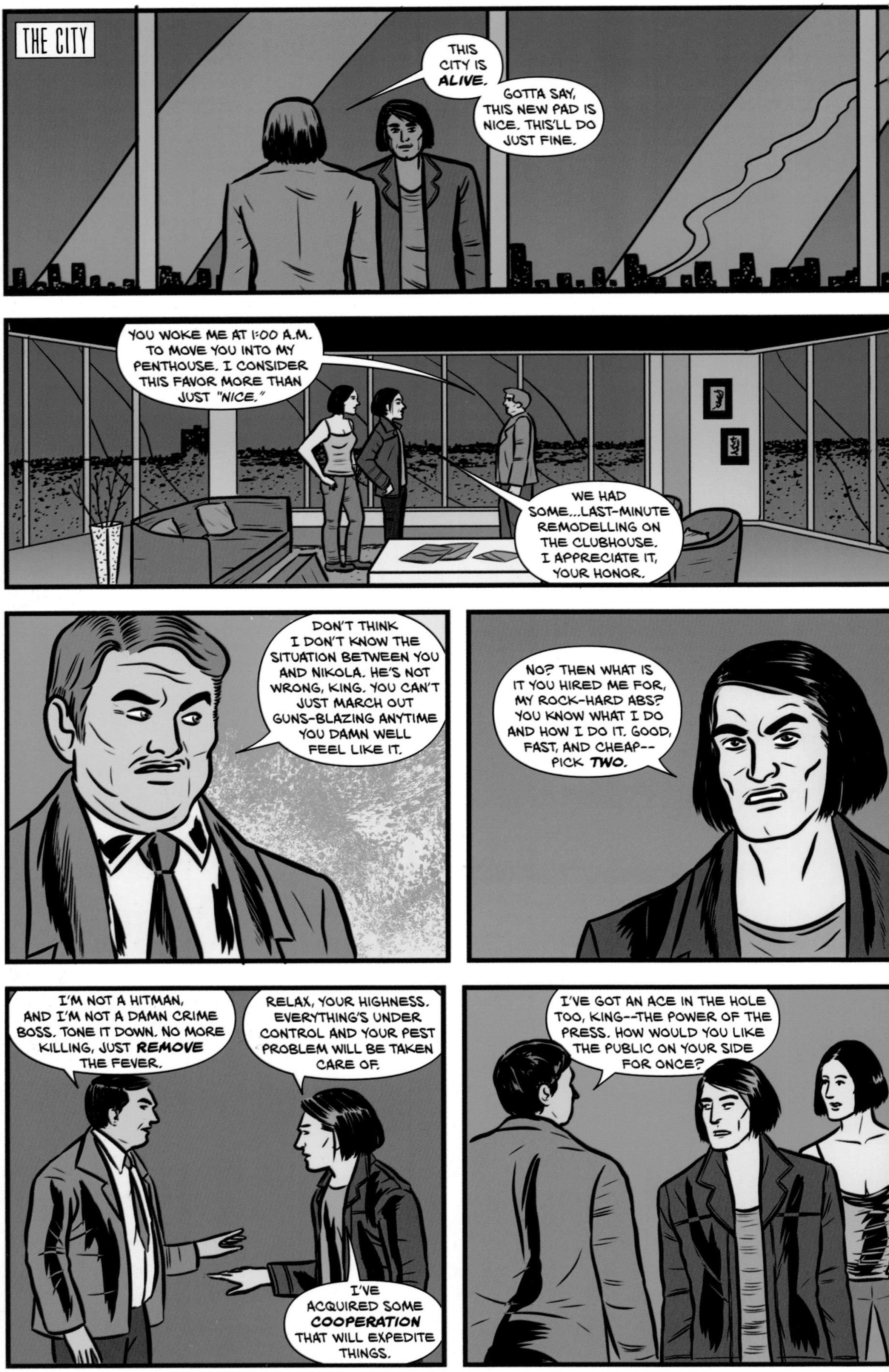
THE CITY
THIS CITY IS **ALIVE.**
GOTTA SAY, THIS NEW PAD IS NICE. THIS'LL DO JUST FINE.
YOU WOKE ME AT 1:00 A.M. TO MOVE YOU INTO MY PENTHOUSE. I CONSIDER THIS FAVOR MORE THAN JUST *"NICE."*
WE HAD SOME...LAST-MINUTE REMODELLING ON THE CLUBHOUSE. I APPRECIATE IT, YOUR HONOR.
DON'T THINK I DON'T KNOW THE SITUATION BETWEEN YOU AND NIKOLA. HE'S NOT WRONG, KING. YOU CAN'T JUST MARCH OUT GUNS-BLAZING ANYTIME YOU DAMN WELL FEEL LIKE IT.
NO? THEN WHAT IS IT YOU HIRED ME FOR, MY ROCK-HARD ABS? YOU KNOW WHAT I DO AND HOW I DO IT. GOOD, FAST, AND CHEAP-- PICK **TWO.**
I'M NOT A HITMAN, AND I'M NOT A DAMN CRIME BOSS. TONE IT DOWN. NO MORE KILLING, JUST **REMOVE** THE FEVER.
RELAX, YOUR HIGHNESS. EVERYTHING'S UNDER CONTROL AND YOUR PEST PROBLEM WILL BE TAKEN CARE OF.
I'VE ACQUIRED SOME ***COOPERATION*** THAT WILL EXPEDITE THINGS.
I'VE GOT AN ACE IN THE HOLE TOO, KING--THE POWER OF THE PRESS. HOW WOULD YOU LIKE THE PUBLIC ON YOUR SIDE FOR ONCE?

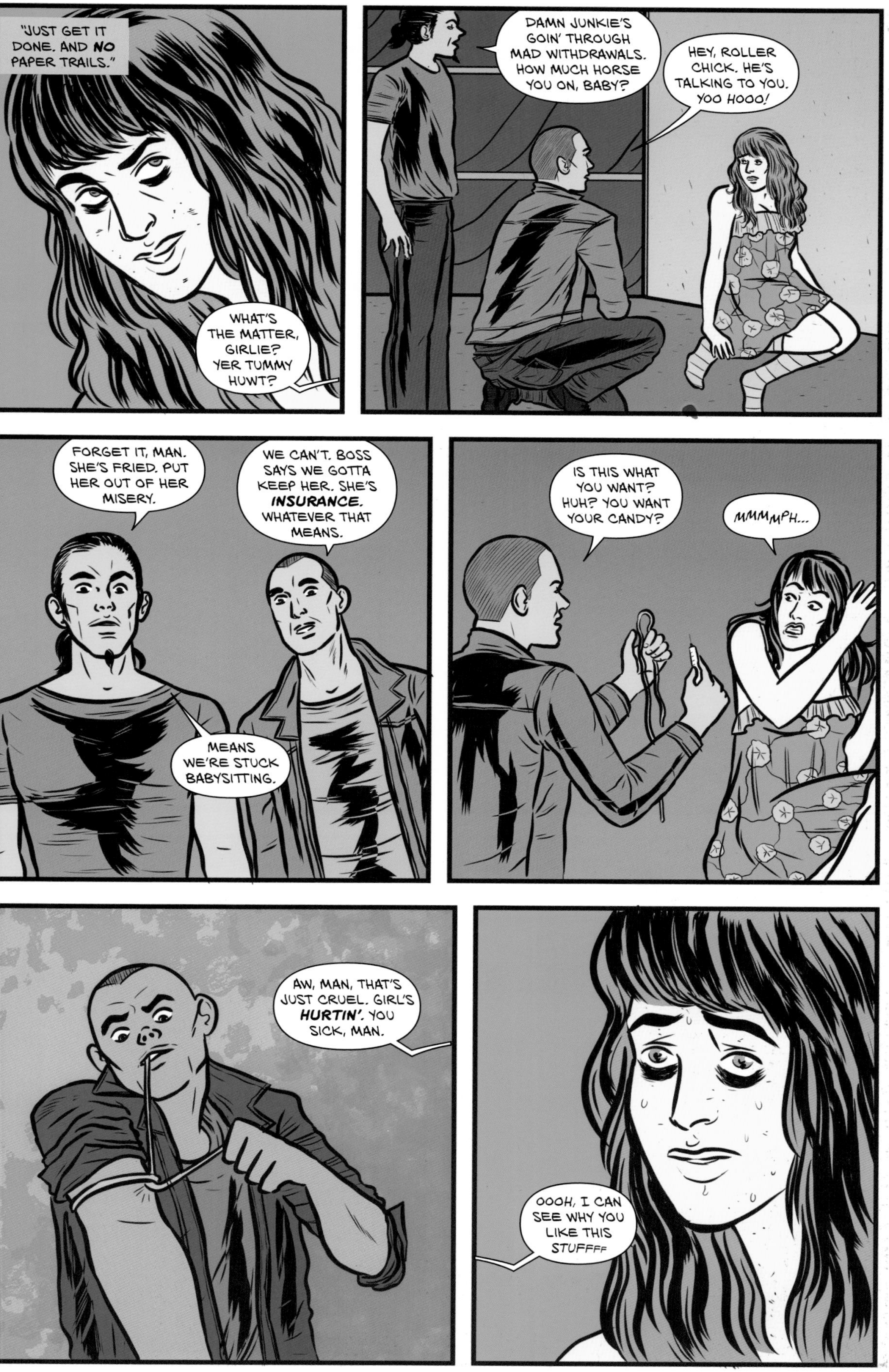
"JUST GET IT DONE. AND NO PAPER TRAILS."
WHAT'S THE MATTER, GIRLIE? YER TUMMY HUWT?
DAMN JUNKIE'S GOIN' THROUGH MAD WITHDRAWALS. HOW MUCH HORSE YOU ON, BABY?
HEY, ROLLER CHICK. HE'S TALKING TO YOU. YOO HOOO!
FORGET IT, MAN. SHE'S FRIED. PUT HER OUT OF HER MISERY.
WE CAN'T. BOSS SAYS WE GOTTA KEEP HER. SHE'S INSURANCE. WHATEVER THAT MEANS.
MEANS WE'RE STUCK BABYSITTING.
IS THIS WHAT YOU WANT? HUH? YOU WANT YOUR CANDY?
MMMMPH...
AW, MAN, THAT'S JUST CRUEL. GIRL'S HURTIN'. YOU SICK, MAN.
OOOH, I CAN SEE WHY YOU LIKE THIS STUFFFF

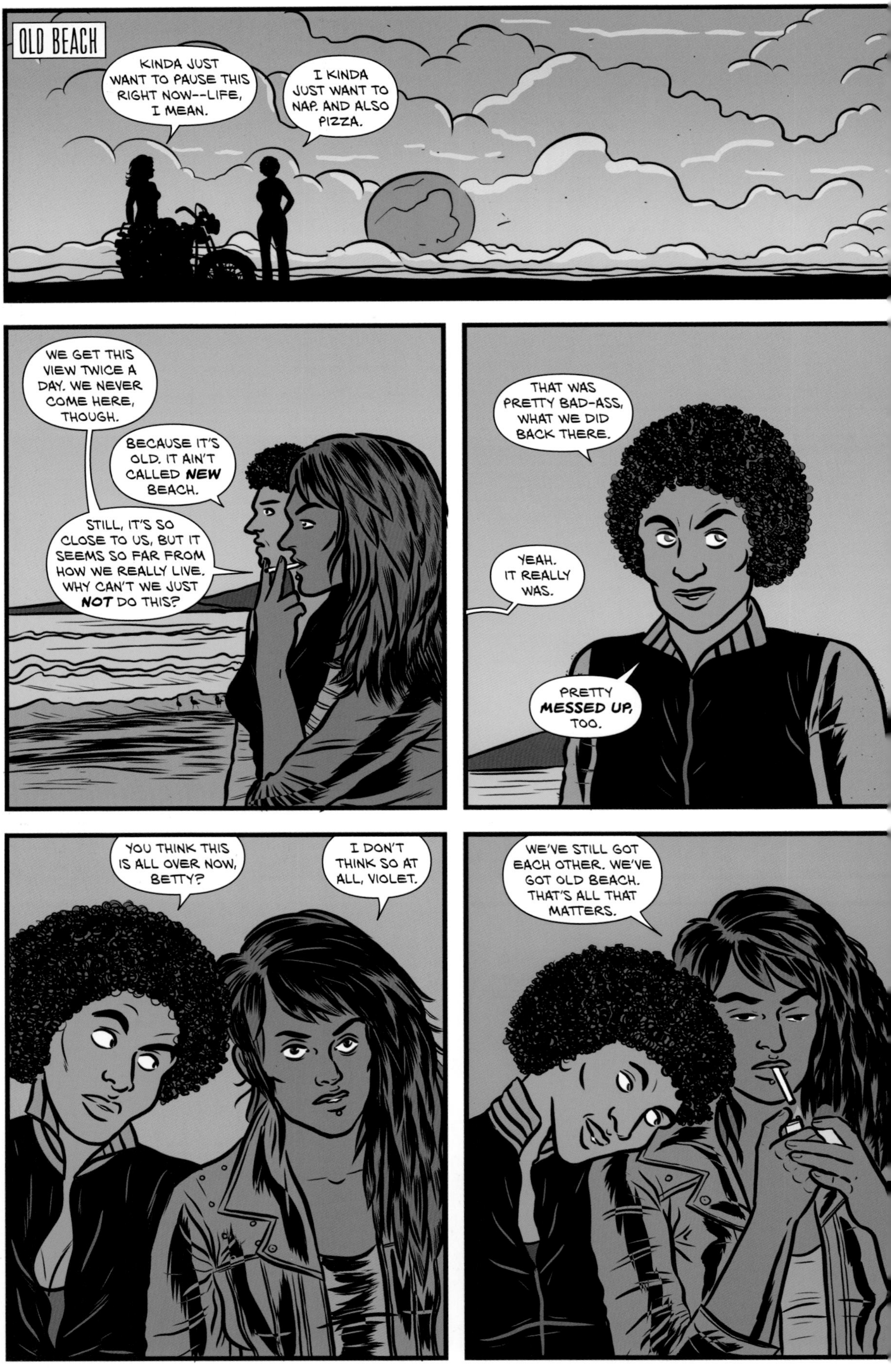
OLD BEACH
KINDA JUST WANT TO PAUSE THIS RIGHT NOW--LIFE, I MEAN.
I KINDA JUST WANT TO NAP. AND ALSO PIZZA.
WE GET THIS VIEW TWICE A DAY. WE NEVER COME HERE, THOUGH.
BECAUSE IT'S OLD. IT AIN'T CALLED NEW BEACH.
STILL, IT'S SO CLOSE TO US, BUT IT SEEMS SO FAR FROM HOW WE REALLY LIVE. WHY CAN'T WE JUST NOT DO THIS?
THAT WAS PRETTY BAD-ASS, WHAT WE DID BACK THERE.
YEAH. IT REALLY WAS.
PRETTY MESSED UP, TOO.
YOU THINK THIS IS ALL OVER NOW, BETTY?
I DON'T THINK SO AT ALL, VIOLET.
WE'VE STILL GOT EACH OTHER. WE'VE GOT OLD BEACH. THAT'S ALL THAT MATTERS.

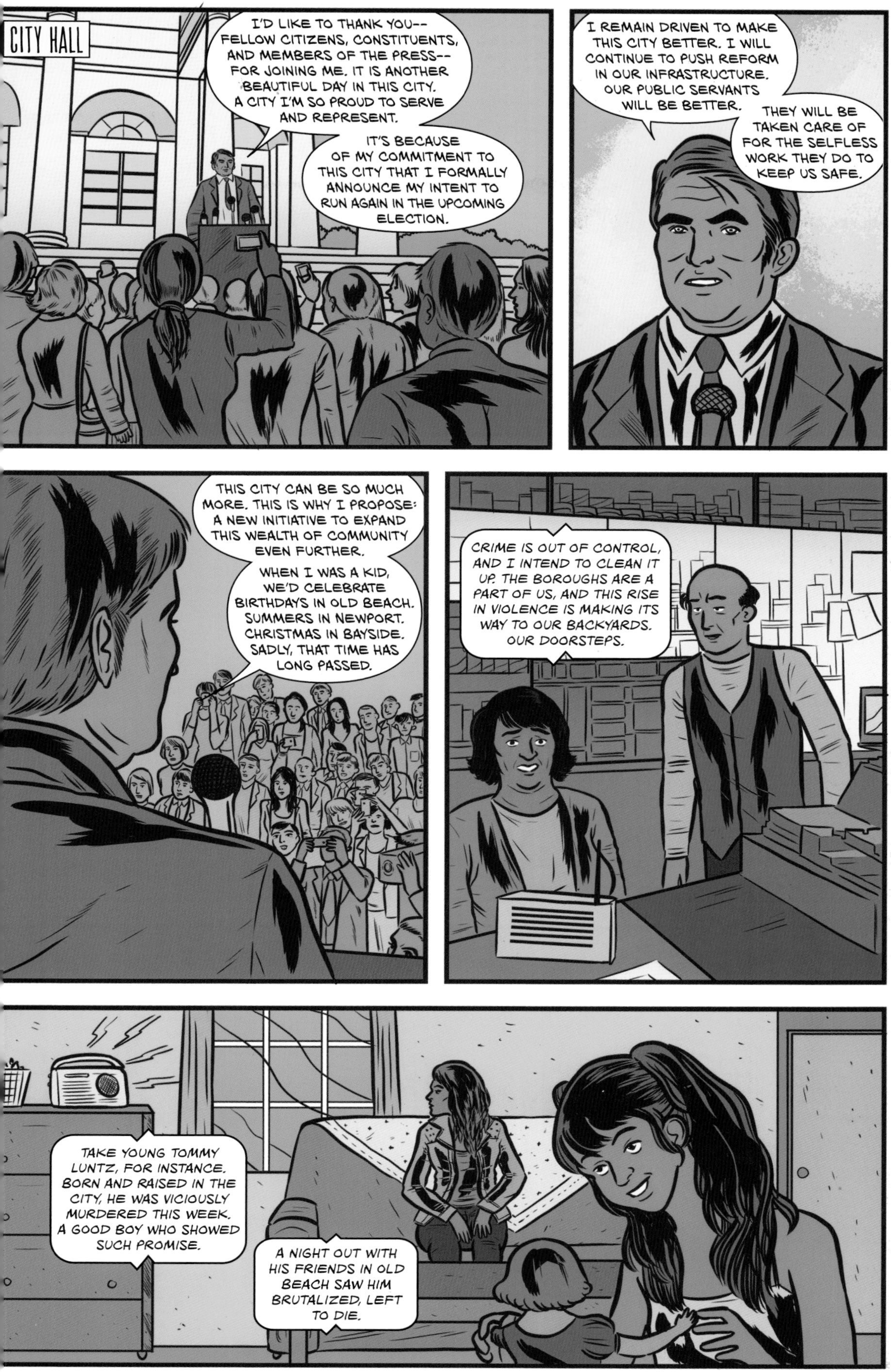
CITY HALL
I'D LIKE TO THANK YOU-- FELLOW CITIZENS, CONSTITUENTS, AND MEMBERS OF THE PRESS-- FOR JOINING ME. IT IS ANOTHER BEAUTIFUL DAY IN THIS CITY. A CITY I'M SO PROUD TO SERVE AND REPRESENT.
IT'S BECAUSE OF MY COMMITMENT TO THIS CITY THAT I FORMALLY ANNOUNCE MY INTENT TO RUN AGAIN IN THE UPCOMING ELECTION.
I REMAIN DRIVEN TO MAKE THIS CITY BETTER. I WILL CONTINUE TO PUSH REFORM IN OUR INFRASTRUCTURE. OUR PUBLIC SERVANTS WILL BE BETTER.
THEY WILL BE TAKEN CARE OF FOR THE SELFLESS WORK THEY DO TO KEEP US SAFE.
THIS CITY CAN BE SO MUCH MORE. THIS IS WHY I PROPOSE: A NEW INITIATIVE TO EXPAND THIS WEALTH OF COMMUNITY EVEN FURTHER.
WHEN I WAS A KID, WE'D CELEBRATE BIRTHDAYS IN OLD BEACH. SUMMERS IN NEWPORT. CHRISTMAS IN BAYSIDE. SADLY, THAT TIME HAS LONG PASSED.
CRIME IS OUT OF CONTROL, AND I INTEND TO CLEAN IT UP. THE BOROUGHS ARE A PART OF US, AND THIS RISE IN VIOLENCE IS MAKING ITS WAY TO OUR BACKYARDS. OUR DOORSTEPS.
TAKE YOUNG TOMMY LUNTZ, FOR INSTANCE. BORN AND RAISED IN THE CITY, HE WAS VICIOUSLY MURDERED THIS WEEK. A GOOD BOY WHO SHOWED SUCH PROMISE.
A NIGHT OUT WITH HIS FRIENDS IN OLD BEACH SAW HIM BRUTALIZED, LEFT TO DIE.

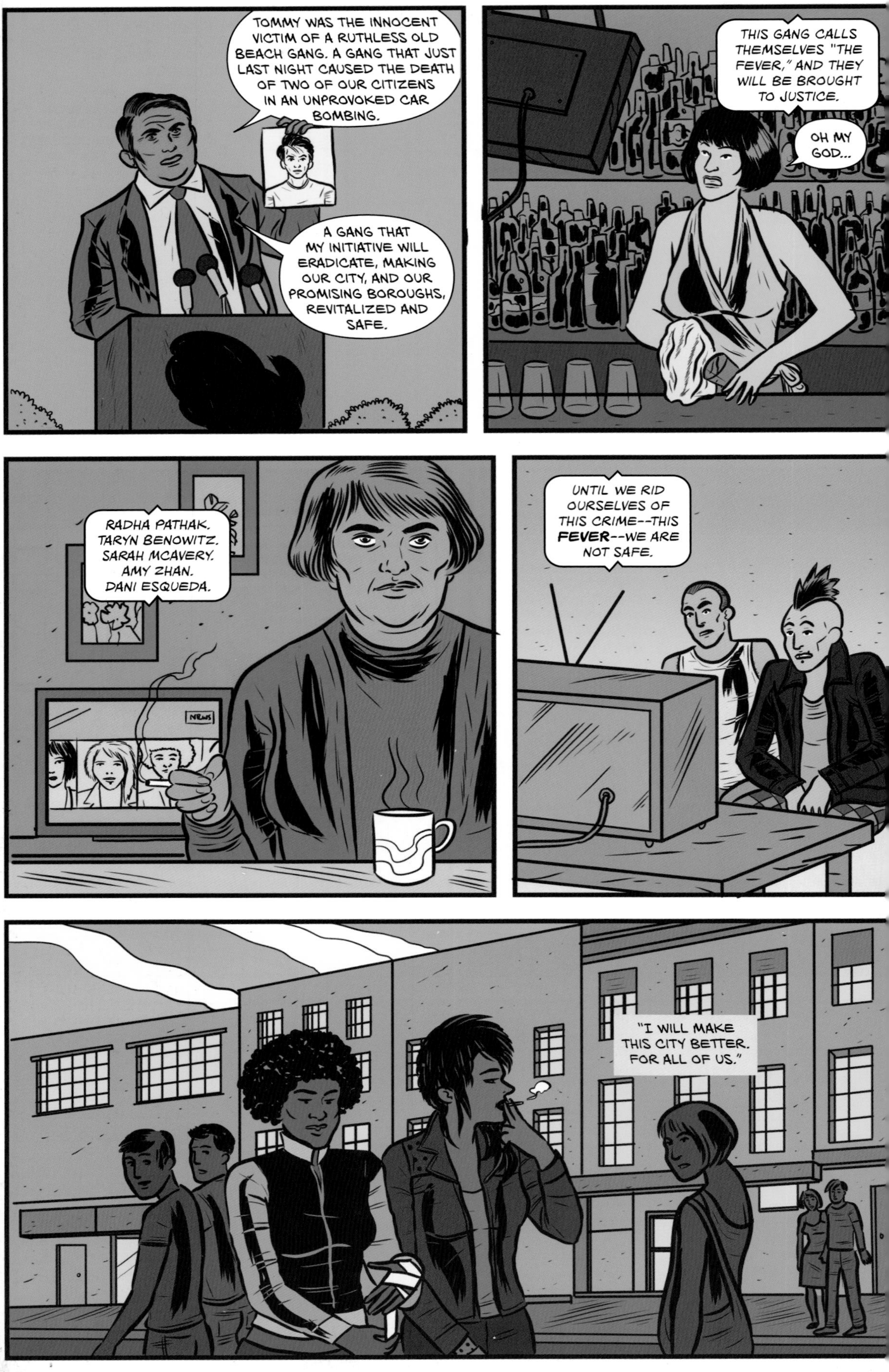
TOMMY WAS THE INNOCENT VICTIM OF A RUTHLESS OLD BEACH GANG. A GANG THAT JUST LAST NIGHT CAUSED THE DEATH OF TWO OF OUR CITIZENS IN AN UNPROVOKED CAR BOMBING.
A GANG THAT MY INITIATIVE WILL ERADICATE, MAKING OUR CITY, AND OUR PROMISING BOROUGHS, REVITALIZED AND SAFE.
THIS GANG CALLS THEMSELVES "THE FEVER," AND THEY WILL BE BROUGHT TO JUSTICE.
OH MY GOD...
RADHA PATHAK. TARYN BENOWITZ. SARAH MCAVERY. AMY ZHAN. DANI ESQUEDA.
NEWS
UNTIL WE RID OURSELVES OF THIS CRIME--THIS **FEVER**--WE ARE NOT SAFE.
"I WILL MAKE THIS CITY BETTER. FOR ALL OF US."

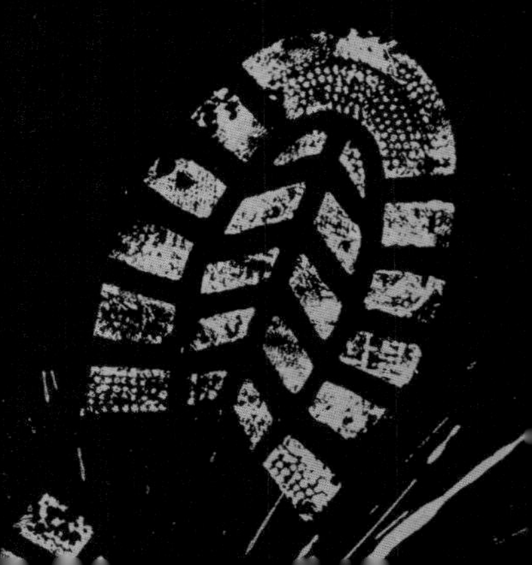

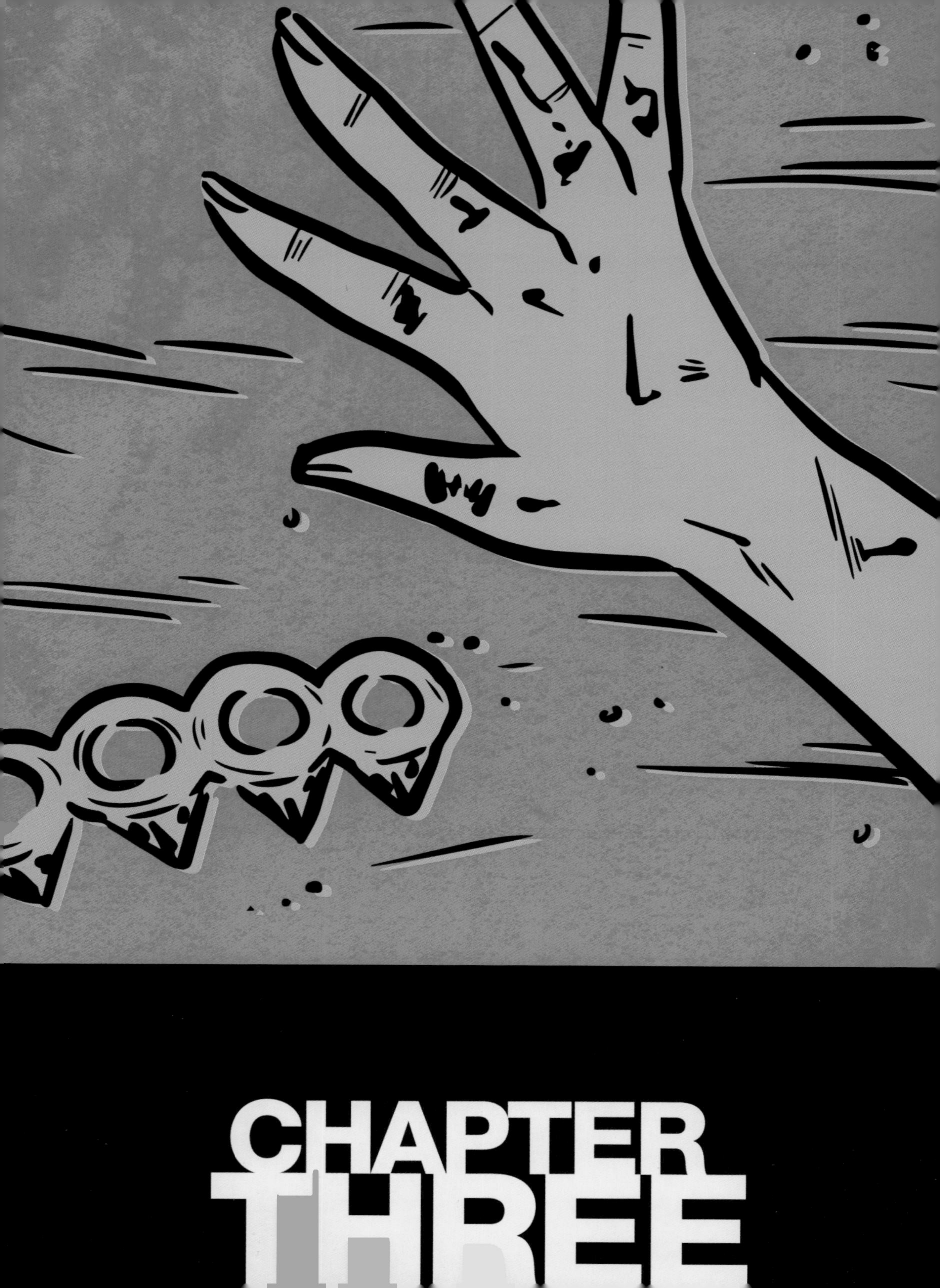

CHAPTER THREE

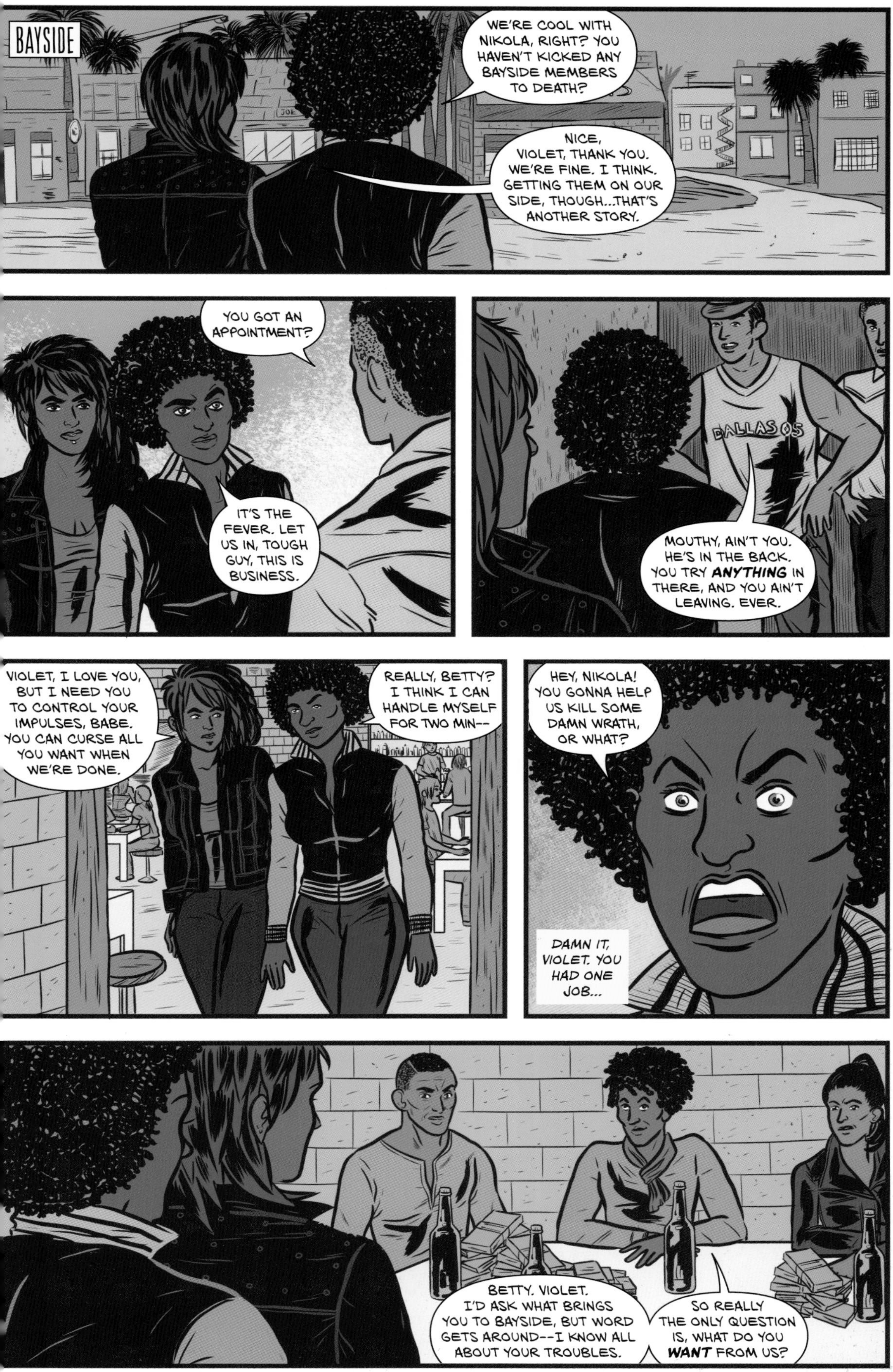
BAYSIDE
WE'RE COOL WITH NIKOLA, RIGHT? YOU HAVEN'T KICKED ANY BAYSIDE MEMBERS TO DEATH?
NICE, VIOLET, THANK YOU. WE'RE FINE. I THINK. GETTING THEM ON OUR SIDE, THOUGH...THAT'S ANOTHER STORY.
YOU GOT AN APPOINTMENT?
IT'S THE FEVER. LET US IN, TOUGH GUY, THIS IS BUSINESS.
MOUTHY, AIN'T YOU. HE'S IN THE BACK. YOU TRY **ANYTHING** IN THERE, AND YOU AIN'T LEAVING. EVER.
VIOLET, I LOVE YOU, BUT I NEED YOU TO CONTROL YOUR IMPULSES, BABE. YOU CAN CURSE ALL YOU WANT WHEN WE'RE DONE.
REALLY, BETTY? I THINK I CAN HANDLE MYSELF FOR TWO MIN--
HEY, NIKOLA! YOU GONNA HELP US KILL SOME DAMN WRATH, OR WHAT?
DAMN IT, VIOLET. YOU HAD ONE JOB...
BETTY. VIOLET. I'D ASK WHAT BRINGS YOU TO BAYSIDE, BUT WORD GETS AROUND--I KNOW ALL ABOUT YOUR TROUBLES.
SO REALLY THE ONLY QUESTION IS, WHAT DO YOU ***WANT*** FROM US?

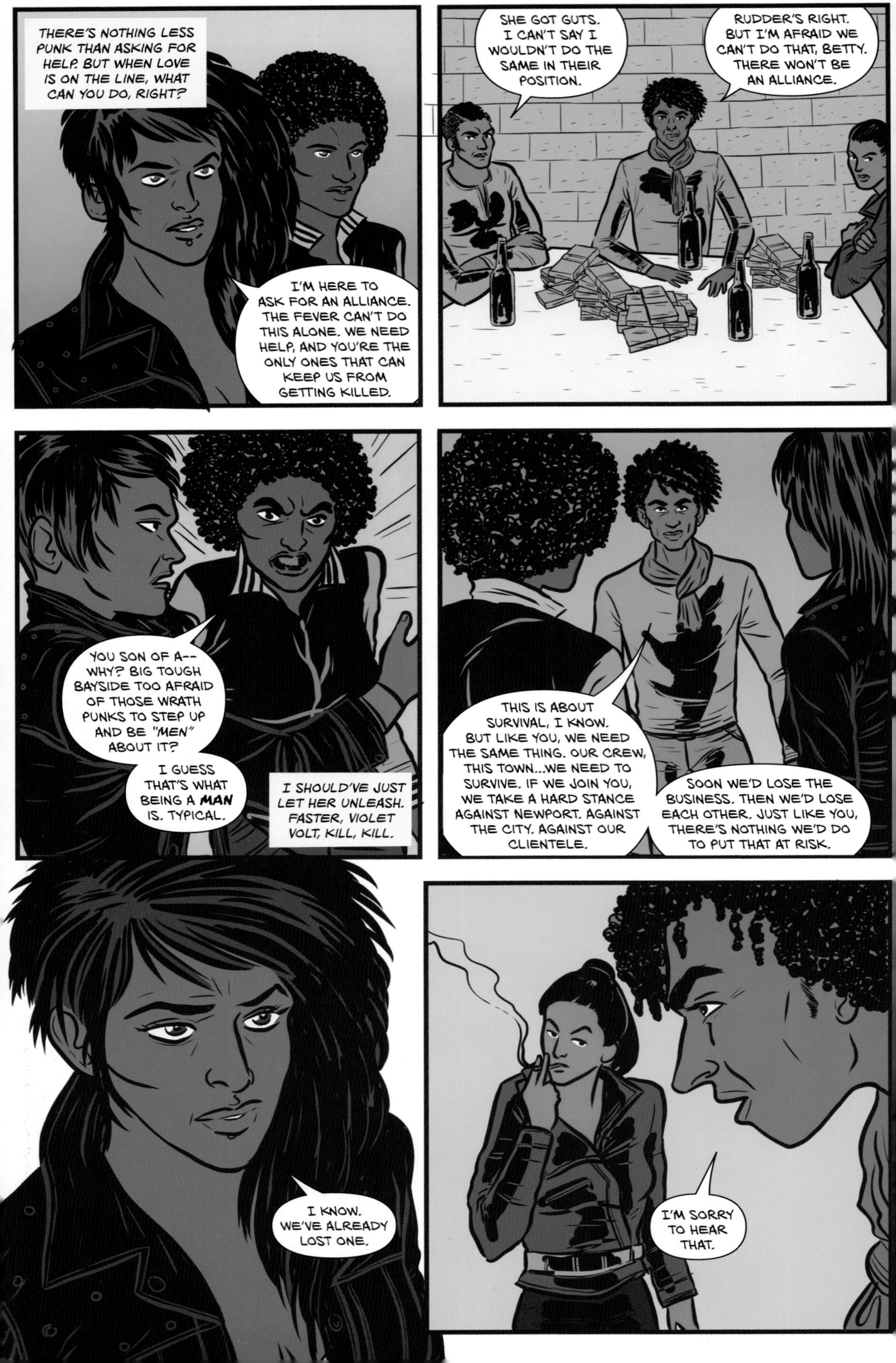
THERE'S NOTHING LESS PUNK THAN ASKING FOR HELP. BUT WHEN LOVE IS ON THE LINE, WHAT CAN YOU DO, RIGHT?
I'M HERE TO ASK FOR AN ALLIANCE. THE FEVER CAN'T DO THIS ALONE. WE NEED HELP, AND YOU'RE THE ONLY ONES THAT CAN KEEP US FROM GETTING KILLED.
SHE GOT GUTS. I CAN'T SAY I WOULDN'T DO THE SAME IN THEIR POSITION.
RUDDER'S RIGHT. BUT I'M AFRAID WE CAN'T DO THAT, BETTY. THERE WON'T BE AN ALLIANCE.
YOU SON OF A-- WHY? BIG TOUGH BAYSIDE TOO AFRAID OF THOSE WRATH PUNKS TO STEP UP AND BE "MEN" ABOUT IT?
I GUESS THAT'S WHAT BEING A **MAN** IS. TYPICAL.
I SHOULD'VE JUST LET HER UNLEASH. FASTER, VIOLET VOLT, KILL, KILL.
THIS IS ABOUT SURVIVAL, I KNOW. BUT LIKE YOU, WE NEED THE SAME THING. OUR CREW, THIS TOWN...WE NEED TO SURVIVE. IF WE JOIN YOU, WE TAKE A HARD STANCE AGAINST NEWPORT. AGAINST THE CITY. AGAINST OUR CLIENTELE.
SOON WE'D LOSE THE BUSINESS. THEN WE'D LOSE EACH OTHER. JUST LIKE YOU, THERE'S NOTHING WE'D DO TO PUT THAT AT RISK.
I KNOW. WE'VE ALREADY LOST ONE.
I'M SORRY TO HEAR THAT.

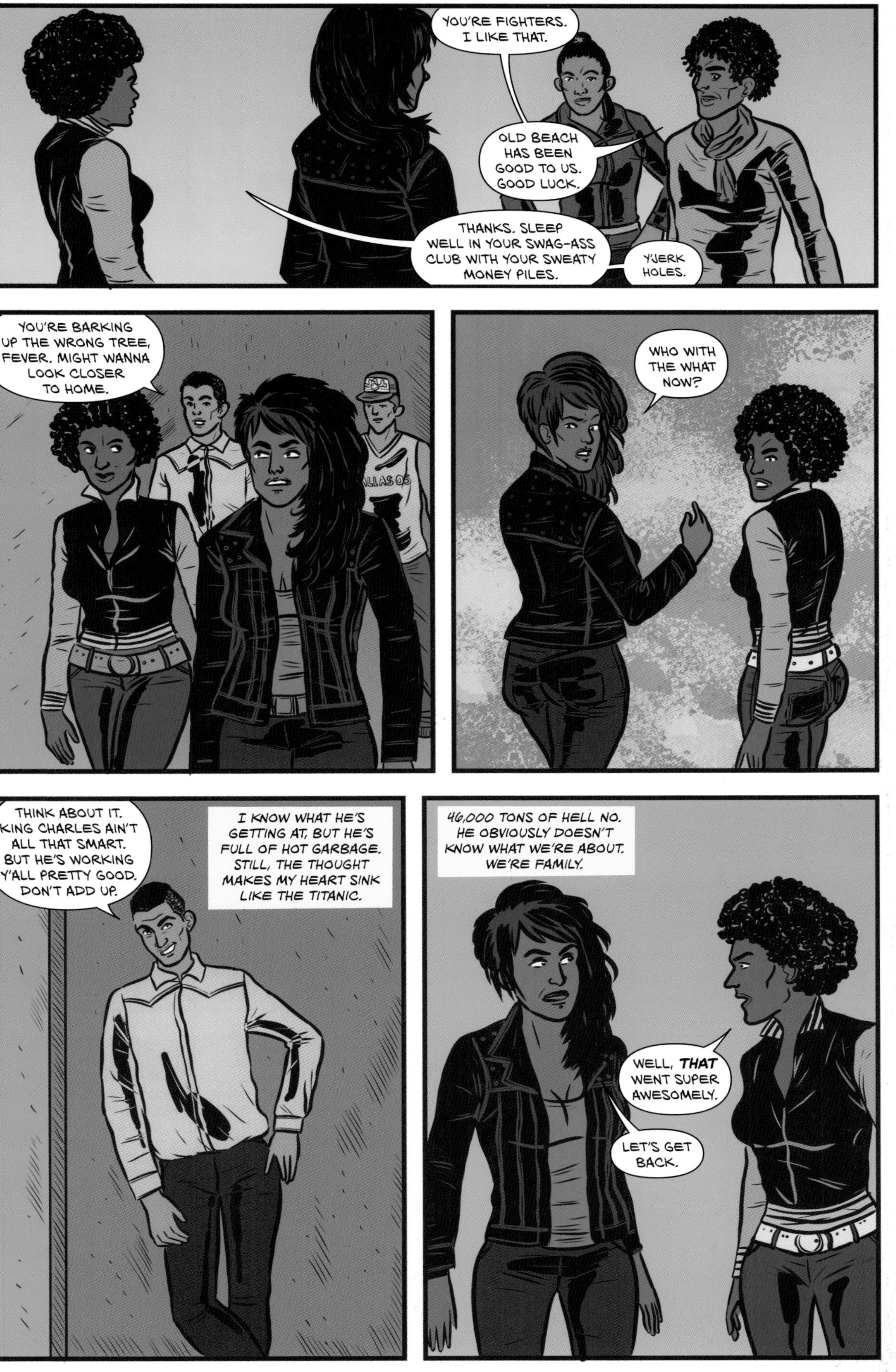
YOU'RE FIGHTERS. I LIKE THAT.
OLD BEACH HAS BEEN GOOD TO US. GOOD LUCK.
THANKS. SLEEP WELL IN YOUR SWAG-ASS CLUB WITH YOUR SWEATY MONEY PILES.
Y'JERK HOLES.
YOU'RE BARKING UP THE WRONG TREE, FEVER. MIGHT WANNA LOOK CLOSER TO HOME.
WHO WITH THE WHAT NOW?
THINK ABOUT IT. KING CHARLES AIN'T ALL THAT SMART. BUT HE'S WORKING Y'ALL PRETTY GOOD. DON'T ADD UP.
I KNOW WHAT HE'S GETTING AT, BUT HE'S FULL OF HOT GARBAGE. STILL, THE THOUGHT MAKES MY HEART SINK LIKE THE TITANIC.
46,000 TONS OF HELL NO. HE OBVIOUSLY DOESN'T KNOW WHAT WE'RE ABOUT. WE'RE FAMILY.
WELL, **THAT** WENT SUPER AWESOMELY.
LET'S GET BACK.

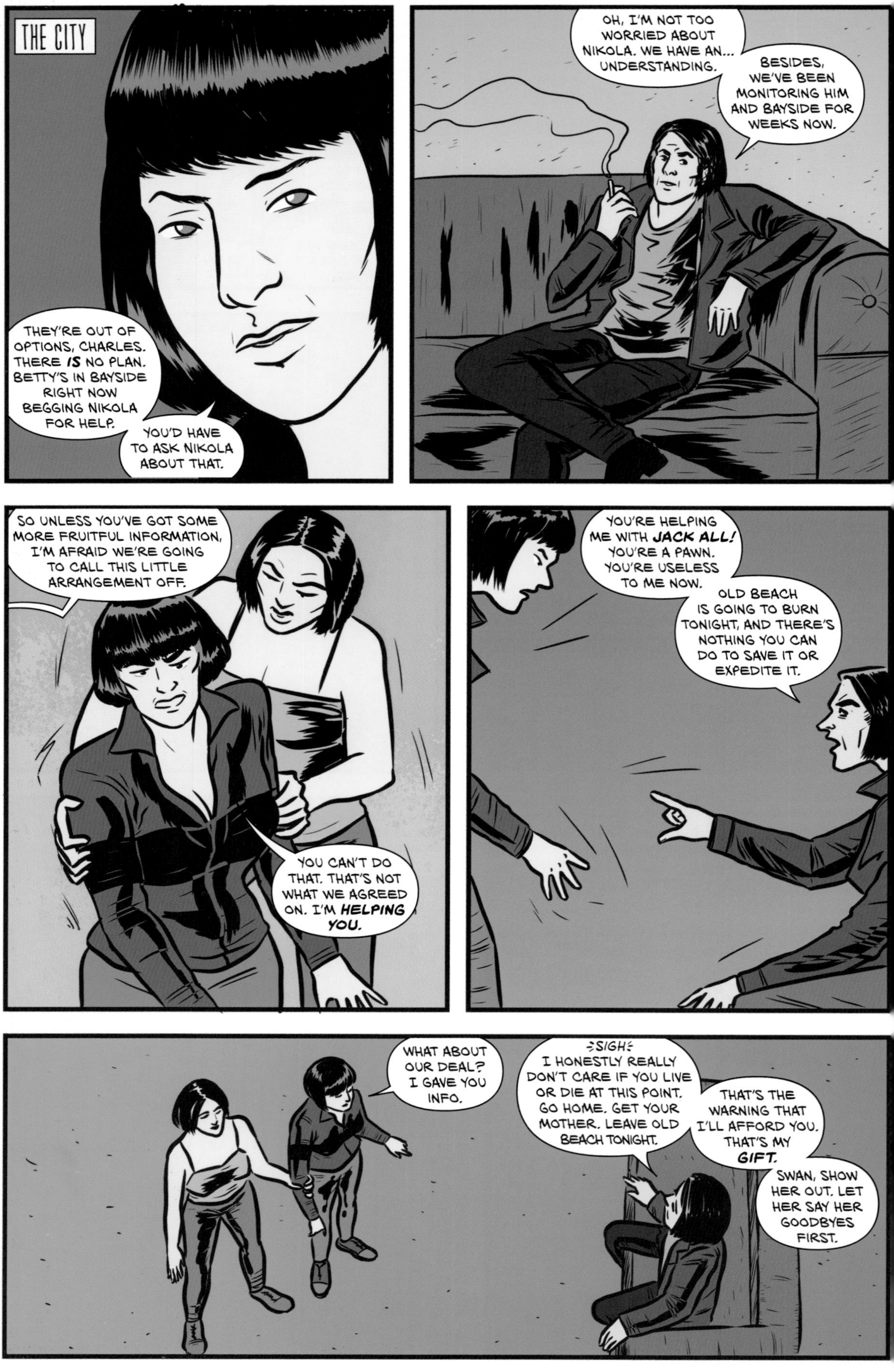
THE CITY
THEY'RE OUT OF OPTIONS, CHARLES. THERE IS NO PLAN. BETTY'S IN BAYSIDE RIGHT NOW BEGGING NIKOLA FOR HELP.
YOU'D HAVE TO ASK NIKOLA ABOUT THAT.
OH, I'M NOT TOO WORRIED ABOUT NIKOLA. WE HAVE AN... UNDERSTANDING.
BESIDES, WE'VE BEEN MONITORING HIM AND BAYSIDE FOR WEEKS NOW.
SO UNLESS YOU'VE GOT SOME MORE FRUITFUL INFORMATION, I'M AFRAID WE'RE GOING TO CALL THIS LITTLE ARRANGEMENT OFF.
YOU CAN'T DO THAT. THAT'S NOT WHAT WE AGREED ON. I'M HELPING YOU.
YOU'RE HELPING ME WITH JACK ALL! YOU'RE A PAWN. YOU'RE USELESS TO ME NOW.
OLD BEACH IS GOING TO BURN TONIGHT, AND THERE'S NOTHING YOU CAN DO TO SAVE IT OR EXPEDITE IT.
WHAT ABOUT OUR DEAL? I GAVE YOU INFO.
SIGH
I HONESTLY REALLY DON'T CARE IF YOU LIVE OR DIE AT THIS POINT. GO HOME. GET YOUR MOTHER. LEAVE OLD BEACH TONIGHT.
THAT'S THE WARNING THAT I'LL AFFORD YOU. THAT'S MY GIFT.
SWAN, SHOW HER OUT. LET HER SAY HER GOODBYES FIRST.

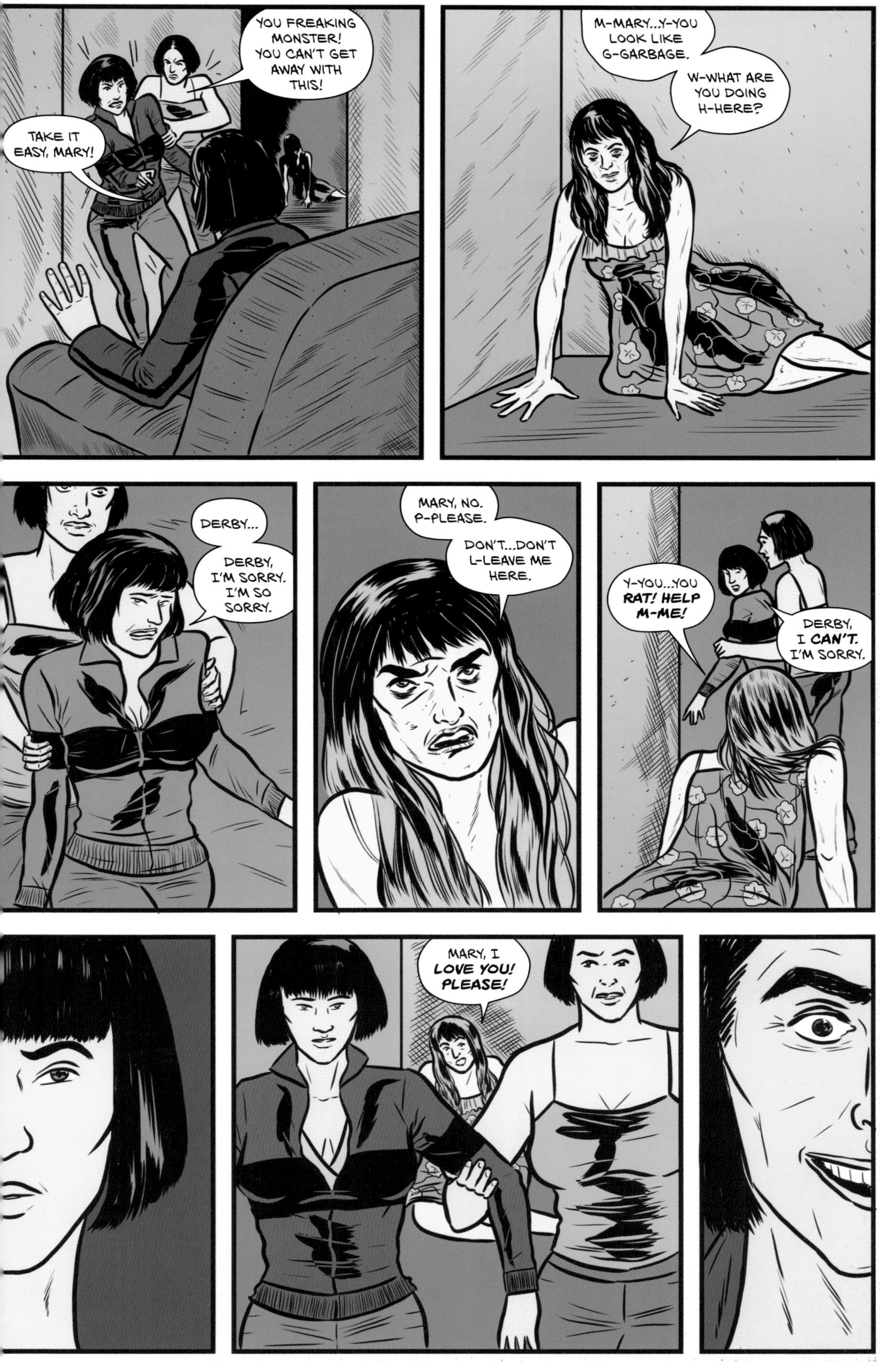
YOU FREAKING MONSTER! YOU CAN'T GET AWAY WITH THIS!
TAKE IT EASY, MARY!
M-MARY...Y-YOU LOOK LIKE G-GARBAGE.
W-WHAT ARE YOU DOING H-HERE?
DERBY...
DERBY, I'M SORRY. I'M SO SORRY.
MARY, NO. P-PLEASE.
DON'T...DON'T L-LEAVE ME HERE.
Y-YOU...YOU RAT! HELP M-ME!
DERBY, I CAN'T. I'M SORRY.
MARY, I LOVE YOU! PLEASE!

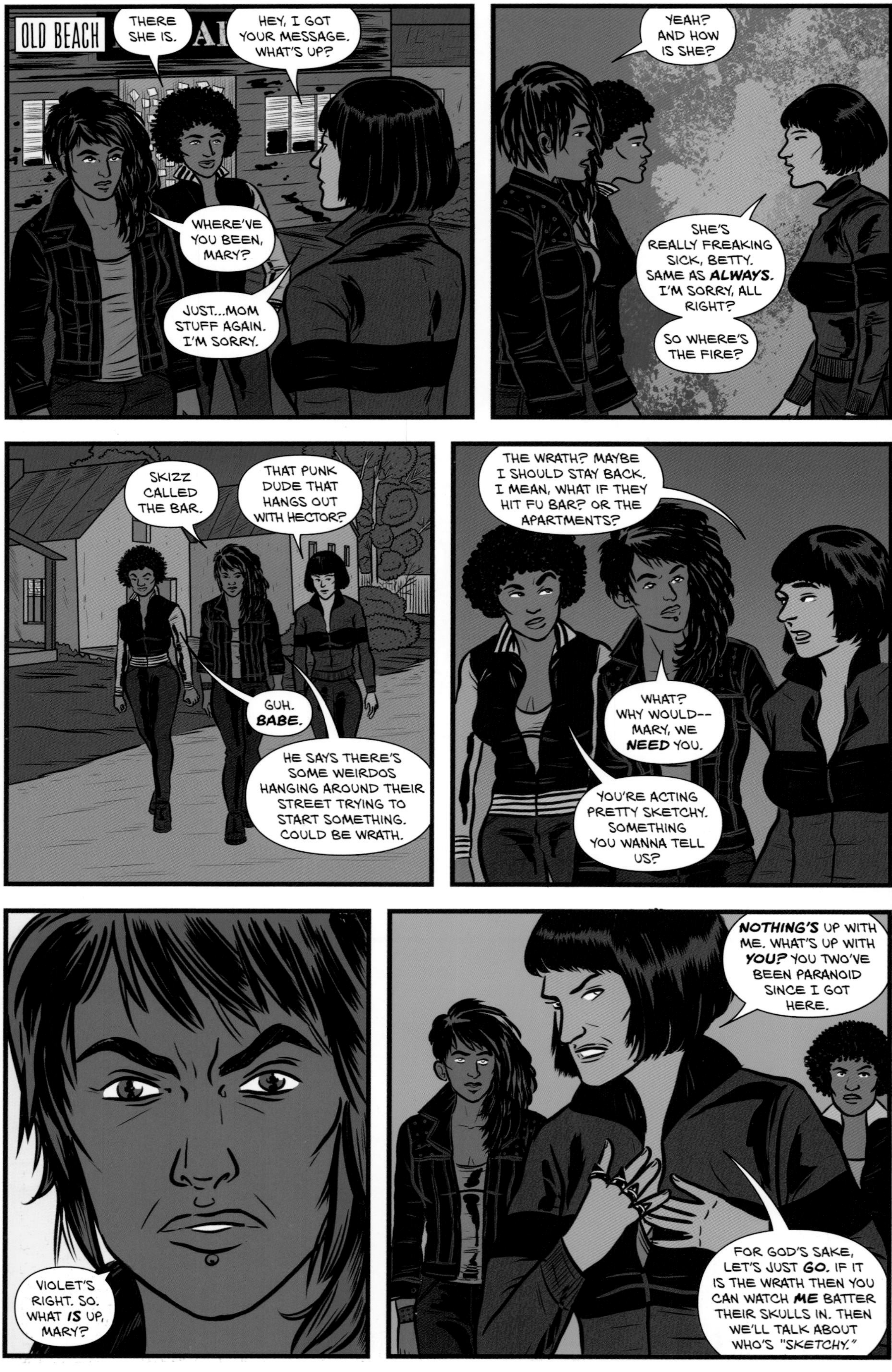
OLD BEACH
THERE SHE IS.
HEY, I GOT YOUR MESSAGE. WHAT'S UP?
WHERE'VE YOU BEEN, MARY?
JUST...MOM STUFF AGAIN. I'M SORRY.
YEAH? AND HOW IS SHE?
SHE'S REALLY FREAKING SICK, BETTY. SAME AS **ALWAYS.** I'M SORRY, ALL RIGHT?
SO WHERE'S THE FIRE?
SKIZZ CALLED THE BAR.
THAT PUNK DUDE THAT HANGS OUT WITH HECTOR?
GUH. ***BABE.***
HE SAYS THERE'S SOME WEIRDOS HANGING AROUND THEIR STREET TRYING TO START SOMETHING. COULD BE WRATH.
THE WRATH? MAYBE I SHOULD STAY BACK. I MEAN, WHAT IF THEY HIT FU BAR? OR THE APARTMENTS?
WHAT? WHY WOULD-- MARY, WE **NEED** YOU.
YOU'RE ACTING PRETTY SKETCHY. SOMETHING YOU WANNA TELL US?
VIOLET'S RIGHT. SO. WHAT ***IS*** UP, MARY?
NOTHING'S UP WITH ME. WHAT'S UP WITH ***YOU?*** YOU TWO'VE BEEN PARANOID SINCE I GOT HERE.
FOR GOD'S SAKE, LET'S JUST ***GO.*** IF IT IS THE WRATH THEN YOU CAN WATCH ***ME*** BATTER THEIR SKULLS IN. THEN WE'LL TALK ABOUT WHO'S *"SKETCHY."*

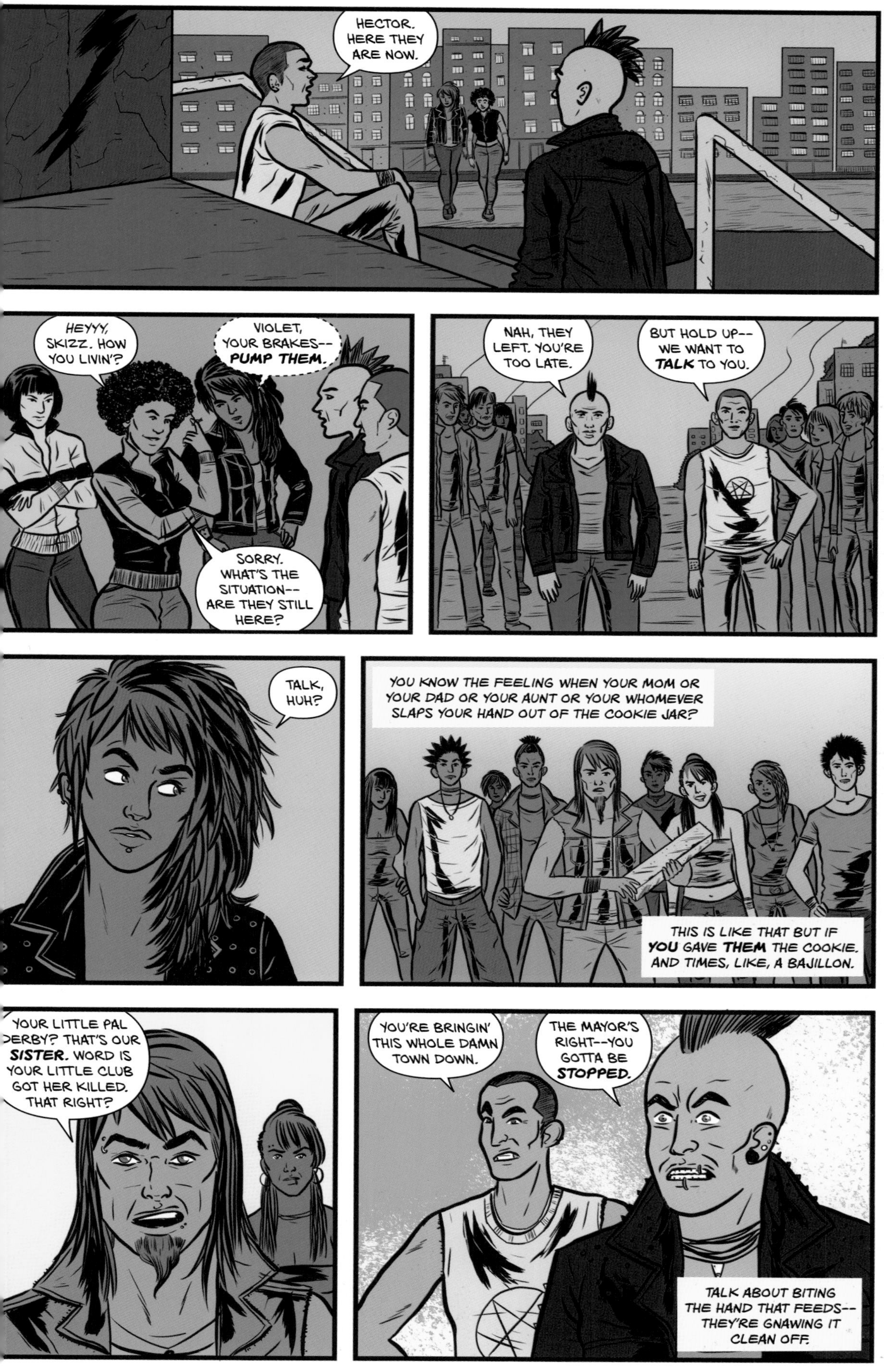
HECTOR. HERE THEY ARE NOW.
HEYYY, SKIZZ. HOW YOU LIVIN'?
VIOLET, YOUR BRAKES-- PUMP THEM.
SORRY. WHAT'S THE SITUATION-- ARE THEY STILL HERE?
NAH, THEY LEFT. YOU'RE TOO LATE.
BUT HOLD UP-- WE WANT TO TALK TO YOU.
TALK, HUH?
YOU KNOW THE FEELING WHEN YOUR MOM OR YOUR DAD OR YOUR AUNT OR YOUR WHOMEVER SLAPS YOUR HAND OUT OF THE COOKIE JAR?
THIS IS LIKE THAT BUT IF YOU GAVE THEM THE COOKIE. AND TIMES, LIKE, A BAJILLON.
YOUR LITTLE PAL DERBY? THAT'S OUR SISTER. WORD IS YOUR LITTLE CLUB GOT HER KILLED. THAT RIGHT?
YOU'RE BRINGIN' THIS WHOLE DAMN TOWN DOWN.
THE MAYOR'S RIGHT--YOU GOTTA BE STOPPED.
TALK ABOUT BITING THE HAND THAT FEEDS-- THEY'RE GNAWING IT CLEAN OFF.

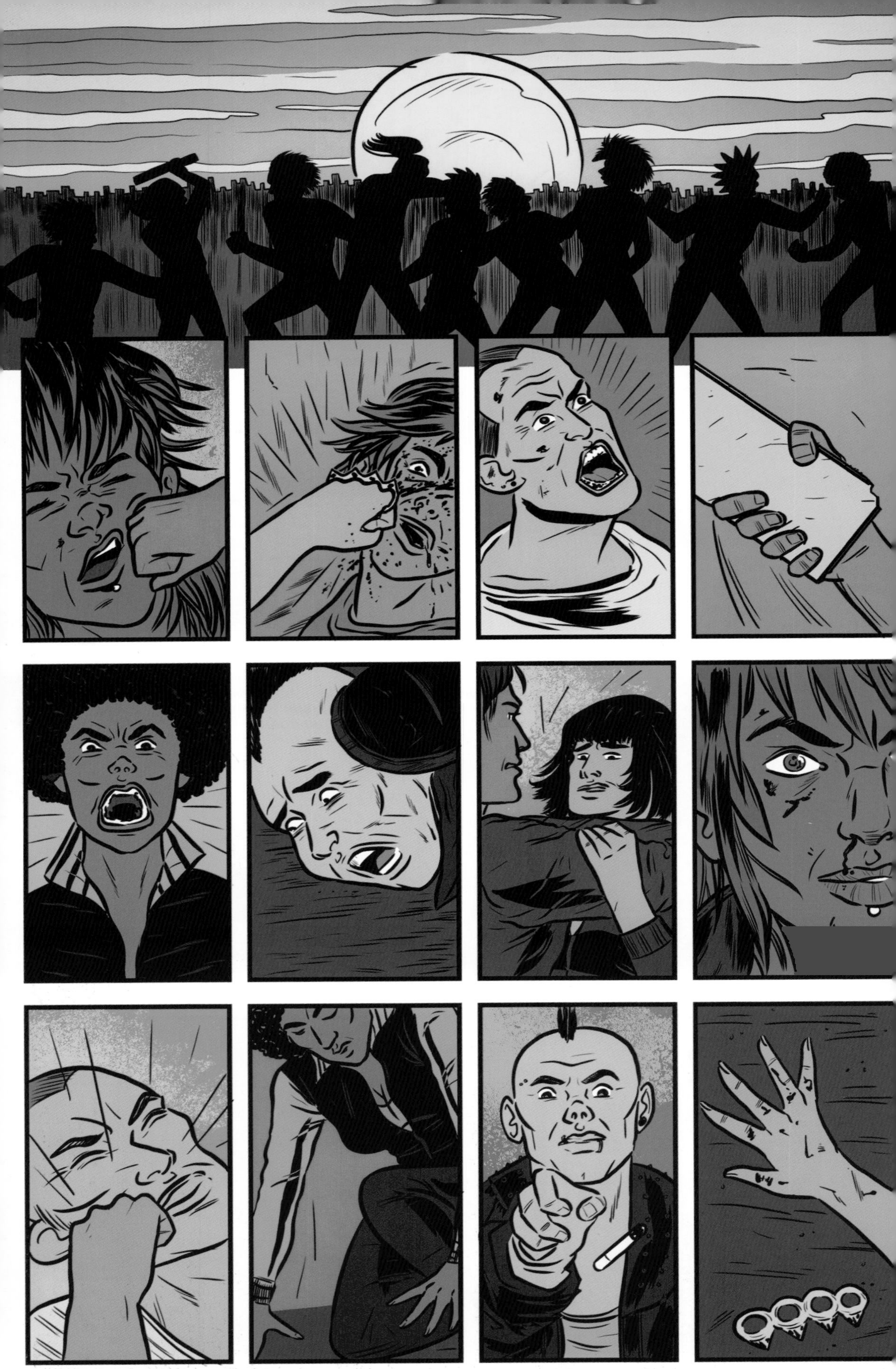

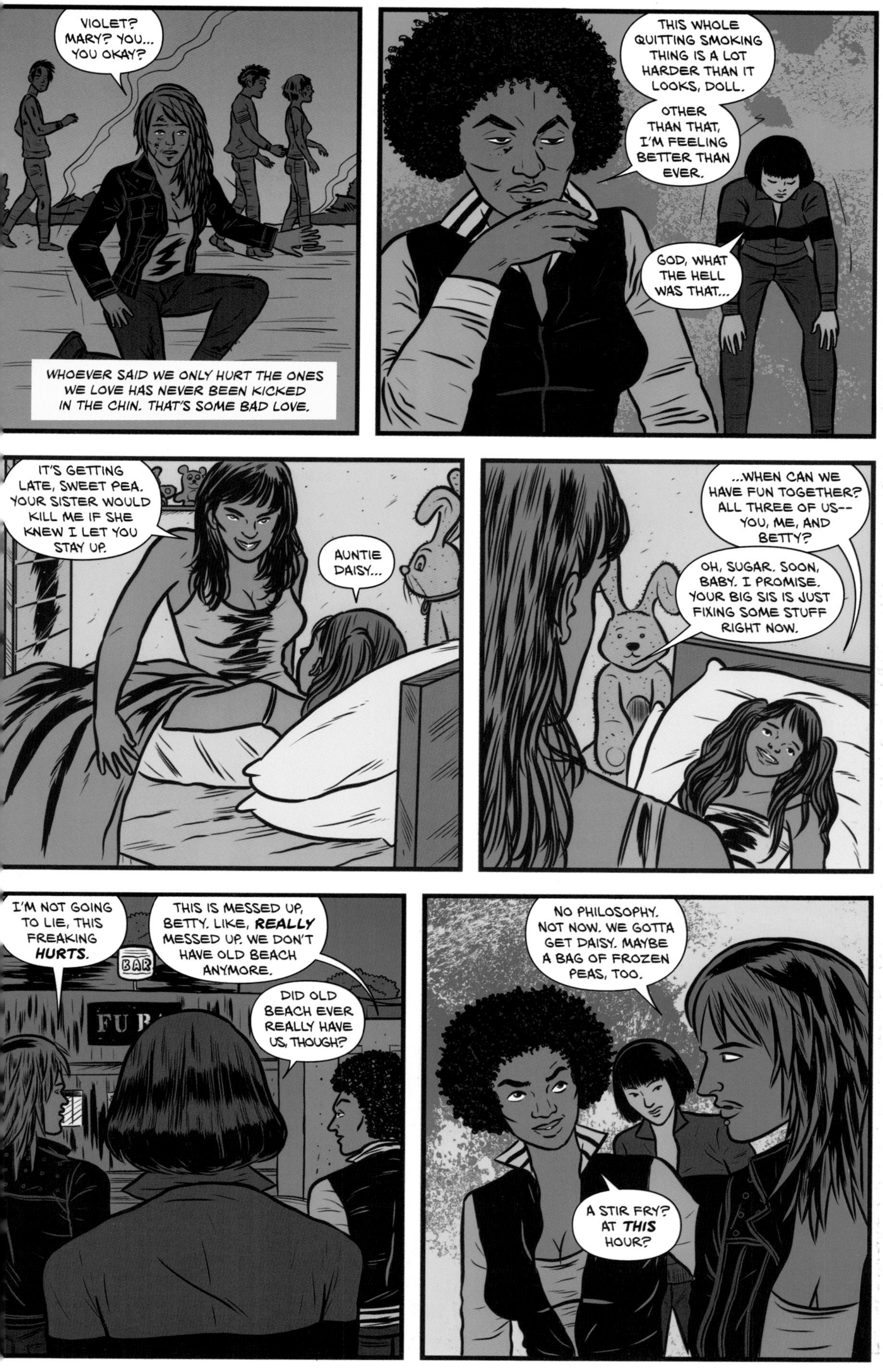

VIOLET? MARY? YOU... YOU OKAY?
WHOEVER SAID WE ONLY HURT THE ONES WE LOVE HAS NEVER BEEN KICKED IN THE CHIN. THAT'S SOME BAD LOVE.
THIS WHOLE QUITTING SMOKING THING IS A LOT HARDER THAN IT LOOKS, DOLL.
OTHER THAN THAT, I'M FEELING BETTER THAN EVER.
GOD, WHAT THE HELL WAS THAT...
IT'S GETTING LATE, SWEET PEA. YOUR SISTER WOULD KILL ME IF SHE KNEW I LET YOU STAY UP.
AUNTIE DAISY...
...WHEN CAN WE HAVE FUN TOGETHER? ALL THREE OF US-- YOU, ME, AND BETTY?
OH, SUGAR. SOON, BABY. I PROMISE. YOUR BIG SIS IS JUST FIXING SOME STUFF RIGHT NOW.
I'M NOT GOING TO LIE, THIS FREAKING **HURTS**.
THIS IS MESSED UP, BETTY. LIKE, **REALLY** MESSED UP. WE DON'T HAVE OLD BEACH ANYMORE.
BAR
DID OLD BEACH EVER REALLY HAVE US, THOUGH?
NO PHILOSOPHY. NOT NOW. WE GOTTA GET DAISY. MAYBE A BAG OF FROZEN PEAS, TOO.
A STIR FRY? AT **THIS** HOUR?

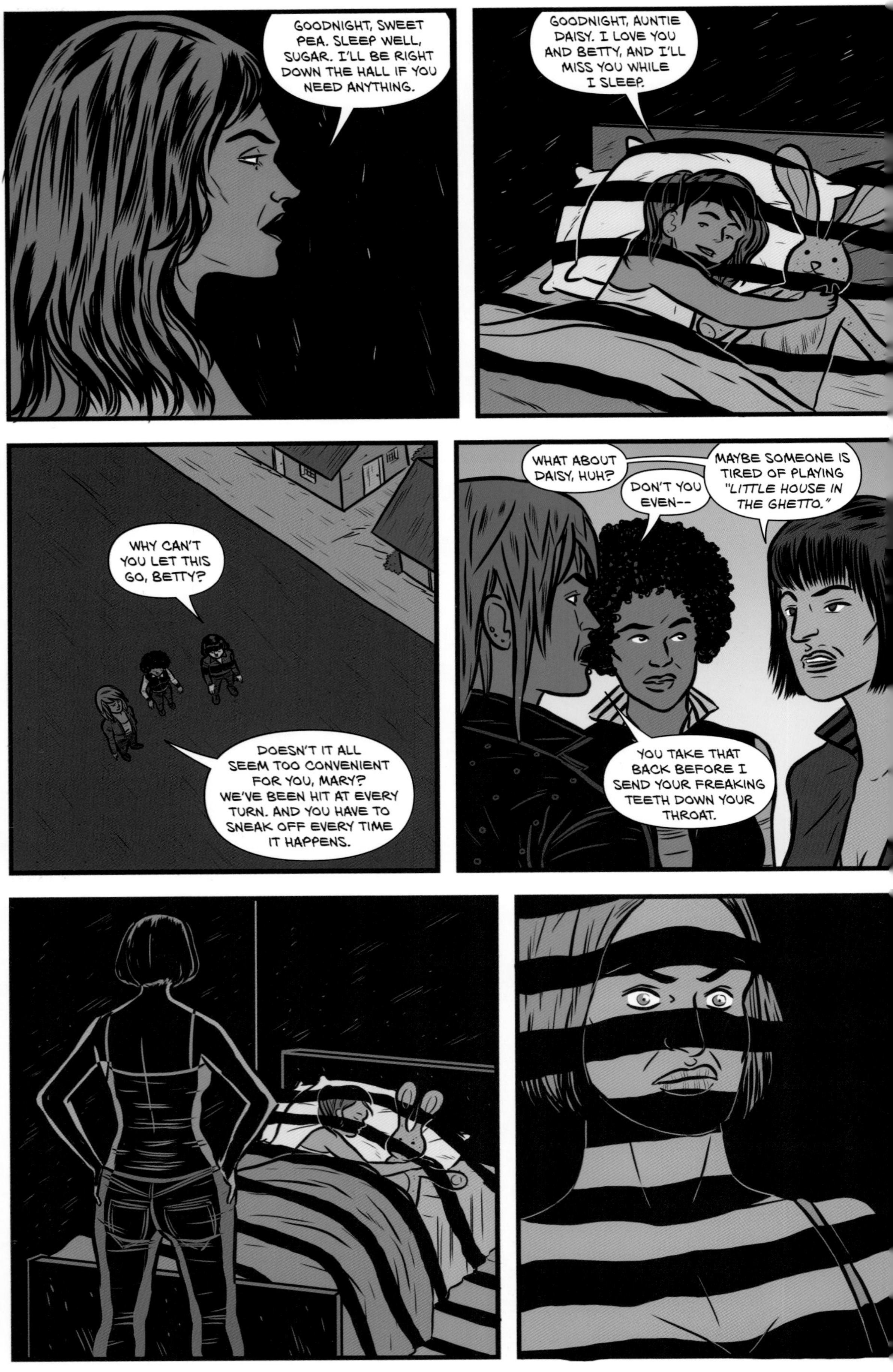
GOODNIGHT, SWEET PEA. SLEEP WELL, SUGAR. I'LL BE RIGHT DOWN THE HALL IF YOU NEED ANYTHING.
GOODNIGHT, AUNTIE DAISY. I LOVE YOU AND BETTY, AND I'LL MISS YOU WHILE I SLEEP.
WHY CAN'T YOU LET THIS GO, BETTY?
DOESN'T IT ALL SEEM TOO CONVENIENT FOR YOU, MARY? WE'VE BEEN HIT AT EVERY TURN. AND YOU HAVE TO SNEAK OFF EVERY TIME IT HAPPENS.
WHAT ABOUT DAISY, HUH?
MAYBE SOMEONE IS TIRED OF PLAYING "LITTLE HOUSE IN THE GHETTO."
DON'T YOU EVEN--
YOU TAKE THAT BACK BEFORE I SEND YOUR FREAKING TEETH DOWN YOUR THROAT.

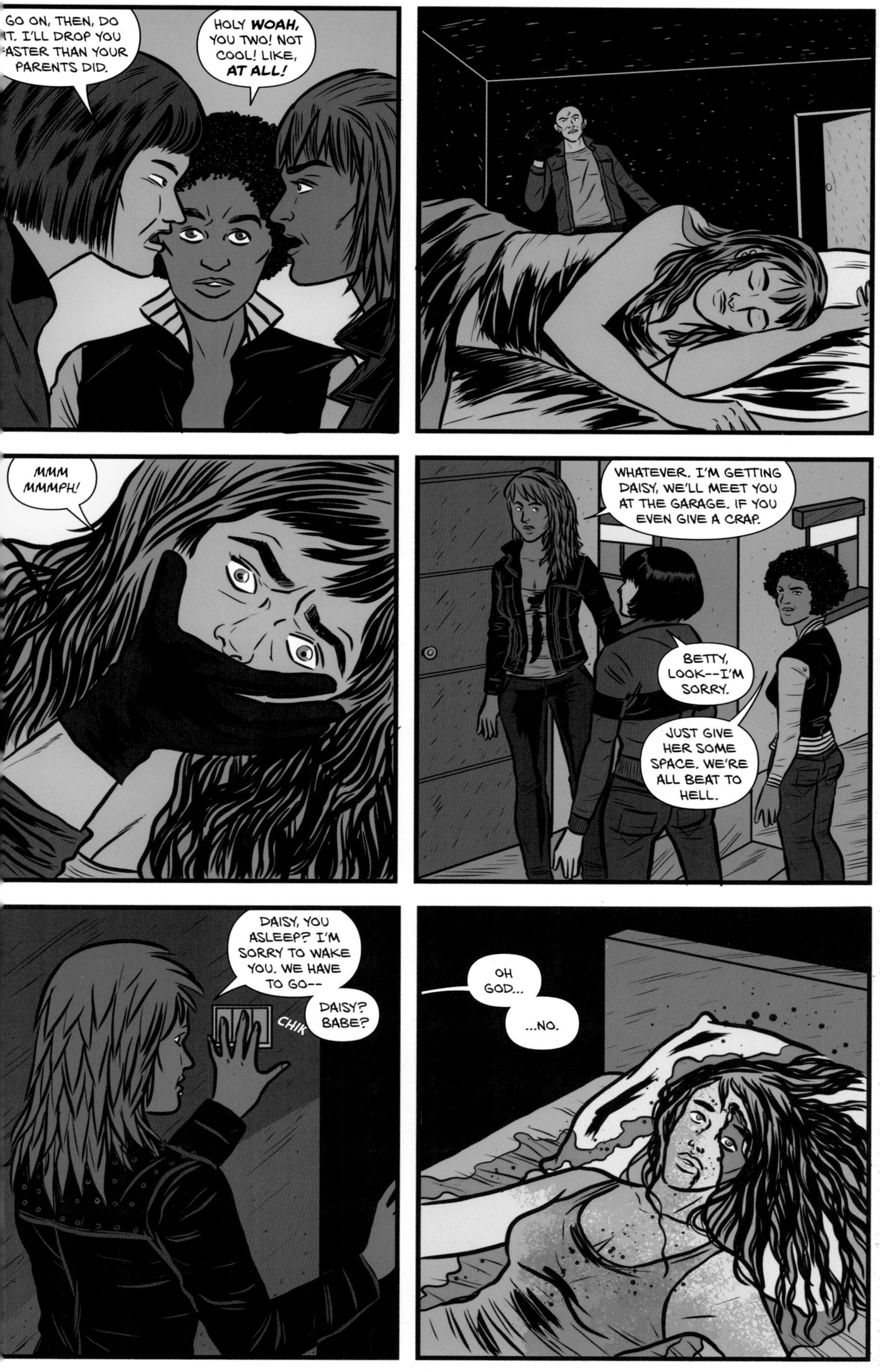
GO ON, THEN, DO IT. I'LL DROP YOU FASTER THAN YOUR PARENTS DID.
HOLY WOAH, YOU TWO! NOT COOL! LIKE, AT ALL!
MMM MMMPH!
WHATEVER. I'M GETTING DAISY, WE'LL MEET YOU AT THE GARAGE. IF YOU EVEN GIVE A CRAP.
BETTY, LOOK--I'M SORRY.
JUST GIVE HER SOME SPACE. WE'RE ALL BEAT TO HELL.
DAISY, YOU ASLEEP? I'M SORRY TO WAKE YOU. WE HAVE TO GO--
CHIK
DAISY? BABE?
OH GOD...
...NO.

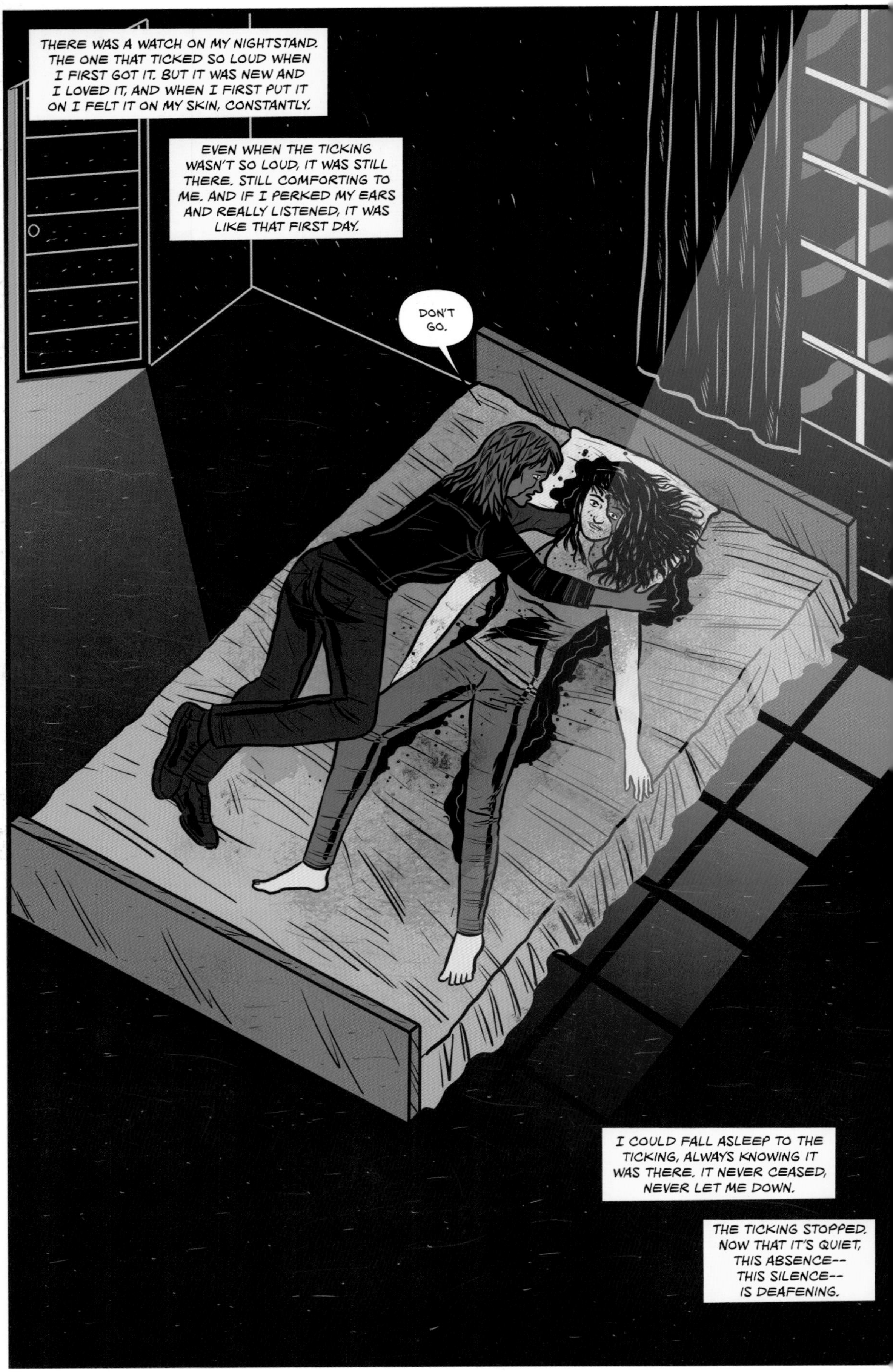
THERE WAS A WATCH ON MY NIGHTSTAND. THE ONE THAT TICKED SO LOUD WHEN I FIRST GOT IT. BUT IT WAS NEW AND I LOVED IT, AND WHEN I FIRST PUT IT ON I FELT IT ON MY SKIN, CONSTANTLY.
EVEN WHEN THE TICKING WASN'T SO LOUD, IT WAS STILL THERE. STILL COMFORTING TO ME. AND IF I PERKED MY EARS AND REALLY LISTENED, IT WAS LIKE THAT FIRST DAY.
DON'T GO.
I COULD FALL ASLEEP TO THE TICKING, ALWAYS KNOWING IT WAS THERE. IT NEVER CEASED, NEVER LET ME DOWN.
THE TICKING STOPPED. NOW THAT IT'S QUIET, THIS ABSENCE-- THIS SILENCE-- IS DEAFENING.

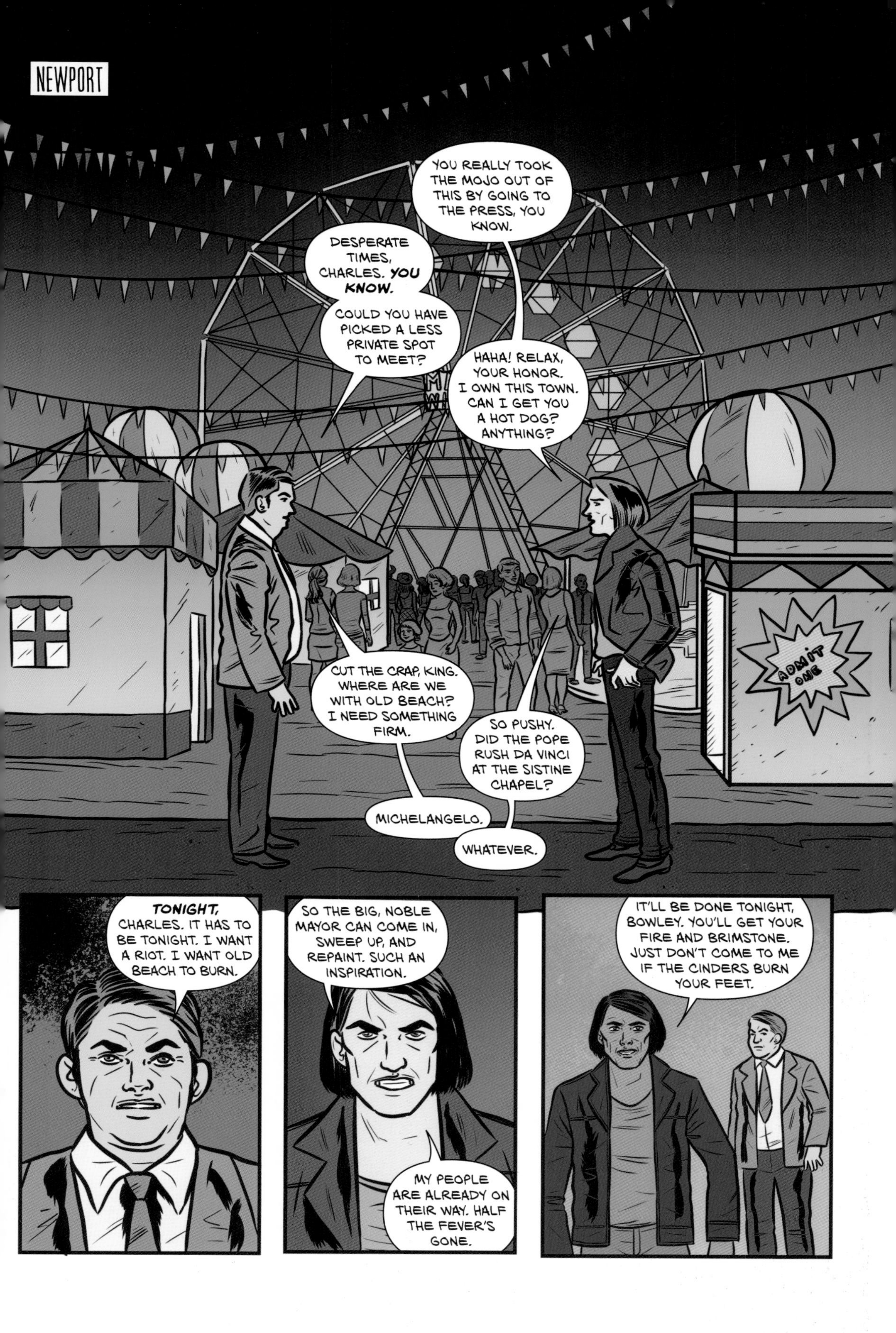
NEWPORT
YOU REALLY TOOK THE MOJO OUT OF THIS BY GOING TO THE PRESS, YOU KNOW.
DESPERATE TIMES, CHARLES. YOU KNOW.
COULD YOU HAVE PICKED A LESS PRIVATE SPOT TO MEET?
HAHA! RELAX, YOUR HONOR. I OWN THIS TOWN. CAN I GET YOU A HOT DOG? ANYTHING?
ADMIT ONE
CUT THE CRAP, KING. WHERE ARE WE WITH OLD BEACH? I NEED SOMETHING FIRM.
SO PUSHY. DID THE POPE RUSH DA VINCI AT THE SISTINE CHAPEL?
MICHELANGELO.
WHATEVER.
TONIGHT, CHARLES. IT HAS TO BE TONIGHT. I WANT A RIOT. I WANT OLD BEACH TO BURN.
SO THE BIG, NOBLE MAYOR CAN COME IN, SWEEP UP, AND REPAINT. SUCH AN INSPIRATION.
MY PEOPLE ARE ALREADY ON THEIR WAY. HALF THE FEVER'S GONE.
IT'LL BE DONE TONIGHT, BOWLEY. YOU'LL GET YOUR FIRE AND BRIMSTONE. JUST DON'T COME TO ME IF THE CINDERS BURN YOUR FEET.

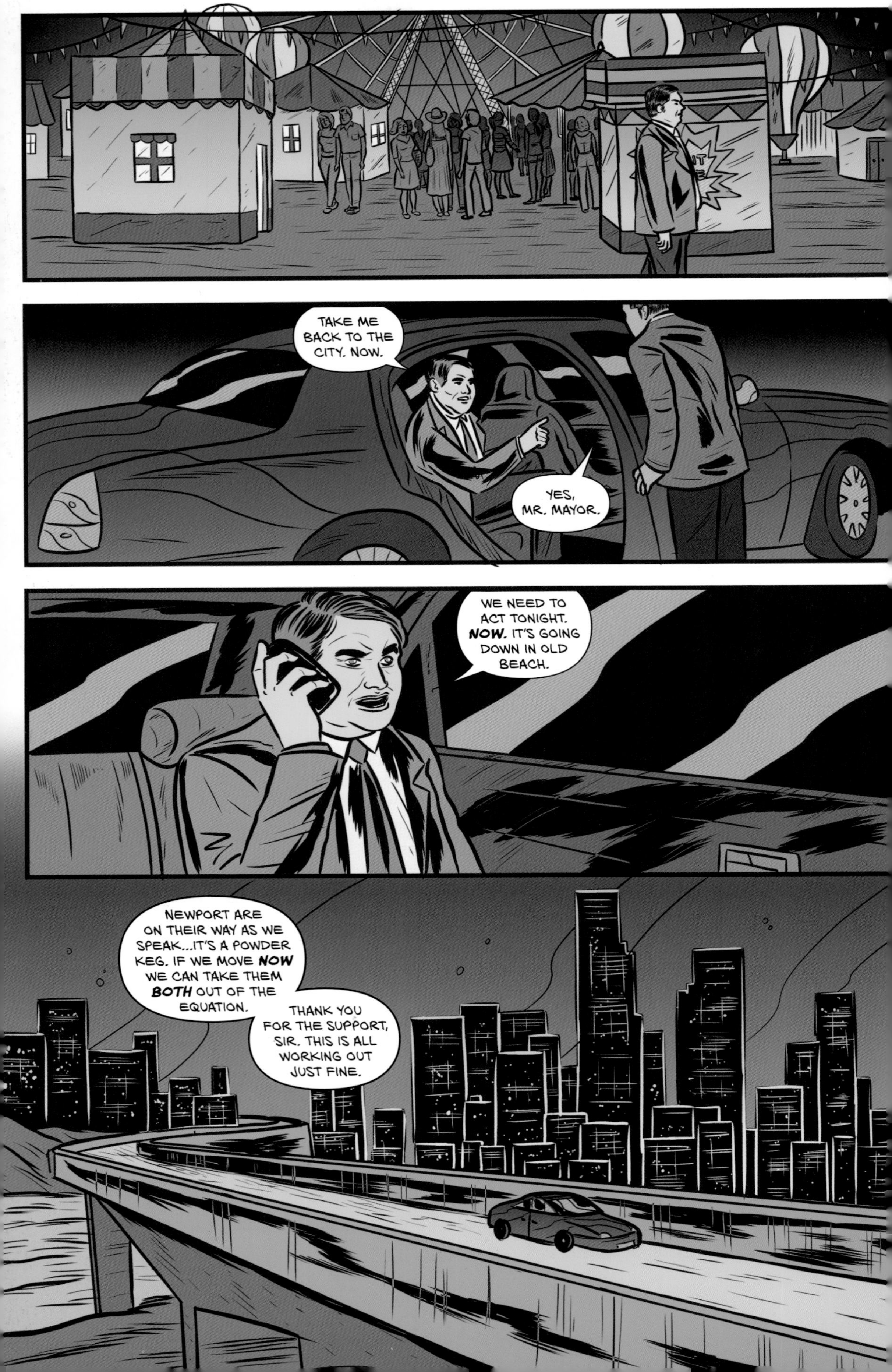
TAKE ME BACK TO THE CITY. NOW.
YES, MR. MAYOR.
WE NEED TO ACT TONIGHT. NOW. IT'S GOING DOWN IN OLD BEACH.
NEWPORT ARE ON THEIR WAY AS WE SPEAK...IT'S A POWDER KEG. IF WE MOVE NOW WE CAN TAKE THEM BOTH OUT OF THE EQUATION.
THANK YOU FOR THE SUPPORT, SIR. THIS IS ALL WORKING OUT JUST FINE.

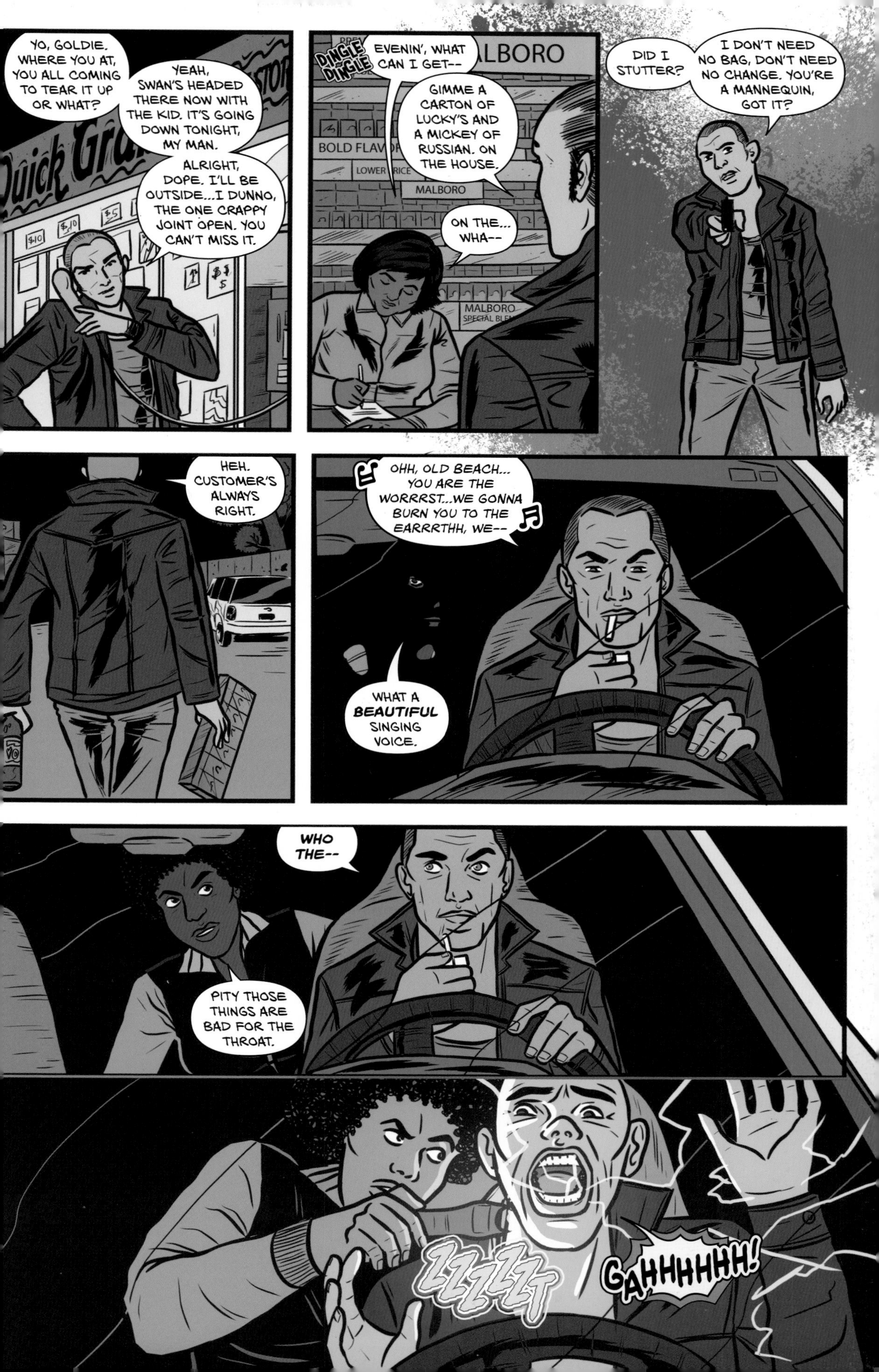
YO, GOLDIE. WHERE YOU AT, YOU ALL COMING TO TEAR IT UP OR WHAT?
YEAH, SWAN'S HEADED THERE NOW WITH THE KID. IT'S GOING DOWN TONIGHT, MY MAN.
ALRIGHT, DOPE. I'LL BE OUTSIDE... I DUNNO, THE ONE CRAPPY JOINT OPEN. YOU CAN'T MISS IT.
DINGLE DINGLE
EVENIN', WHAT CAN I GET--
GIMME A CARTON OF LUCKY'S AND A MICKEY OF RUSSIAN. ON THE HOUSE.
ON THE... WHA--
DID I STUTTER?
I DON'T NEED NO BAG, DON'T NEED NO CHANGE. YOU'RE A MANNEQUIN, GOT IT?
HEH. CUSTOMER'S ALWAYS RIGHT.
OHH, OLD BEACH... YOU ARE THE WORRRST... WE GONNA BURN YOU TO THE EARRRTHH, WE--
WHAT A BEAUTIFUL SINGING VOICE.
WHO THE--
PITY THOSE THINGS ARE BAD FOR THE THROAT.
ZZZZZT
GAHHHHHH!

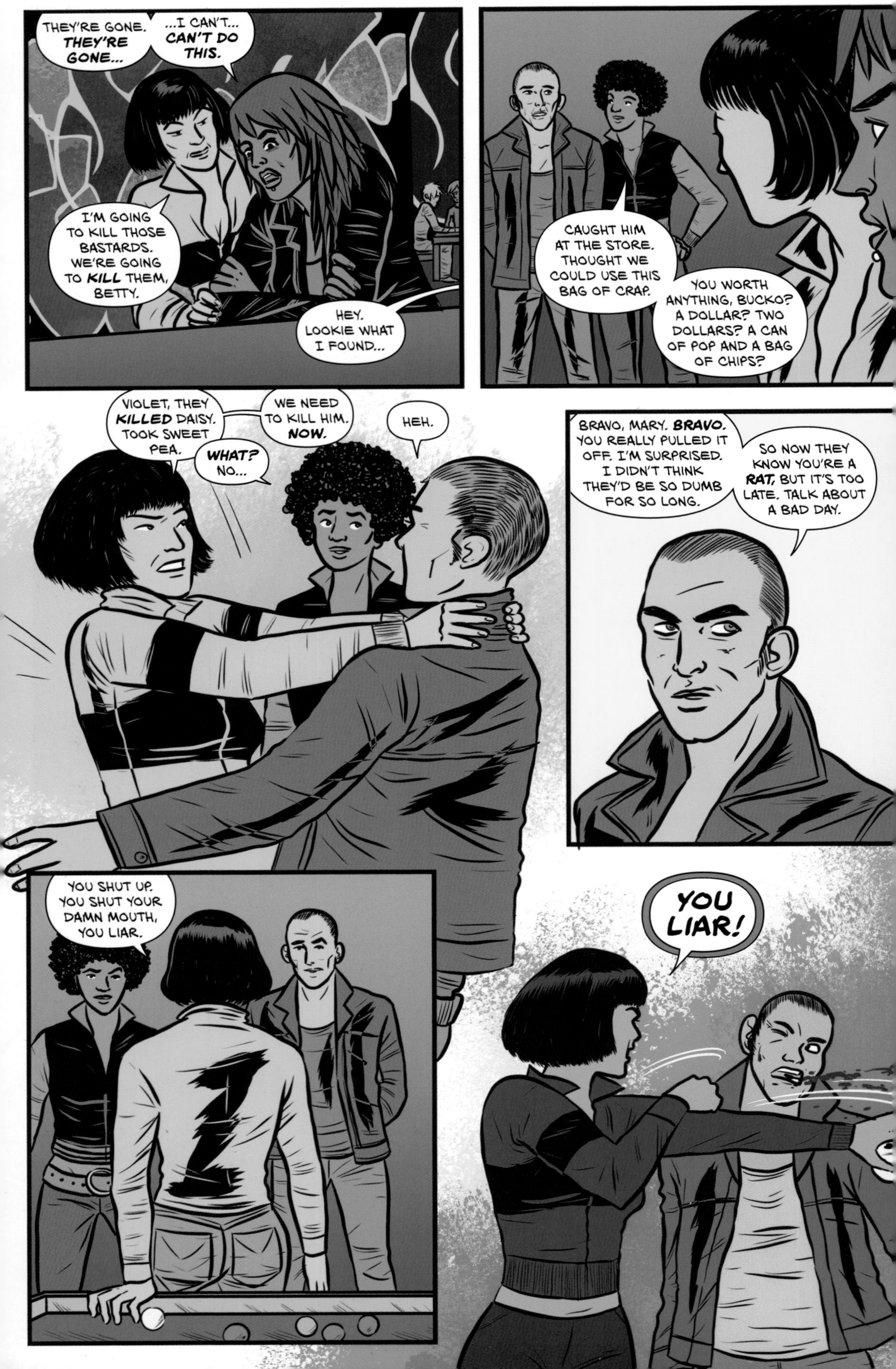
THEY'RE GONE. THEY'RE GONE...
...I CAN'T... CAN'T DO THIS.
I'M GOING TO KILL THOSE BASTARDS. WE'RE GOING TO KILL THEM, BETTY.
HEY. LOOKIE WHAT I FOUND...
CAUGHT HIM AT THE STORE. THOUGHT WE COULD USE THIS BAG OF CRAP.
YOU WORTH ANYTHING, BUCKO? A DOLLAR? TWO DOLLARS? A CAN OF POP AND A BAG OF CHIPS?
VIOLET, THEY KILLED DAISY. TOOK SWEET PEA.
WE NEED TO KILL HIM. NOW.
WHAT? NO...
HEH.
BRAVO, MARY. BRAVO. YOU REALLY PULLED IT OFF. I'M SURPRISED. I DIDN'T THINK THEY'D BE SO DUMB FOR SO LONG.
SO NOW THEY KNOW YOU'RE A RAT, BUT IT'S TOO LATE. TALK ABOUT A BAD DAY.
YOU SHUT UP. YOU SHUT YOUR DAMN MOUTH, YOU LIAR.
YOU LIAR!

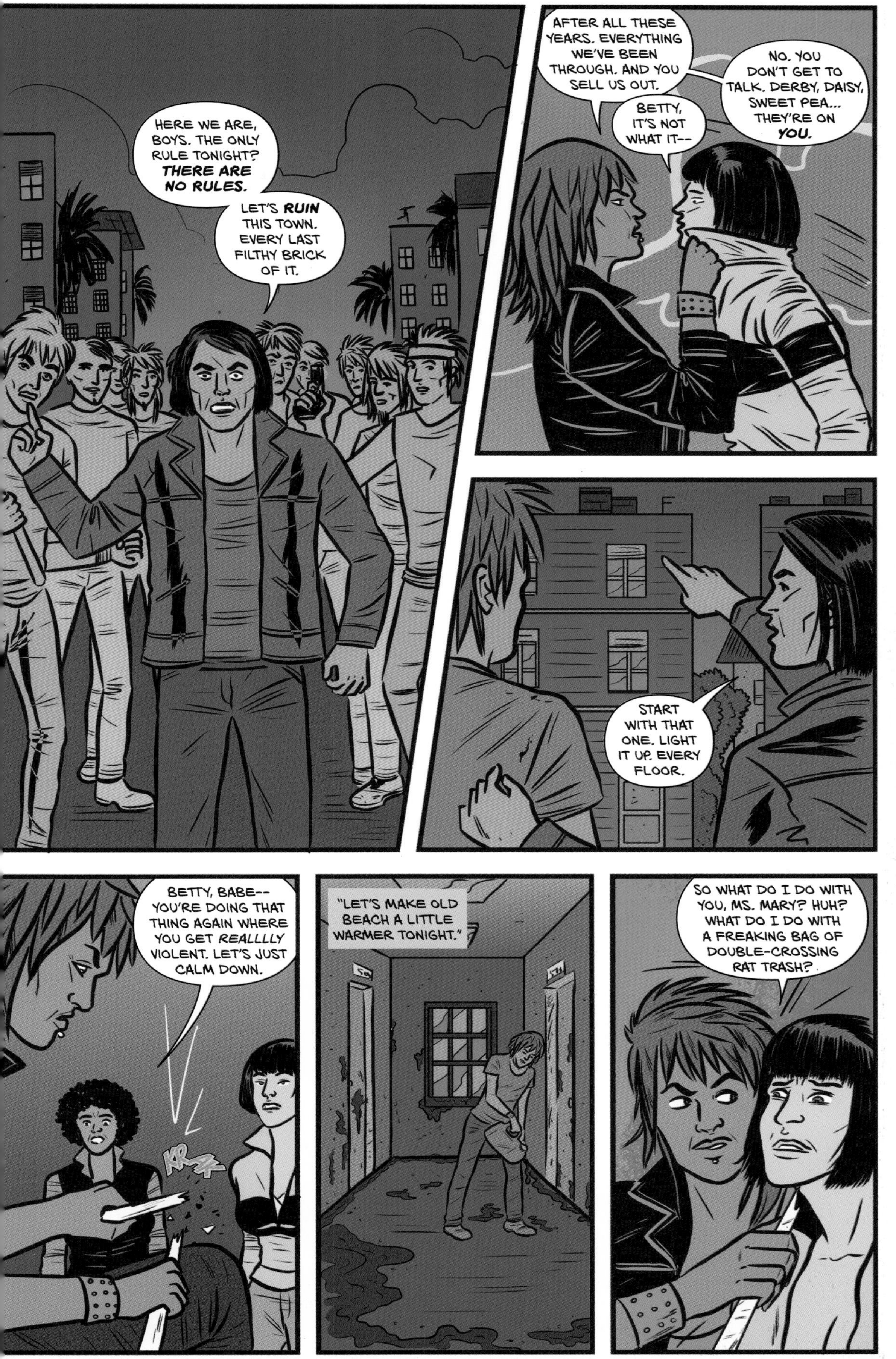
HERE WE ARE, BOYS. THE ONLY RULE TONIGHT? THERE ARE NO RULES.
LET'S RUIN THIS TOWN. EVERY LAST FILTHY BRICK OF IT.
AFTER ALL THESE YEARS. EVERYTHING WE'VE BEEN THROUGH. AND YOU SELL US OUT.
BETTY, IT'S NOT WHAT IT--
NO. YOU DON'T GET TO TALK. DERBY, DAISY, SWEET PEA... THEY'RE ON YOU.
START WITH THAT ONE. LIGHT IT UP. EVERY FLOOR.
BETTY, BABE-- YOU'RE DOING THAT THING AGAIN WHERE YOU GET REALLLLY VIOLENT. LET'S JUST CALM DOWN.
KRAK
"LET'S MAKE OLD BEACH A LITTLE WARMER TONIGHT."
SO WHAT DO I DO WITH YOU, MS. MARY? HUH? WHAT DO I DO WITH A FREAKING BAG OF DOUBLE-CROSSING RAT TRASH?

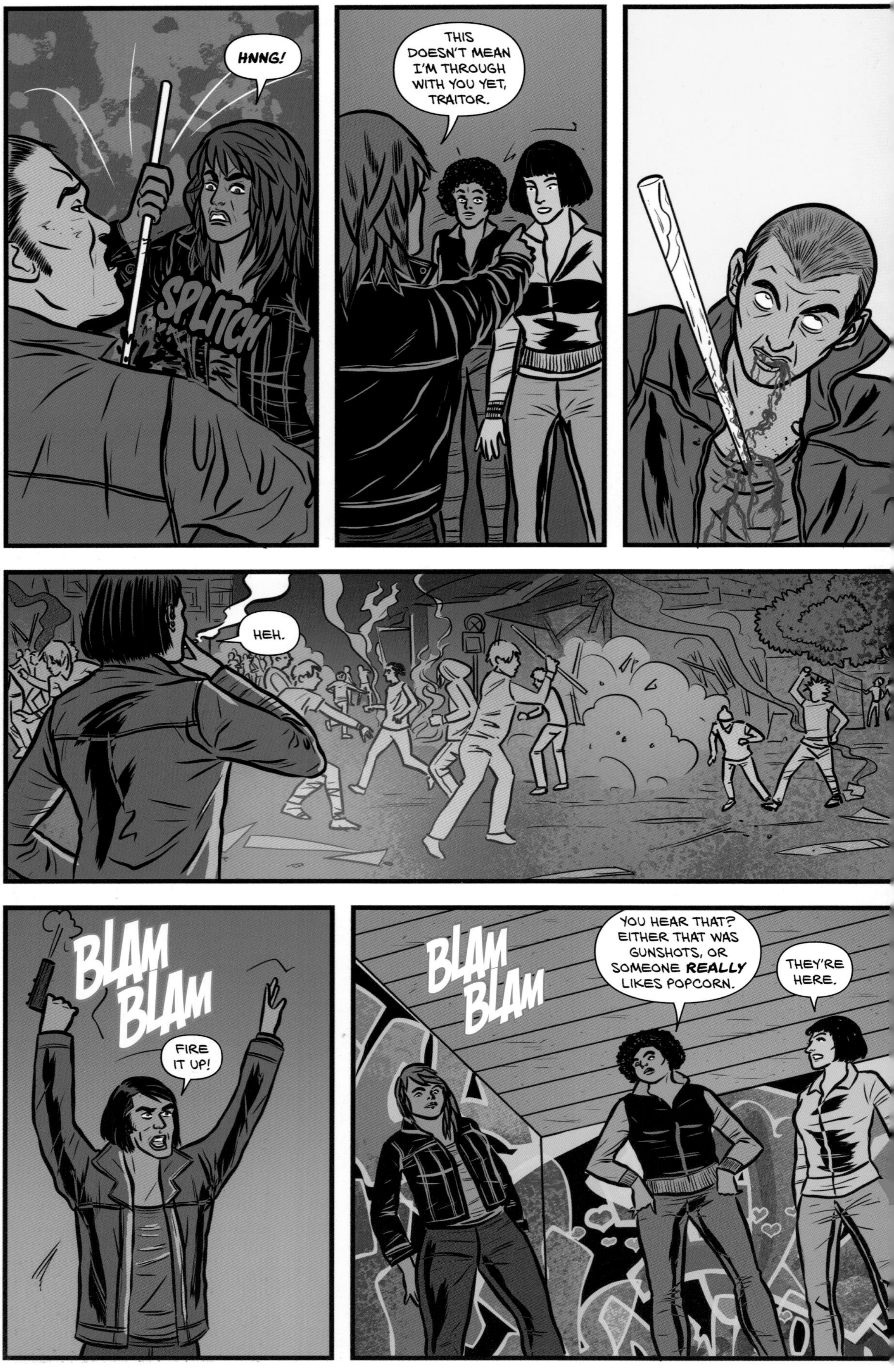
HNNG!
SPLITCH
THIS DOESN'T MEAN I'M THROUGH WITH YOU YET, TRAITOR.
HEH.
BLAM BLAM
FIRE IT UP!
BLAM BLAM
YOU HEAR THAT? EITHER THAT WAS GUNSHOTS, OR SOMEONE **REALLY** LIKES POPCORN.
THEY'RE HERE.

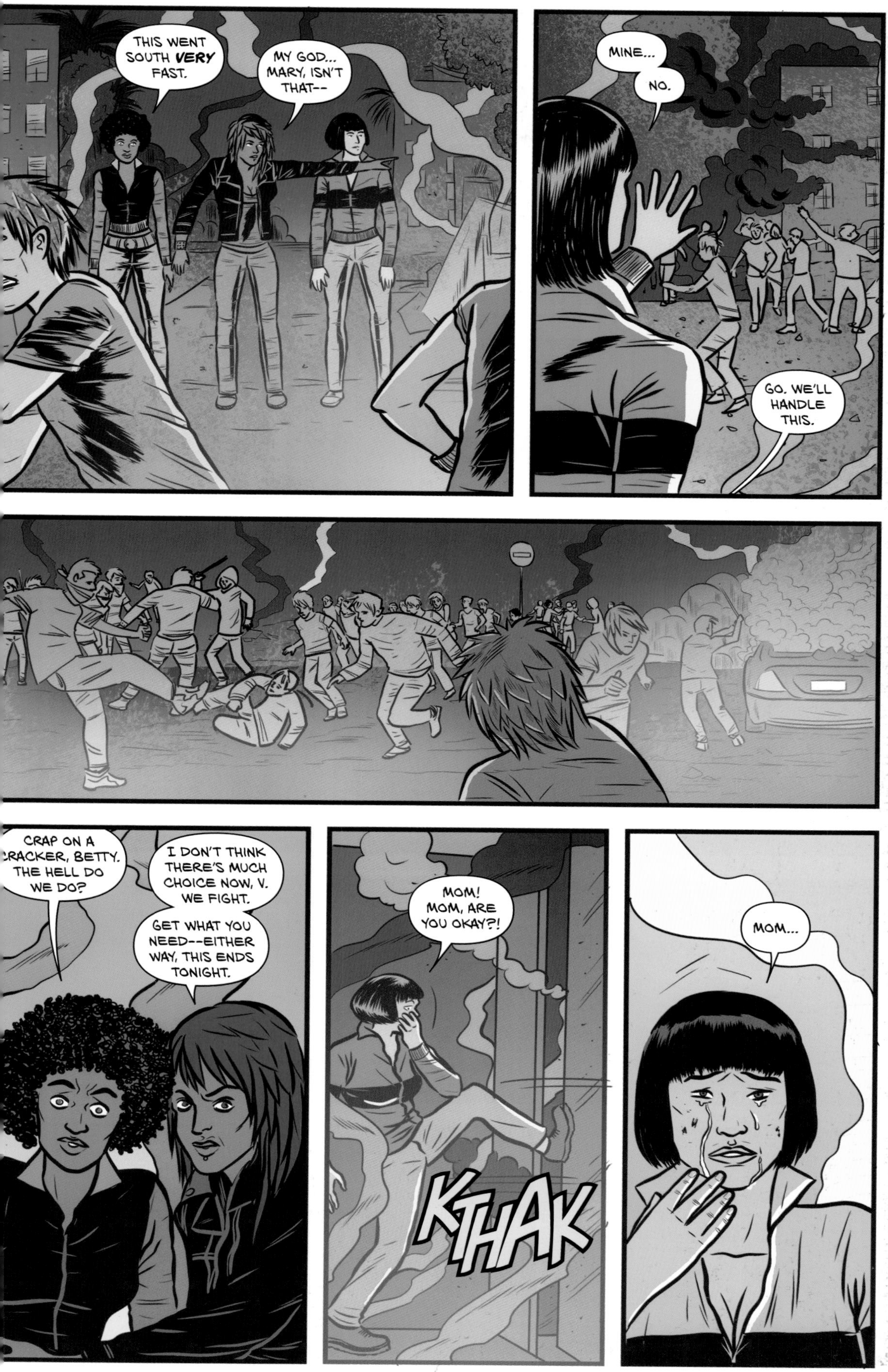
THIS WENT SOUTH VERY FAST.
MY GOD... MARY, ISN'T THAT--
MINE...
NO.
GO. WE'LL HANDLE THIS.
CRAP ON A CRACKER, BETTY. THE HELL DO WE DO?
I DON'T THINK THERE'S MUCH CHOICE NOW, V. WE FIGHT.
GET WHAT YOU NEED--EITHER WAY, THIS ENDS TONIGHT.
MOM! MOM, ARE YOU OKAY?!
KTHAK
MOM...

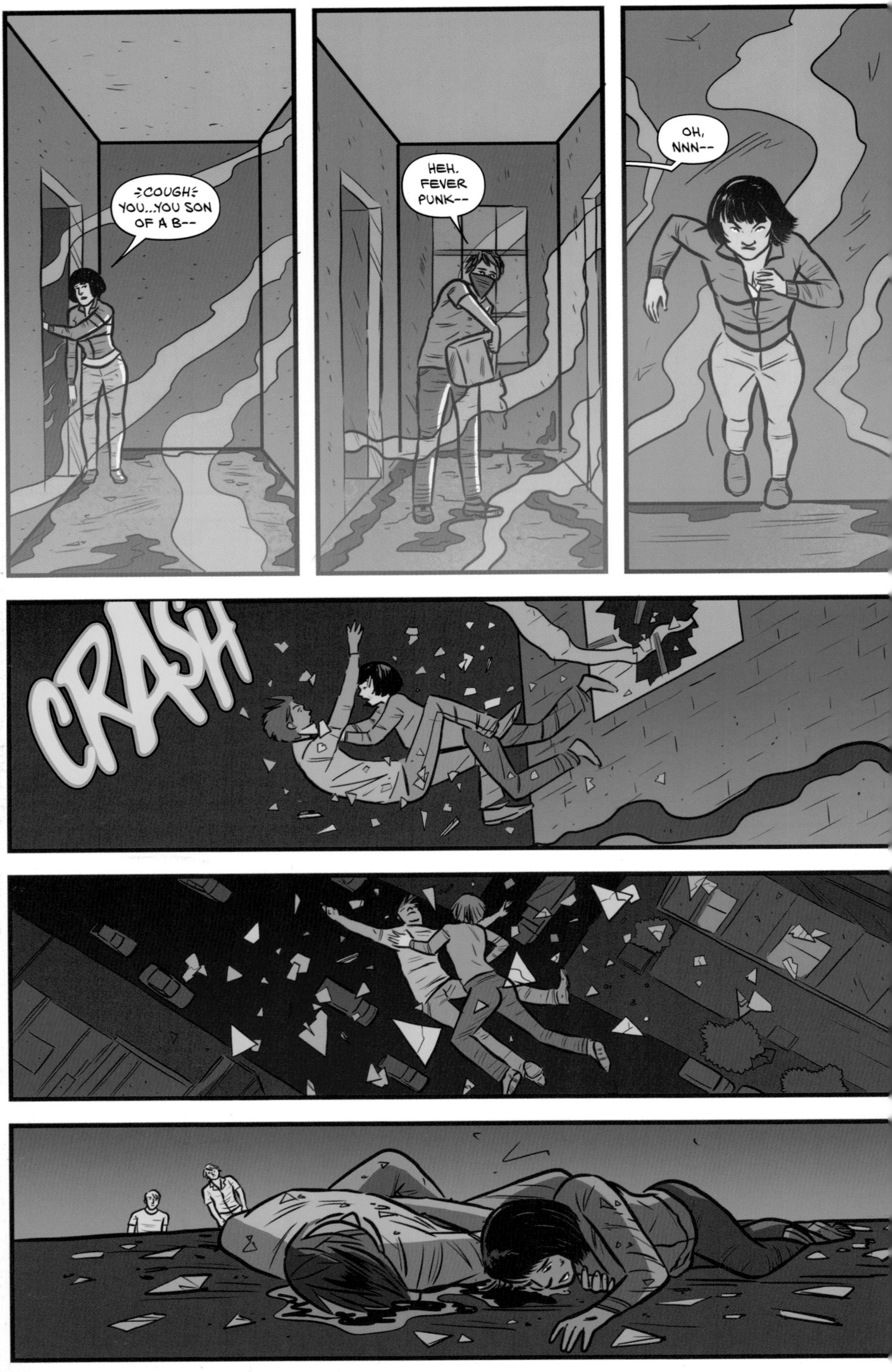

COUGH YOU...YOU SON OF A B--
HEH. FEVER PUNK--
OH, NNN--
CRASH

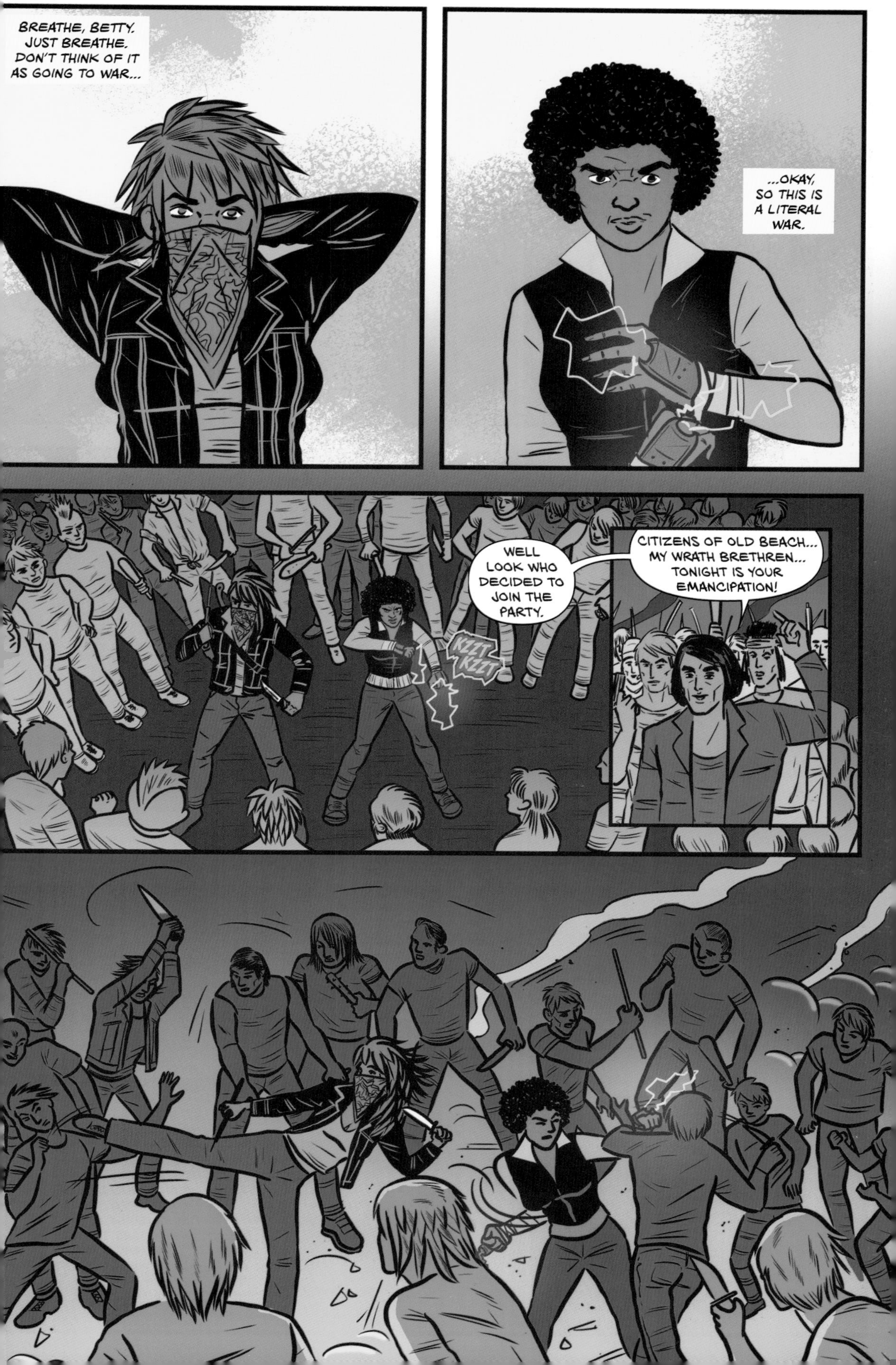

BREATHE, BETTY. JUST BREATHE. DON'T THINK OF IT AS GOING TO WAR...
...OKAY, SO THIS IS A LITERAL WAR.
WELL LOOK WHO DECIDED TO JOIN THE PARTY.
CITIZENS OF OLD BEACH... MY WRATH BRETHREN... TONIGHT IS YOUR EMANCIPATION!
KZZT KZZT

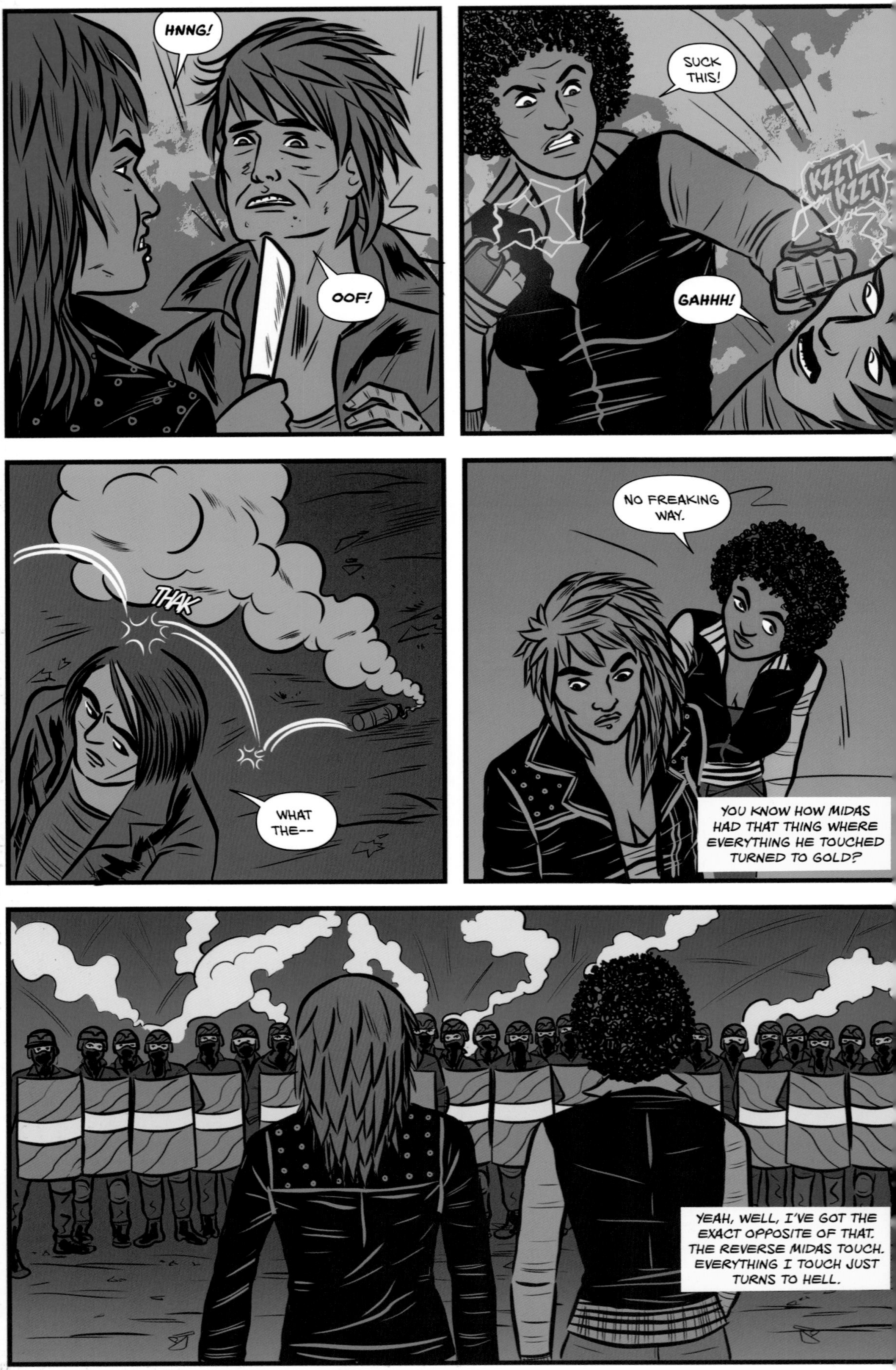
HNNG!
OOF!
SUCK THIS!
KZZT KZZT
GAHHH!
THAK
WHAT THE--
NO FREAKING WAY.
YOU KNOW HOW MIDAS HAD THAT THING WHERE EVERYTHING HE TOUCHED TURNED TO GOLD?
YEAH, WELL, I'VE GOT THE EXACT OPPOSITE OF THAT. THE REVERSE MIDAS TOUCH. EVERYTHING I TOUCH JUST TURNS TO HELL.

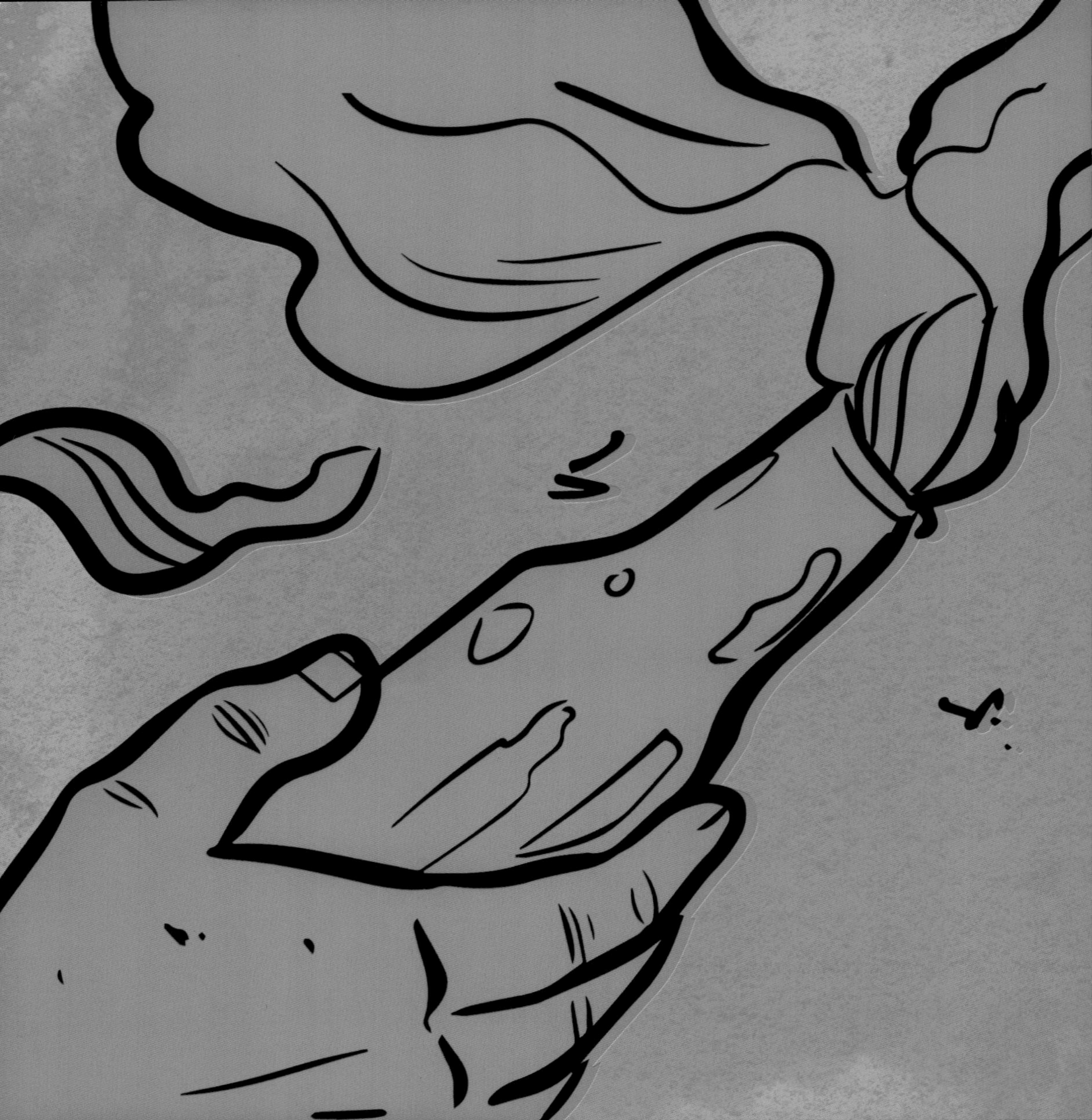

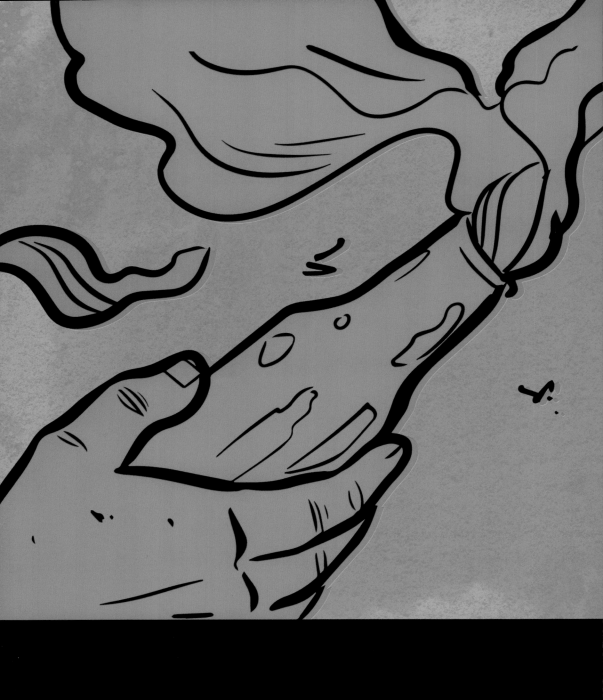

CHAPTER FOUR

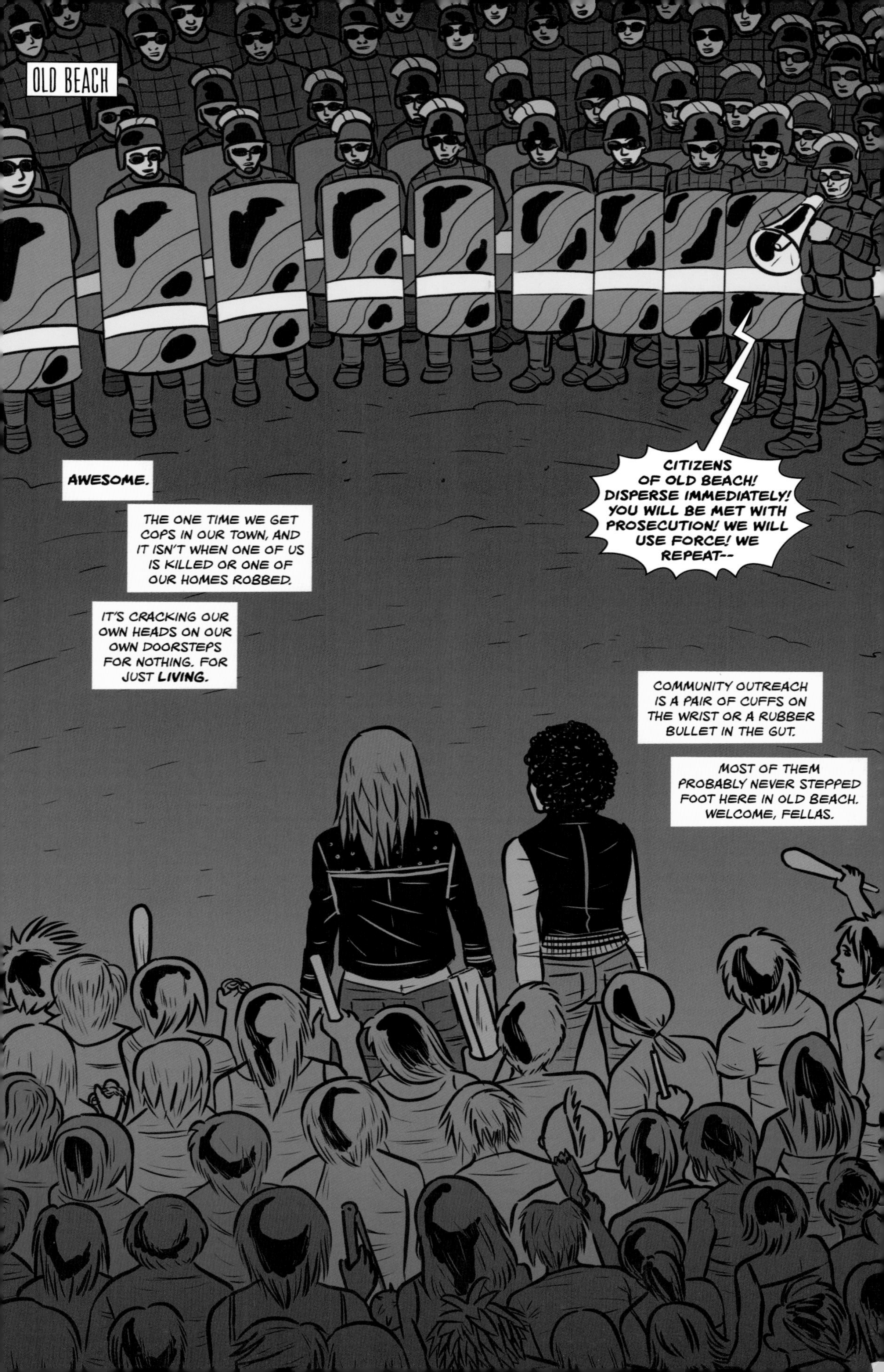
OLD BEACH
CITIZENS OF OLD BEACH! DISPERSE IMMEDIATELY! YOU WILL BE MET WITH PROSECUTION! WE WILL USE FORCE! WE REPEAT--
AWESOME.
THE ONE TIME WE GET COPS IN OUR TOWN, AND IT ISN'T WHEN ONE OF US IS KILLED OR ONE OF OUR HOMES ROBBED.
IT'S CRACKING OUR OWN HEADS ON OUR OWN DOORSTEPS FOR NOTHING. FOR JUST LIVING.
COMMUNITY OUTREACH IS A PAIR OF CUFFS ON THE WRIST OR A RUBBER BULLET IN THE GUT.
MOST OF THEM PROBABLY NEVER STEPPED FOOT HERE IN OLD BEACH. WELCOME, FELLAS.

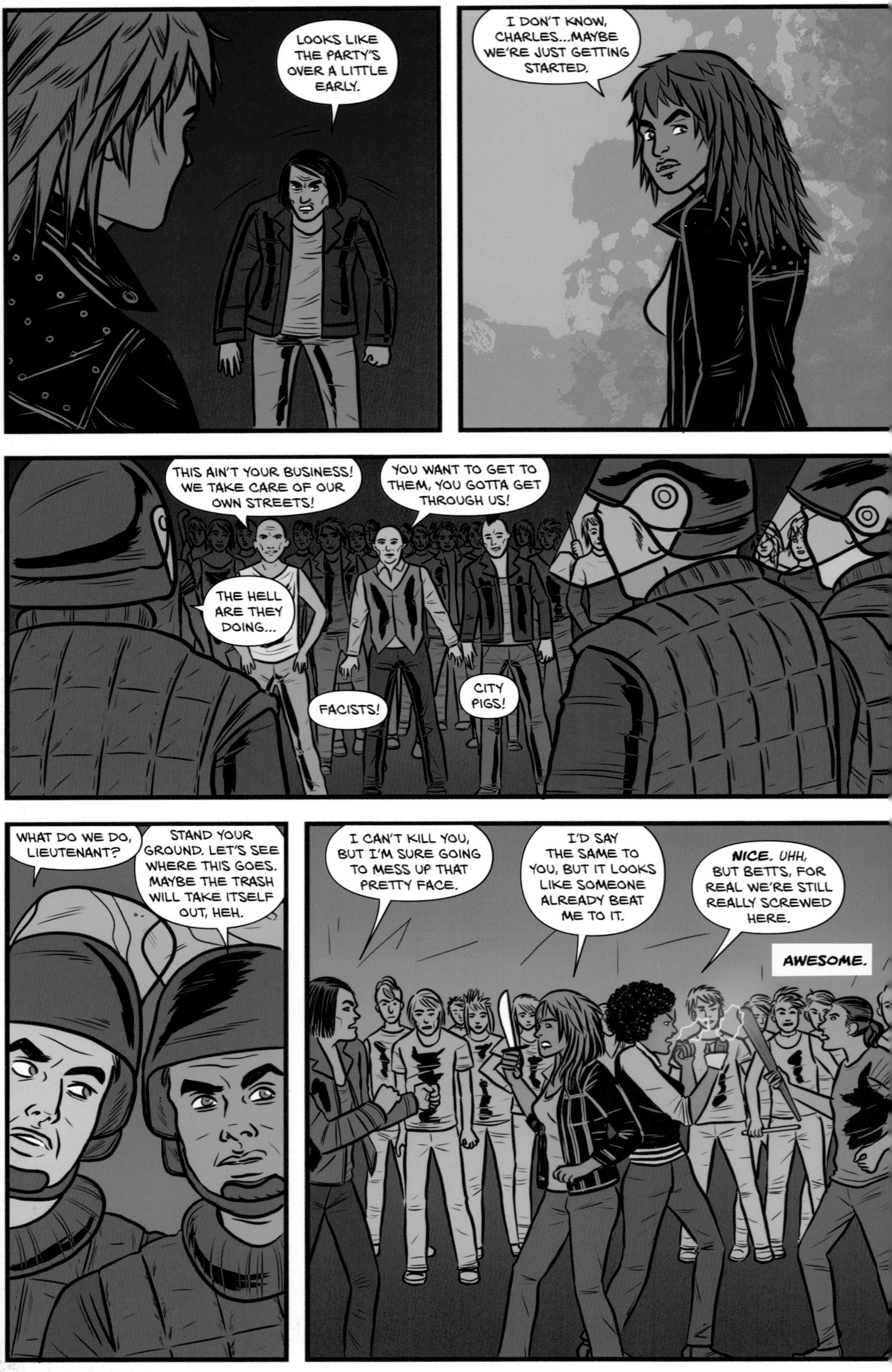
LOOKS LIKE THE PARTY'S OVER A LITTLE EARLY.
I DON'T KNOW, CHARLES...MAYBE WE'RE JUST GETTING STARTED.
THIS AIN'T YOUR BUSINESS! WE TAKE CARE OF OUR OWN STREETS!
YOU WANT TO GET TO THEM, YOU GOTTA GET THROUGH US!
THE HELL ARE THEY DOING...
FACISTS!
CITY PIGS!
WHAT DO WE DO, LIEUTENANT?
STAND YOUR GROUND. LET'S SEE WHERE THIS GOES. MAYBE THE TRASH WILL TAKE ITSELF OUT, HEH.
I CAN'T KILL YOU, BUT I'M SURE GOING TO MESS UP THAT PRETTY FACE.
I'D SAY THE SAME TO YOU, BUT IT LOOKS LIKE SOMEONE ALREADY BEAT ME TO IT.
NICE. UHH, BUT BETTS, FOR REAL WE'RE STILL REALLY SCREWED HERE.
AWESOME.

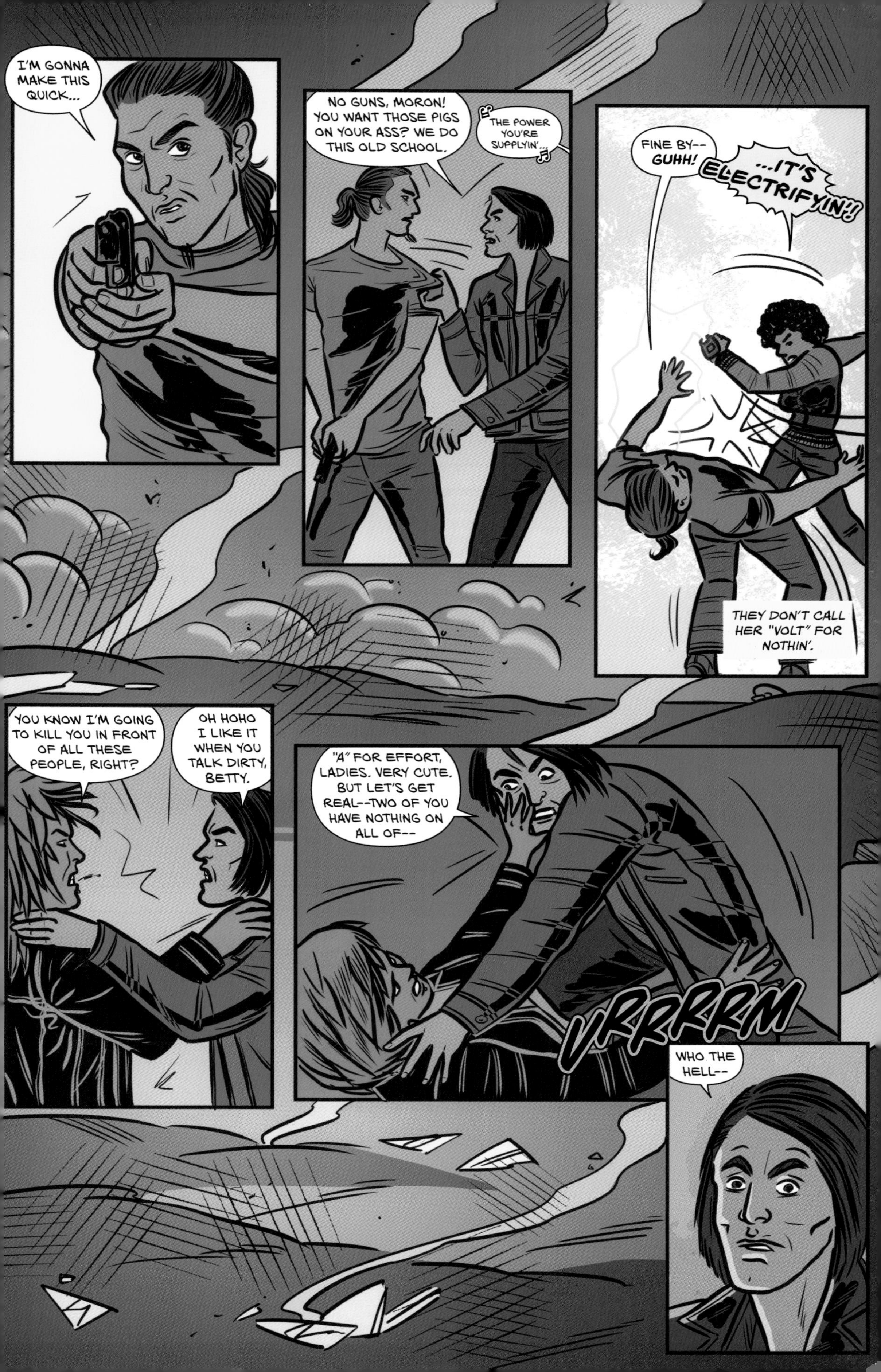

I'M GONNA MAKE THIS QUICK...
NO GUNS, MORON! YOU WANT THOSE PIGS ON YOUR ASS? WE DO THIS OLD SCHOOL.
THE POWER YOU'RE SUPPLYIN'...
FINE BY-- GUHH!
...IT'S ELECTRIFYIN'!
THEY DON'T CALL HER "VOLT" FOR NOTHIN'.
YOU KNOW I'M GOING TO KILL YOU IN FRONT OF ALL THESE PEOPLE, RIGHT?
OH HOHO I LIKE IT WHEN YOU TALK DIRTY, BETTY.
"A" FOR EFFORT, LADIES. VERY CUTE. BUT LET'S GET REAL--TWO OF YOU HAVE NOTHING ON ALL OF--
VRRRRM
WHO THE HELL--

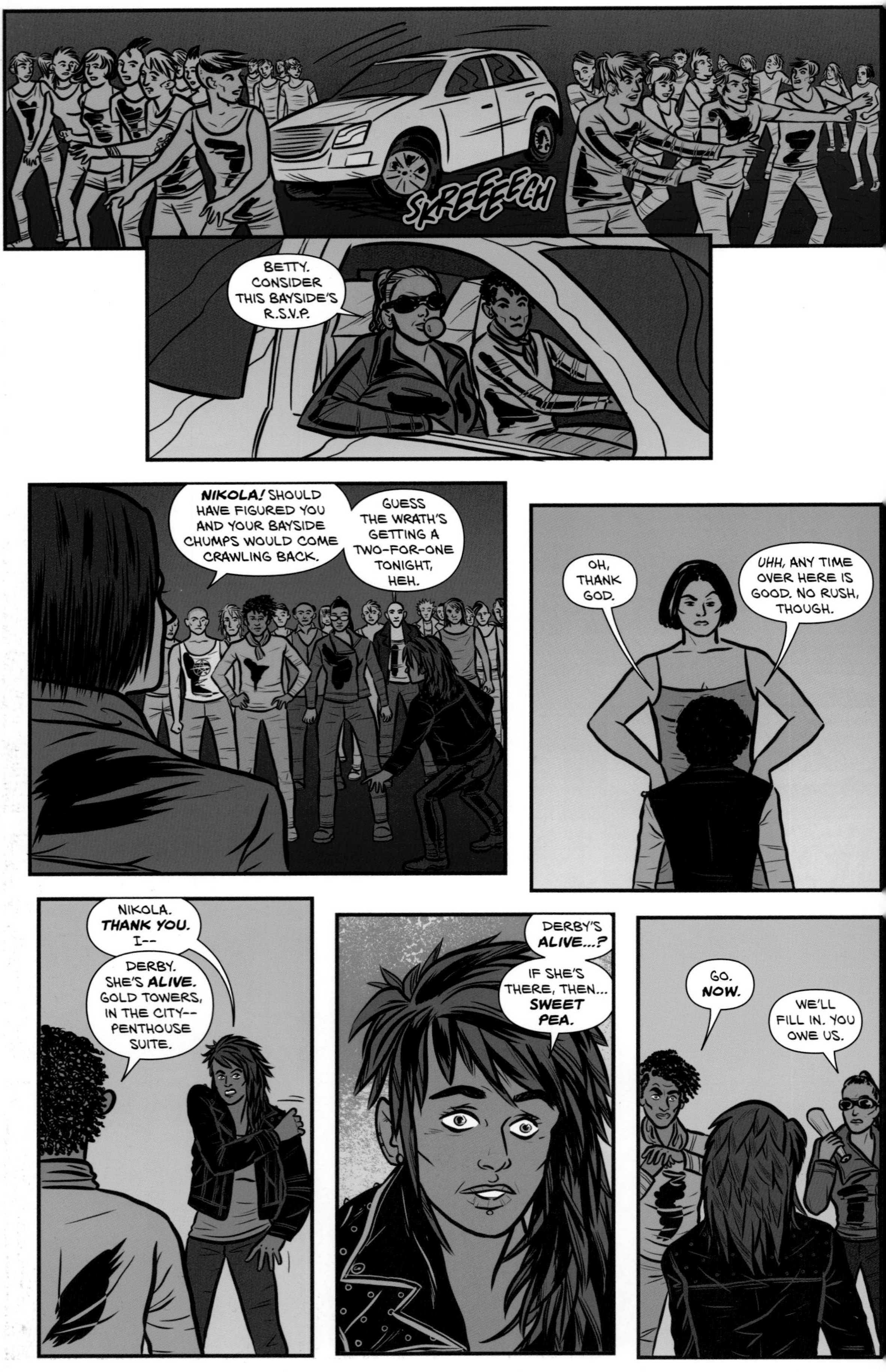
SKREEEEECH
BETTY. CONSIDER THIS BAYSIDE'S R.S.V.P.
NIKOLA! SHOULD HAVE FIGURED YOU AND YOUR BAYSIDE CHUMPS WOULD COME CRAWLING BACK.
GUESS THE WRATH'S GETTING A TWO-FOR-ONE TONIGHT, HEH.
OH, THANK GOD.
UHH, ANY TIME OVER HERE IS GOOD. NO RUSH, THOUGH.
NIKOLA. THANK YOU. I--
DERBY. SHE'S ALIVE. GOLD TOWERS, IN THE CITY-- PENTHOUSE SUITE.
DERBY'S ALIVE...?
IF SHE'S THERE, THEN... SWEET PEA.
GO. NOW.
WE'LL FILL IN. YOU OWE US.

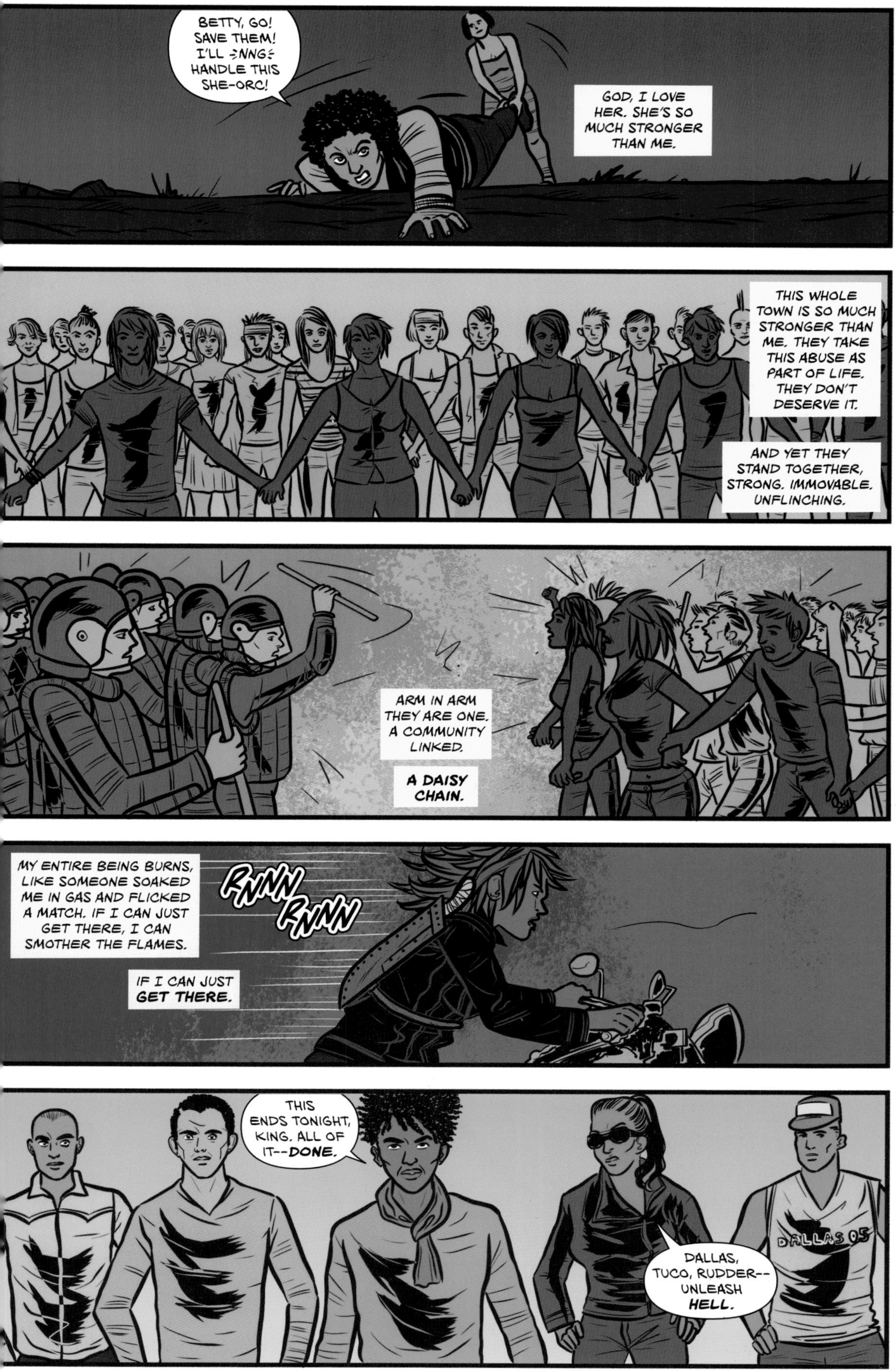
BETTY, GO! SAVE THEM! I'LL -NNG- HANDLE THIS SHE-ORC!
GOD, I LOVE HER. SHE'S SO MUCH STRONGER THAN ME.
THIS WHOLE TOWN IS SO MUCH STRONGER THAN ME. THEY TAKE THIS ABUSE AS PART OF LIFE. THEY DON'T DESERVE IT.
AND YET THEY STAND TOGETHER, STRONG. IMMOVABLE. UNFLINCHING.
ARM IN ARM THEY ARE ONE. A COMMUNITY LINKED.
A DAISY CHAIN.
MY ENTIRE BEING BURNS, LIKE SOMEONE SOAKED ME IN GAS AND FLICKED A MATCH. IF I CAN JUST GET THERE, I CAN SMOTHER THE FLAMES.
RNNN RNNN
IF I CAN JUST **GET THERE.**
THIS ENDS TONIGHT, KING. ALL OF IT--**DONE.**
DALLAS 05
DALLAS, TUCO, RUDDER-- UNLEASH **HELL.**

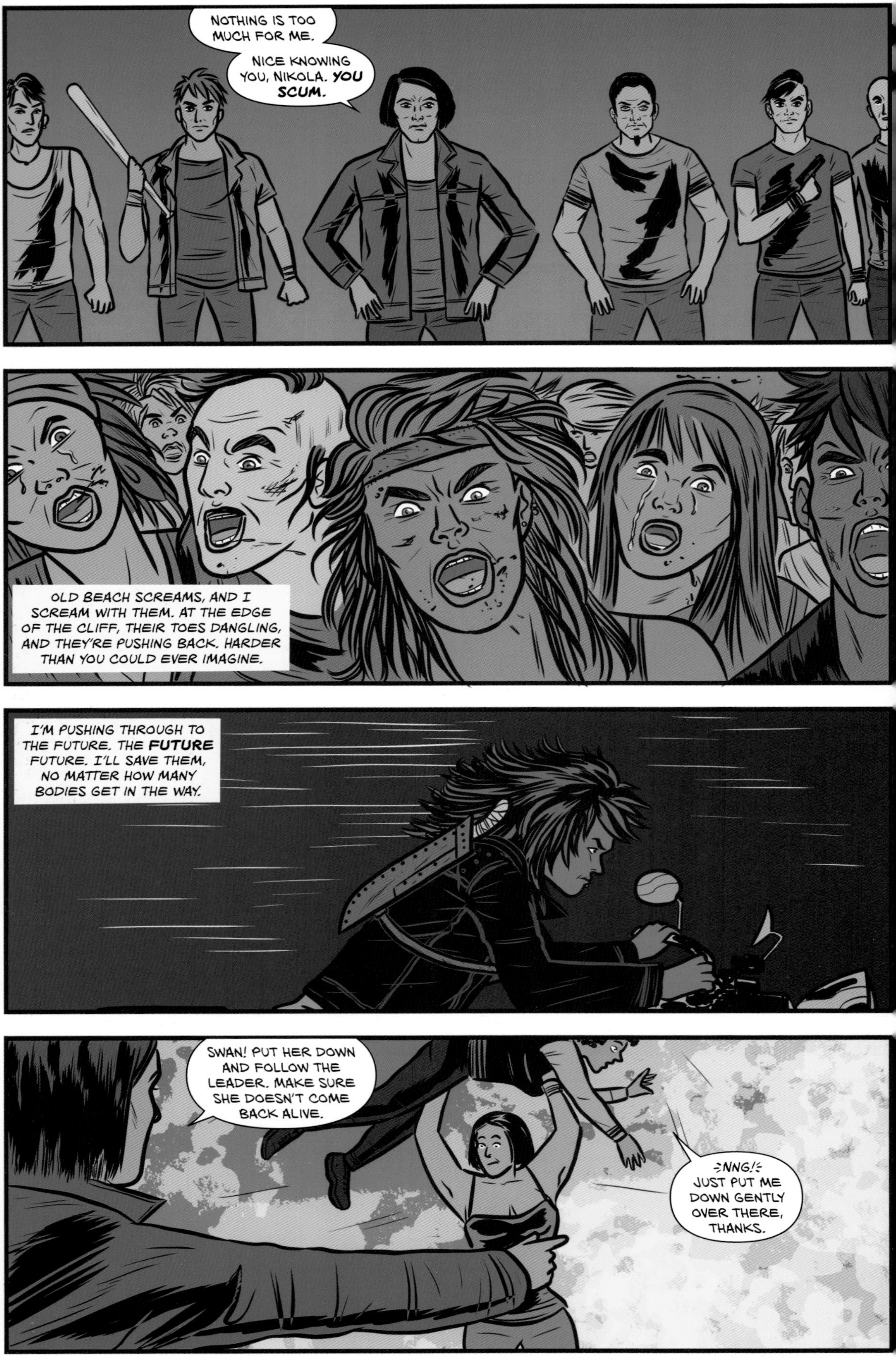
NOTHING IS TOO MUCH FOR ME.
NICE KNOWING YOU, NIKOLA. **YOU SCUM.**
OLD BEACH SCREAMS, AND I SCREAM WITH THEM. AT THE EDGE OF THE CLIFF, THEIR TOES DANGLING, AND THEY'RE PUSHING BACK. HARDER THAN YOU COULD EVER IMAGINE.
I'M PUSHING THROUGH TO THE FUTURE. THE **FUTURE** FUTURE. I'LL SAVE THEM, NO MATTER HOW MANY BODIES GET IN THE WAY.
SWAN! PUT HER DOWN AND FOLLOW THE LEADER. MAKE SURE SHE DOESN'T COME BACK ALIVE.
NNG! JUST PUT ME DOWN GENTLY OVER THERE, THANKS.

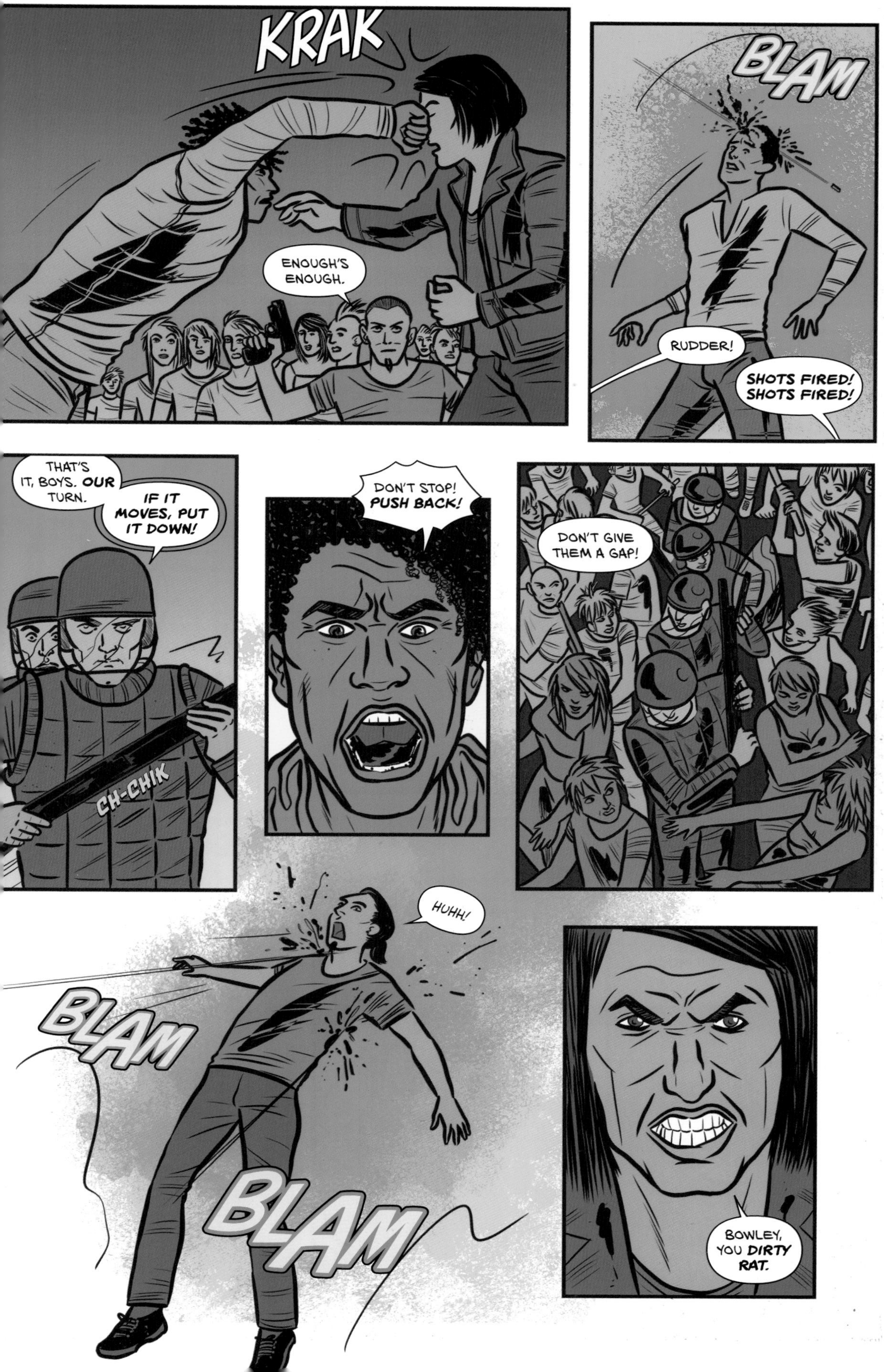
KRAK
ENOUGH'S ENOUGH.
BLAM
RUDDER!
SHOTS FIRED! SHOTS FIRED!
THAT'S IT, BOYS. OUR TURN.
IF IT MOVES, PUT IT DOWN!
CH-CHIK
DON'T STOP! PUSH BACK!
DON'T GIVE THEM A GAP!
HUHH!
BLAM
BLAM
BOWLEY, YOU DIRTY RAT.

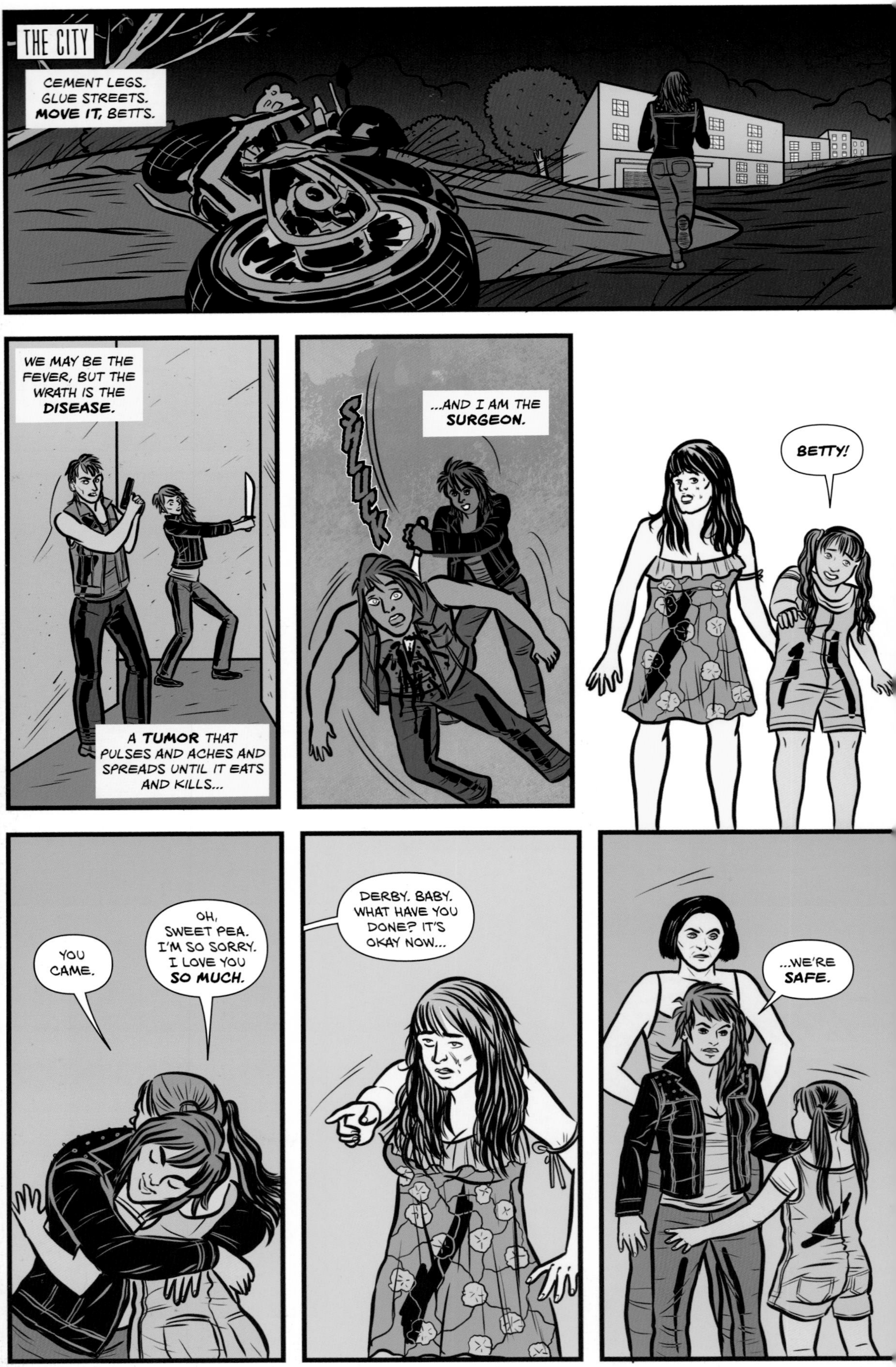
THE CITY
CEMENT LEGS. GLUE STREETS. MOVE IT, BETTS.
WE MAY BE THE FEVER, BUT THE WRATH IS THE DISEASE.
A TUMOR THAT PULSES AND ACHES AND SPREADS UNTIL IT EATS AND KILLS...
SHLUCK
...AND I AM THE SURGEON.
BETTY!
YOU CAME.
OH, SWEET PEA. I'M SO SORRY. I LOVE YOU SO MUCH.
DERBY. BABY. WHAT HAVE YOU DONE? IT'S OKAY NOW...
...WE'RE SAFE.

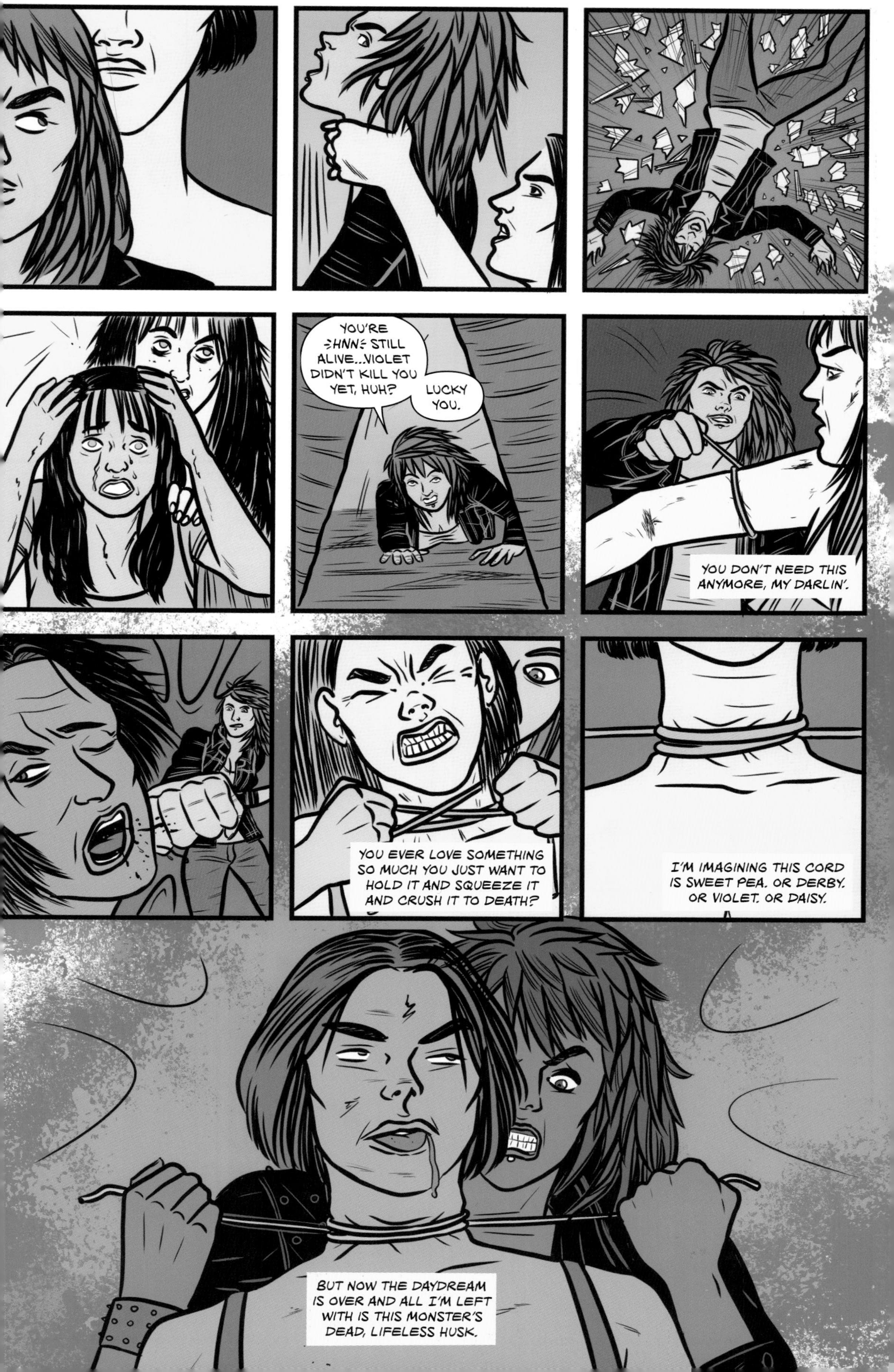
YOU'RE -HNN- STILL ALIVE...VIOLET DIDN'T KILL YOU YET, HUH?
LUCKY YOU.
YOU DON'T NEED THIS ANYMORE, MY DARLIN'.
YOU EVER LOVE SOMETHING SO MUCH YOU JUST WANT TO HOLD IT AND SQUEEZE IT AND CRUSH IT TO DEATH?
I'M IMAGINING THIS CORD IS SWEET PEA. OR DERBY. OR VIOLET. OR DAISY.
BUT NOW THE DAYDREAM IS OVER AND ALL I'M LEFT WITH IS THIS MONSTER'S DEAD, LIFELESS HUSK.

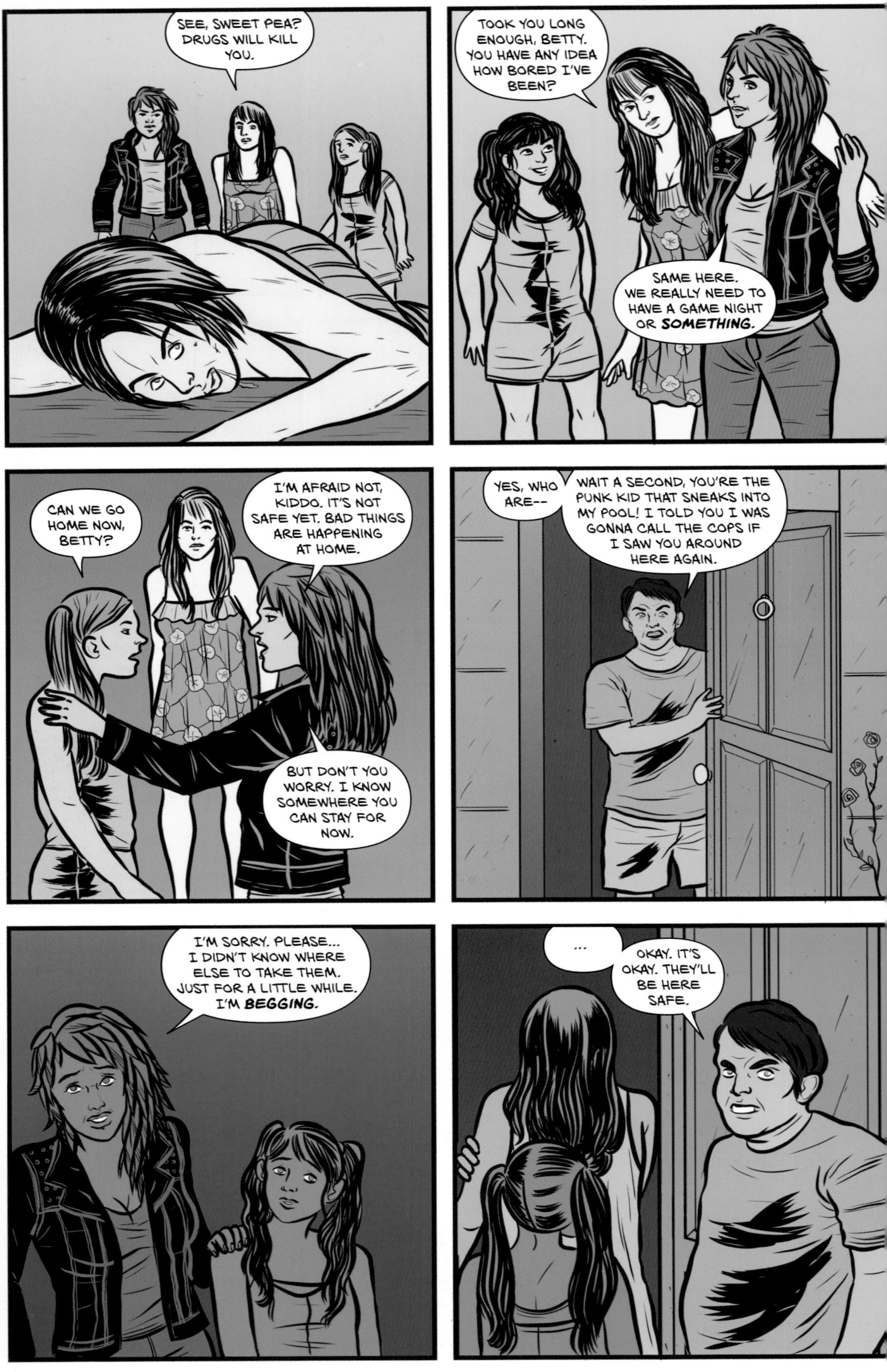
SEE, SWEET PEA? DRUGS WILL KILL YOU.
TOOK YOU LONG ENOUGH, BETTY. YOU HAVE ANY IDEA HOW BORED I'VE BEEN?
SAME HERE. WE REALLY NEED TO HAVE A GAME NIGHT OR **SOMETHING.**
CAN WE GO HOME NOW, BETTY?
I'M AFRAID NOT, KIDDO. IT'S NOT SAFE YET. BAD THINGS ARE HAPPENING AT HOME.
BUT DON'T YOU WORRY. I KNOW SOMEWHERE YOU CAN STAY FOR NOW.
YES, WHO ARE--
WAIT A SECOND, YOU'RE THE PUNK KID THAT SNEAKS INTO MY POOL! I TOLD YOU I WAS GONNA CALL THE COPS IF I SAW YOU AROUND HERE AGAIN.
I'M SORRY. PLEASE... I DIDN'T KNOW WHERE ELSE TO TAKE THEM. JUST FOR A LITTLE WHILE. I'M **BEGGING.**
...
OKAY. IT'S OKAY. THEY'LL BE HERE SAFE.

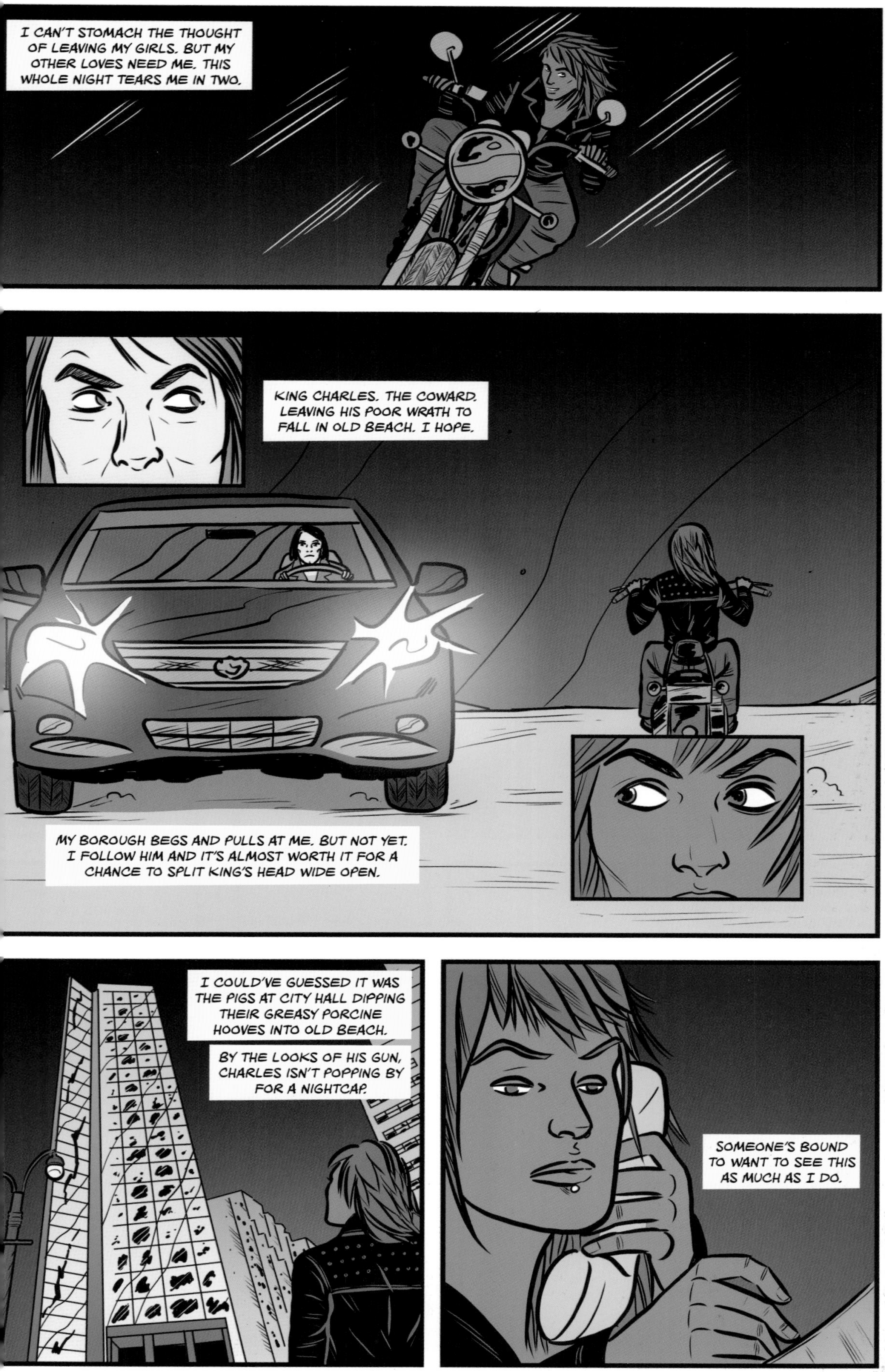
I CAN'T STOMACH THE THOUGHT OF LEAVING MY GIRLS. BUT MY OTHER LOVES NEED ME. THIS WHOLE NIGHT TEARS ME IN TWO.
KING CHARLES. THE COWARD. LEAVING HIS POOR WRATH TO FALL IN OLD BEACH. I HOPE.
MY BOROUGH BEGS AND PULLS AT ME. BUT NOT YET. I FOLLOW HIM AND IT'S ALMOST WORTH IT FOR A CHANCE TO SPLIT KING'S HEAD WIDE OPEN.
I COULD'VE GUESSED IT WAS THE PIGS AT CITY HALL DIPPING THEIR GREASY PORCINE HOOVES INTO OLD BEACH.
BY THE LOOKS OF HIS GUN, CHARLES ISN'T POPPING BY FOR A NIGHTCAP.
SOMEONE'S BOUND TO WANT TO SEE THIS AS MUCH AS I DO.

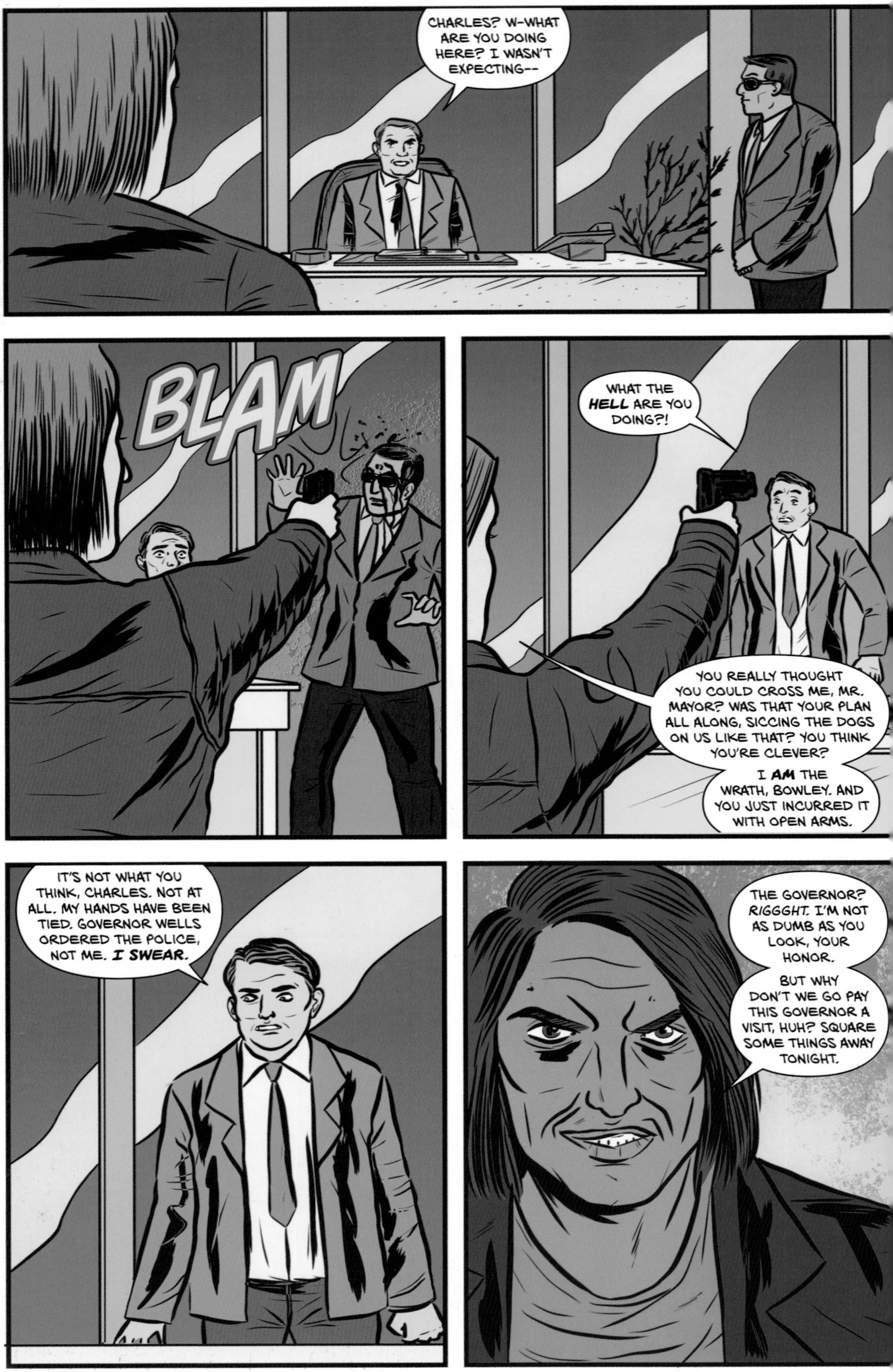
CHARLES? W-WHAT ARE YOU DOING HERE? I WASN'T EXPECTING--
BLAM
WHAT THE HELL ARE YOU DOING?!
YOU REALLY THOUGHT YOU COULD CROSS ME, MR. MAYOR? WAS THAT YOUR PLAN ALL ALONG, SICCING THE DOGS ON US LIKE THAT? YOU THINK YOU'RE CLEVER?
I AM THE WRATH, BOWLEY. AND YOU JUST INCURRED IT WITH OPEN ARMS.
IT'S NOT WHAT YOU THINK, CHARLES. NOT AT ALL. MY HANDS HAVE BEEN TIED. GOVERNOR WELLS ORDERED THE POLICE, NOT ME. I SWEAR.
THE GOVERNOR? RIGGGHT. I'M NOT AS DUMB AS YOU LOOK, YOUR HONOR.
BUT WHY DON'T WE GO PAY THIS GOVERNOR A VISIT, HUH? SQUARE SOME THINGS AWAY TONIGHT.

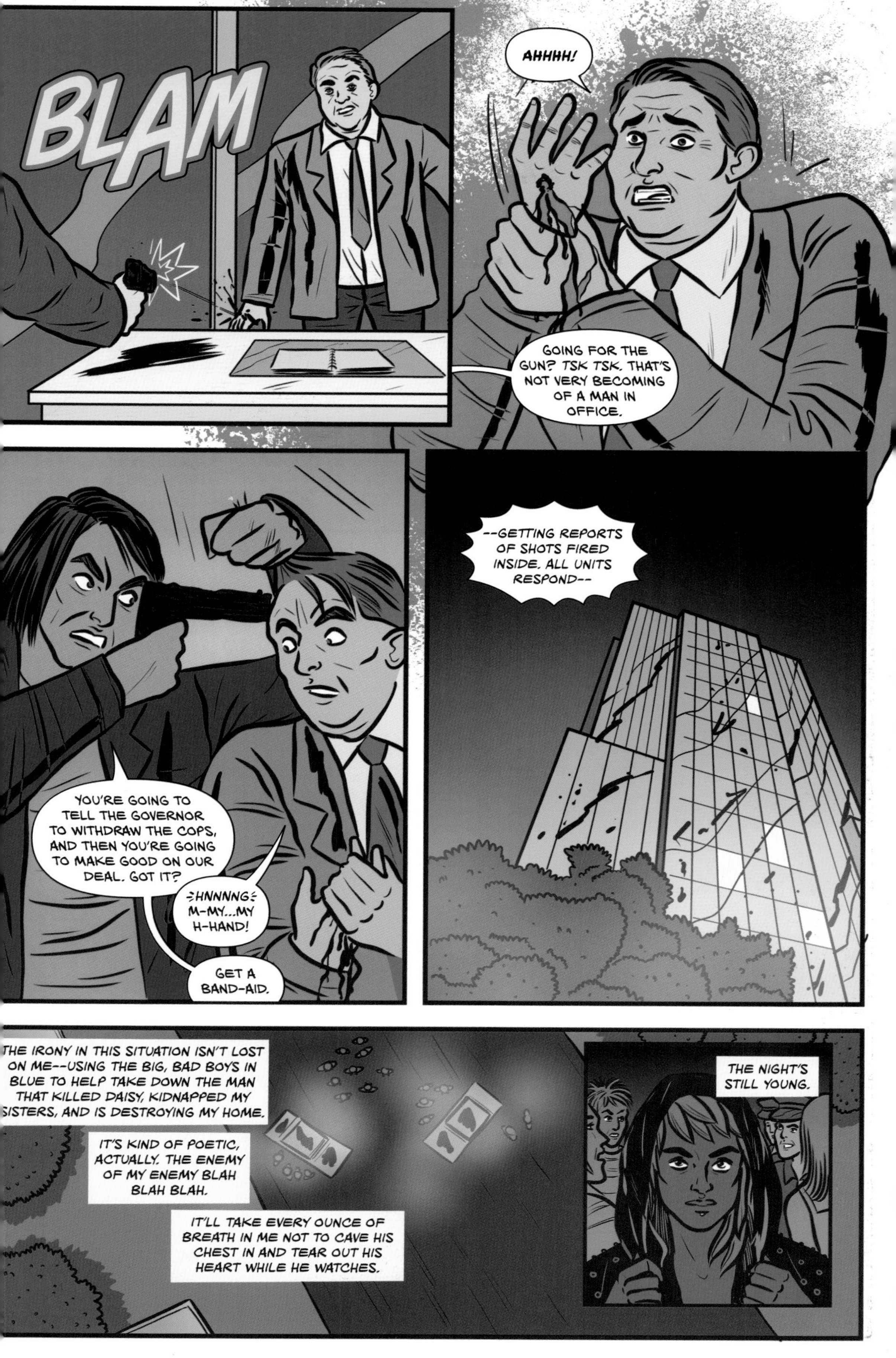
BLAM
AHHHH!
GOING FOR THE GUN? TSK TSK. THAT'S NOT VERY BECOMING OF A MAN IN OFFICE.
YOU'RE GOING TO TELL THE GOVERNOR TO WITHDRAW THE COPS, AND THEN YOU'RE GOING TO MAKE GOOD ON OUR DEAL. GOT IT?
HNNNNG M-MY...MY H-HAND!
GET A BAND-AID.
--GETTING REPORTS OF SHOTS FIRED INSIDE. ALL UNITS RESPOND--
THE IRONY IN THIS SITUATION ISN'T LOST ON ME--USING THE BIG, BAD BOYS IN BLUE TO HELP TAKE DOWN THE MAN THAT KILLED DAISY, KIDNAPPED MY SISTERS, AND IS DESTROYING MY HOME.
IT'S KIND OF POETIC, ACTUALLY. THE ENEMY OF MY ENEMY BLAH BLAH BLAH.
IT'LL TAKE EVERY OUNCE OF BREATH IN ME NOT TO CAVE HIS CHEST IN AND TEAR OUT HIS HEART WHILE HE WATCHES.
THE NIGHT'S STILL YOUNG.

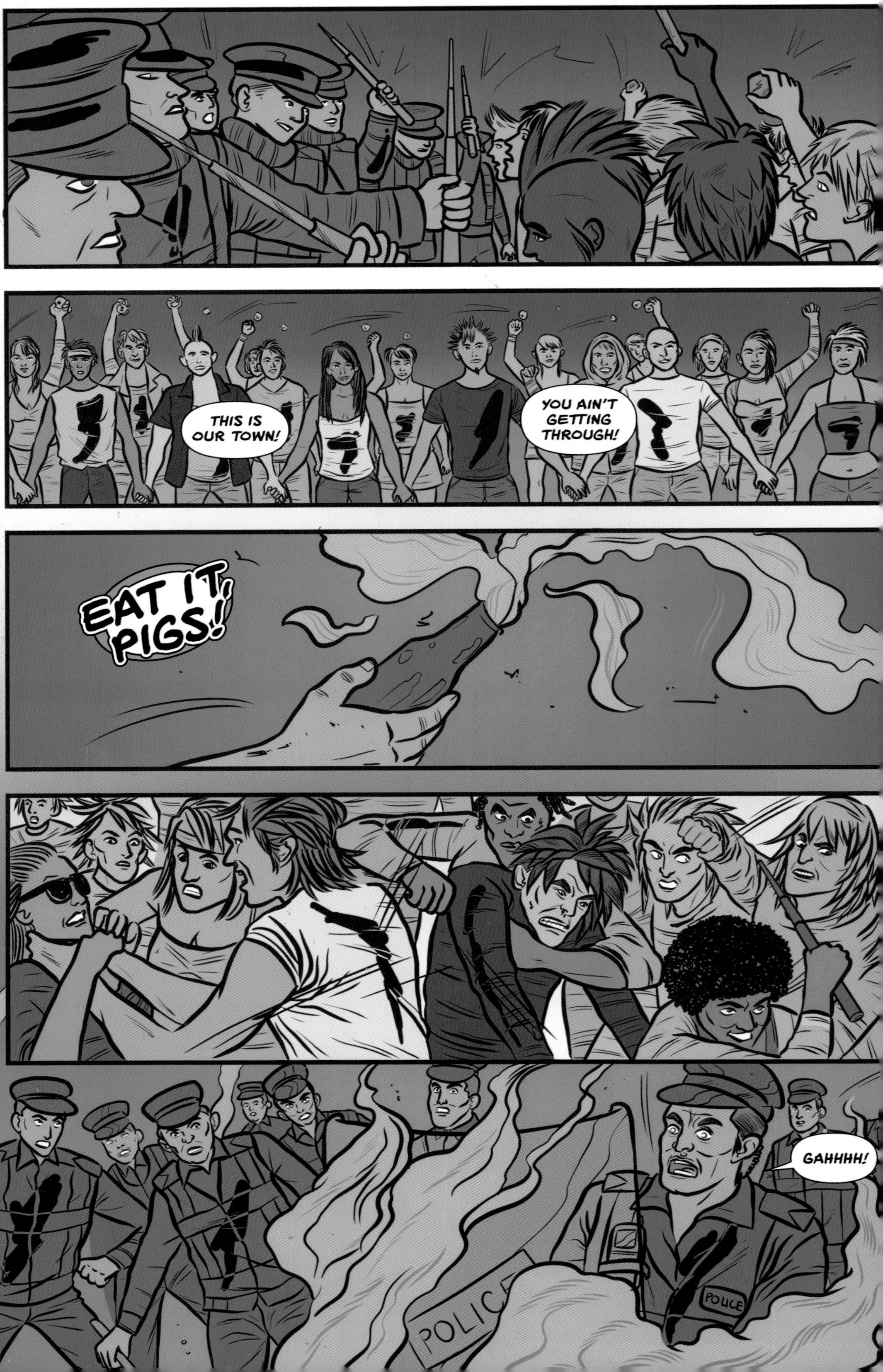
THIS IS OUR TOWN!
YOU AIN'T GETTING THROUGH!
EAT IT, PIGS!
GAHHHH!
POLICE

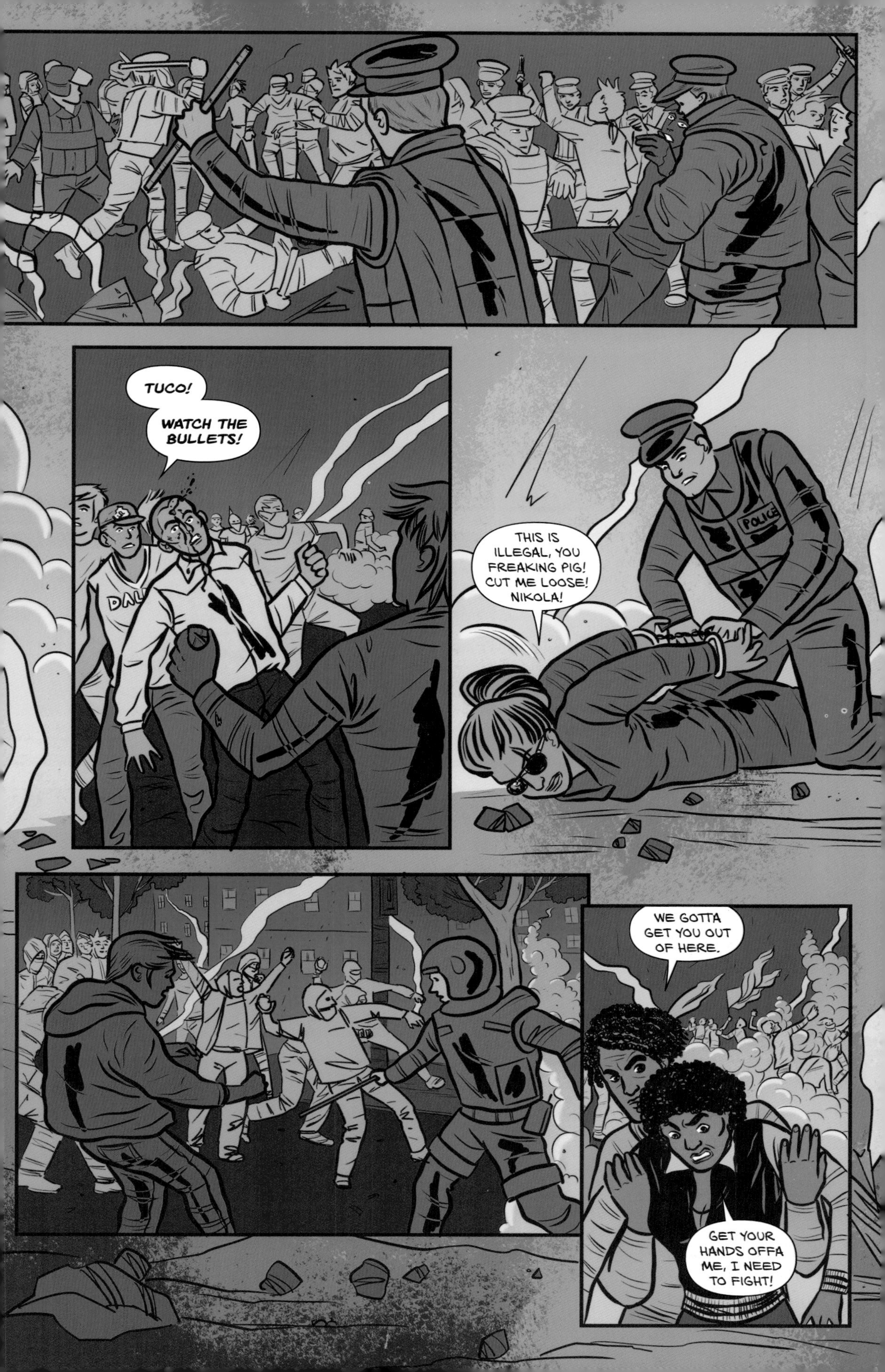
TUCO!
WATCH THE BULLETS!
THIS IS ILLEGAL, YOU FREAKING PIG! CUT ME LOOSE! NIKOLA!
WE GOTTA GET YOU OUT OF HERE.
GET YOUR HANDS OFFA ME, I NEED TO FIGHT!

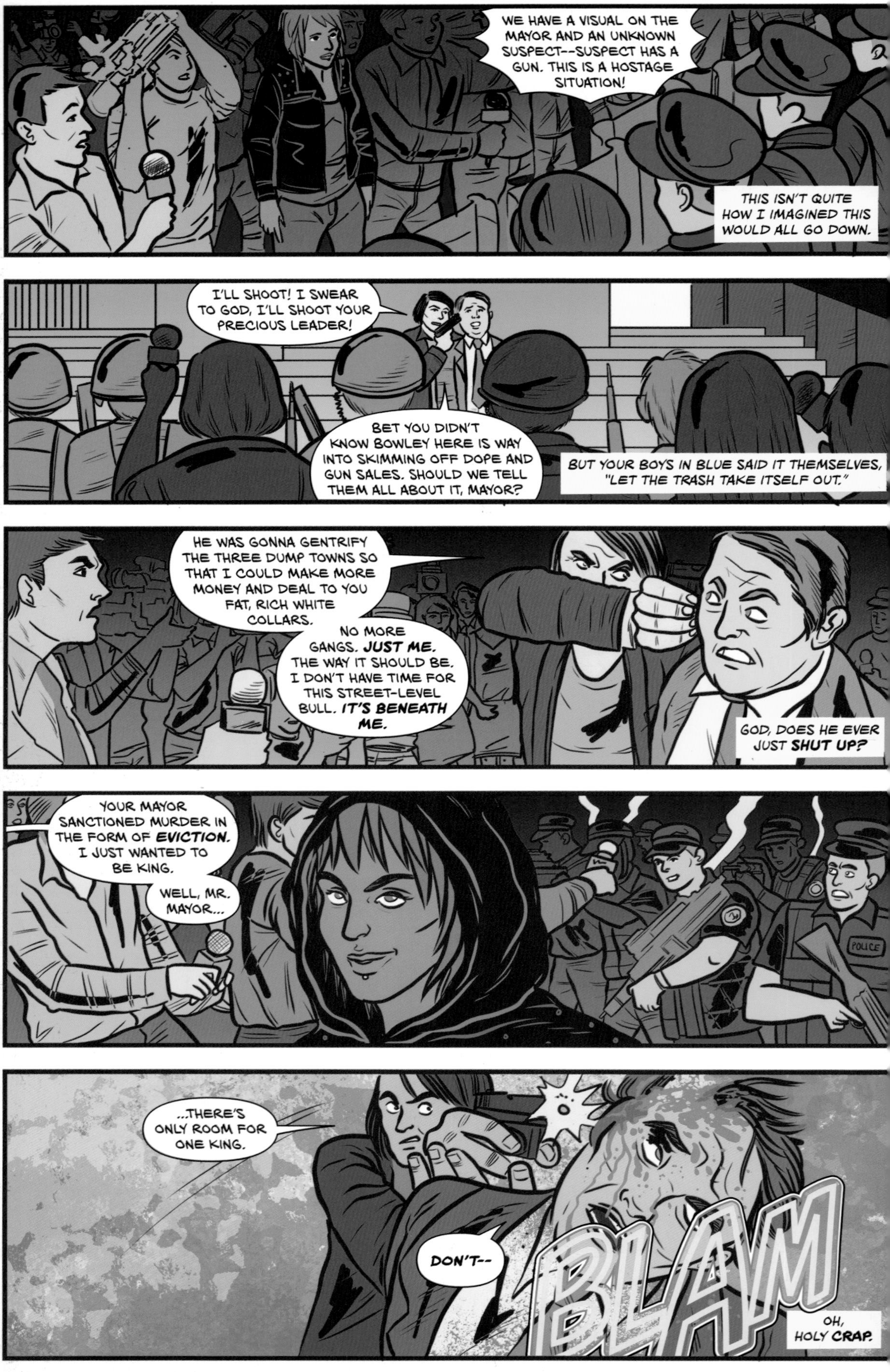
WE HAVE A VISUAL ON THE MAYOR AND AN UNKNOWN SUSPECT--SUSPECT HAS A GUN. THIS IS A HOSTAGE SITUATION!
THIS ISN'T QUITE HOW I IMAGINED THIS WOULD ALL GO DOWN.
I'LL SHOOT! I SWEAR TO GOD, I'LL SHOOT YOUR PRECIOUS LEADER!
BET YOU DIDN'T KNOW BOWLEY HERE IS WAY INTO SKIMMING OFF DOPE AND GUN SALES. SHOULD WE TELL THEM ALL ABOUT IT, MAYOR?
BUT YOUR BOYS IN BLUE SAID IT THEMSELVES, "LET THE TRASH TAKE ITSELF OUT."
HE WAS GONNA GENTRIFY THE THREE DUMP TOWNS SO THAT I COULD MAKE MORE MONEY AND DEAL TO YOU FAT, RICH WHITE COLLARS.
NO MORE GANGS. JUST ME. THE WAY IT SHOULD BE. I DON'T HAVE TIME FOR THIS STREET-LEVEL BULL. IT'S BENEATH ME.
GOD, DOES HE EVER JUST SHUT UP?
YOUR MAYOR SANCTIONED MURDER IN THE FORM OF EVICTION. I JUST WANTED TO BE KING.
WELL, MR. MAYOR...
POLICE
...THERE'S ONLY ROOM FOR ONE KING.
DON'T--
BLAM
OH, HOLY CRAP.

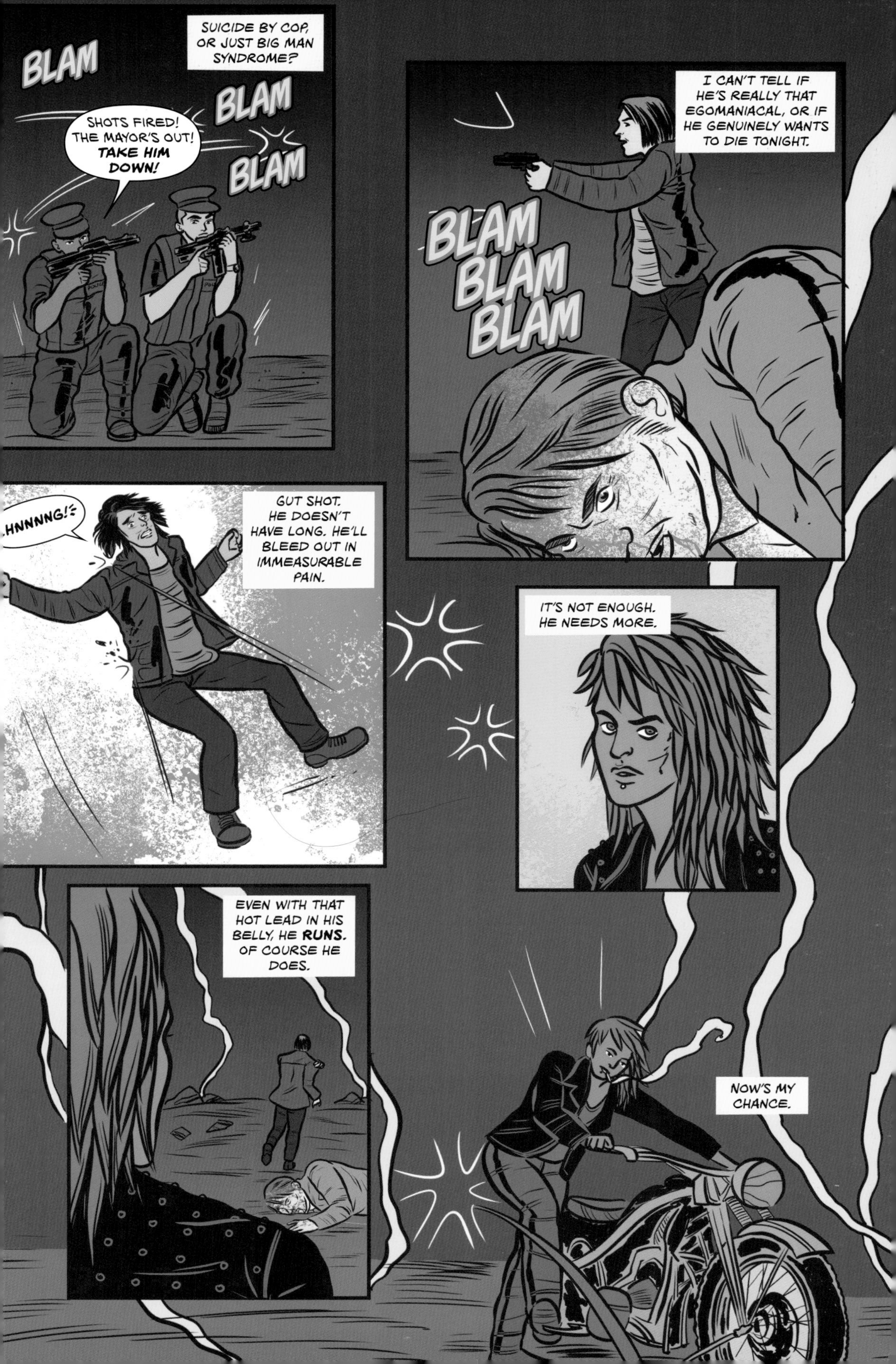
SUICIDE BY COP, OR JUST BIG MAN SYNDROME?
BLAM
BLAM
BLAM
SHOTS FIRED! THE MAYOR'S OUT! **TAKE HIM DOWN!**
I CAN'T TELL IF HE'S REALLY THAT EGOMANIACAL, OR IF HE GENUINELY WANTS TO DIE TONIGHT.
BLAM BLAM BLAM
HNNNNG!
GUT SHOT. HE DOESN'T HAVE LONG. HE'LL BLEED OUT IN IMMEASURABLE PAIN.
IT'S NOT ENOUGH. HE NEEDS MORE.
EVEN WITH THAT HOT LEAD IN HIS BELLY, HE **RUNS.** OF COURSE HE DOES.
NOW'S MY CHANCE.

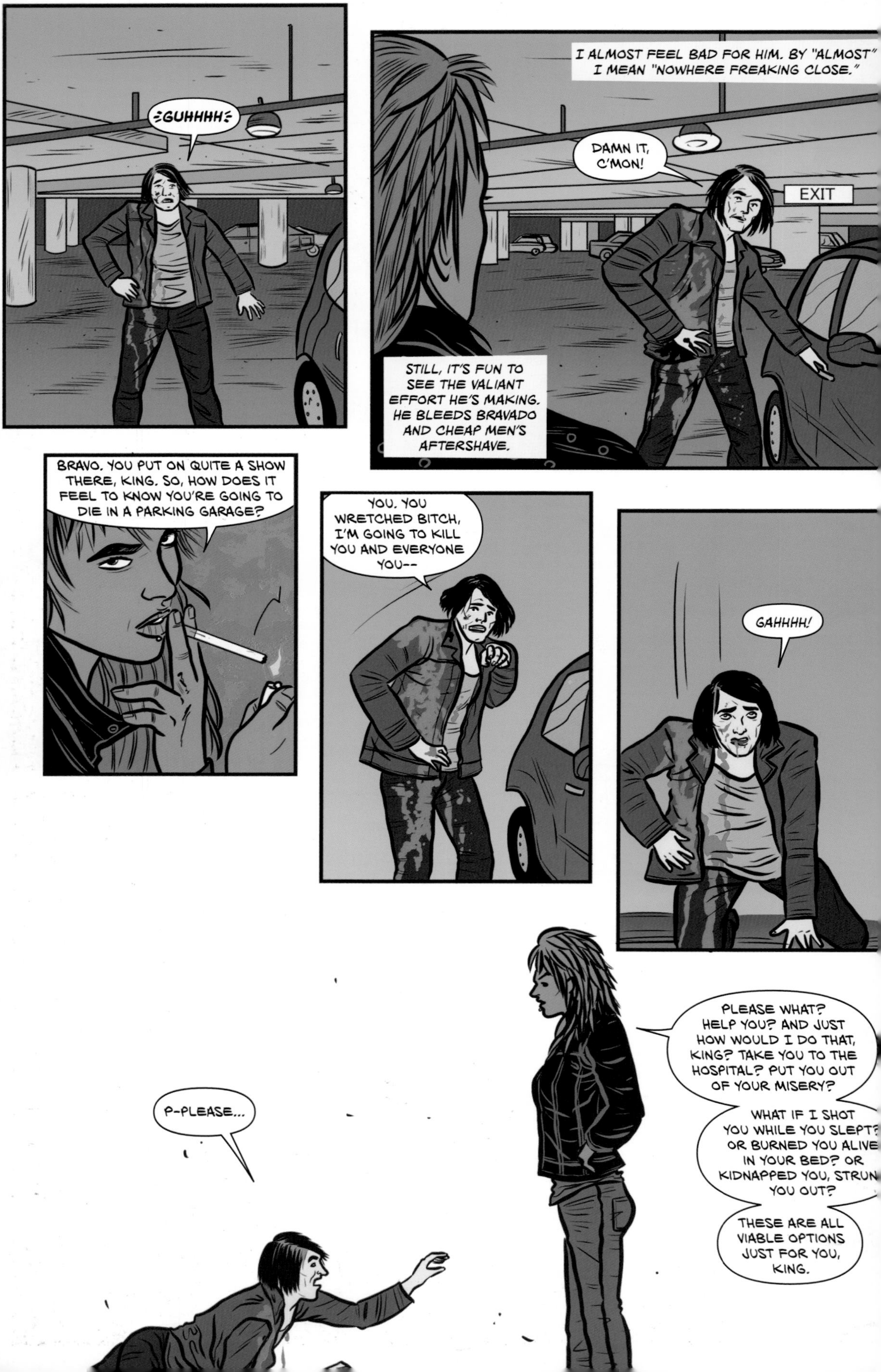
GUHHHH
I ALMOST FEEL BAD FOR HIM. BY "ALMOST" I MEAN "NOWHERE FREAKING CLOSE."
DAMN IT, C'MON!
EXIT
STILL, IT'S FUN TO SEE THE VALIANT EFFORT HE'S MAKING. HE BLEEDS BRAVADO AND CHEAP MEN'S AFTERSHAVE.
BRAVO. YOU PUT ON QUITE A SHOW THERE, KING. SO, HOW DOES IT FEEL TO KNOW YOU'RE GOING TO DIE IN A PARKING GARAGE?
YOU. YOU WRETCHED BITCH, I'M GOING TO KILL YOU AND EVERYONE YOU--
GAHHHH!
P-PLEASE...
PLEASE WHAT? HELP YOU? AND JUST HOW WOULD I DO THAT, KING? TAKE YOU TO THE HOSPITAL? PUT YOU OUT OF YOUR MISERY?
WHAT IF I SHOT YOU WHILE YOU SLEPT? OR BURNED YOU ALIVE IN YOUR BED? OR KIDNAPPED YOU, STRUN YOU OUT?
THESE ARE ALL VIABLE OPTIONS JUST FOR YOU, KING.

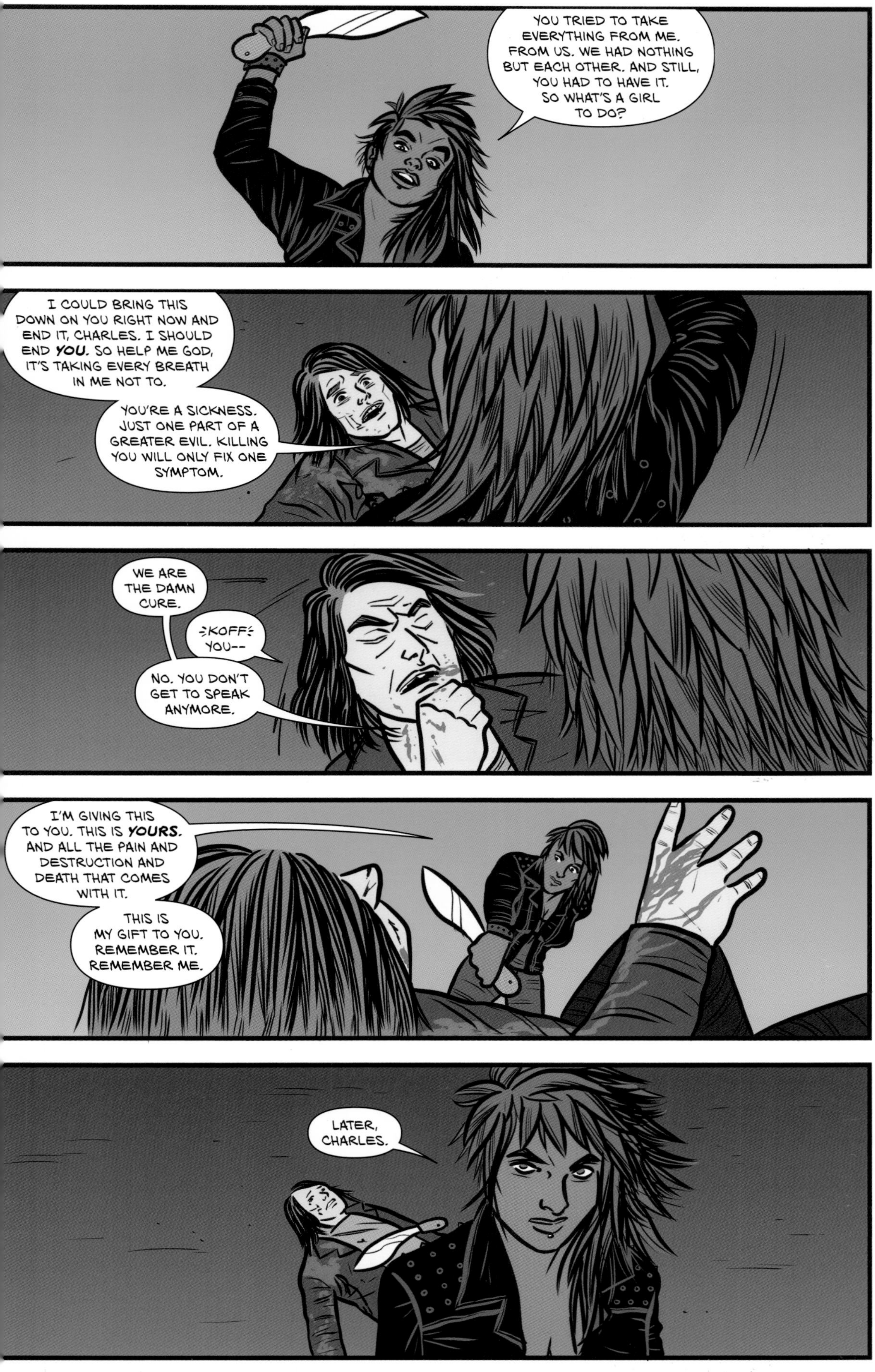
YOU TRIED TO TAKE EVERYTHING FROM ME. FROM US. WE HAD NOTHING BUT EACH OTHER. AND STILL, YOU HAD TO HAVE IT. SO WHAT'S A GIRL TO DO?
I COULD BRING THIS DOWN ON YOU RIGHT NOW AND END IT, CHARLES. I SHOULD END *YOU.* SO HELP ME GOD, IT'S TAKING EVERY BREATH IN ME NOT TO.
YOU'RE A SICKNESS. JUST ONE PART OF A GREATER EVIL. KILLING YOU WILL ONLY FIX ONE SYMPTOM.
WE ARE THE DAMN CURE.
KOFF YOU--
NO. YOU DON'T GET TO SPEAK ANYMORE.
I'M GIVING THIS TO YOU. THIS IS *YOURS.* AND ALL THE PAIN AND DESTRUCTION AND DEATH THAT COMES WITH IT.
THIS IS MY GIFT TO YOU. REMEMBER IT. REMEMBER ME.
LATER, CHARLES.

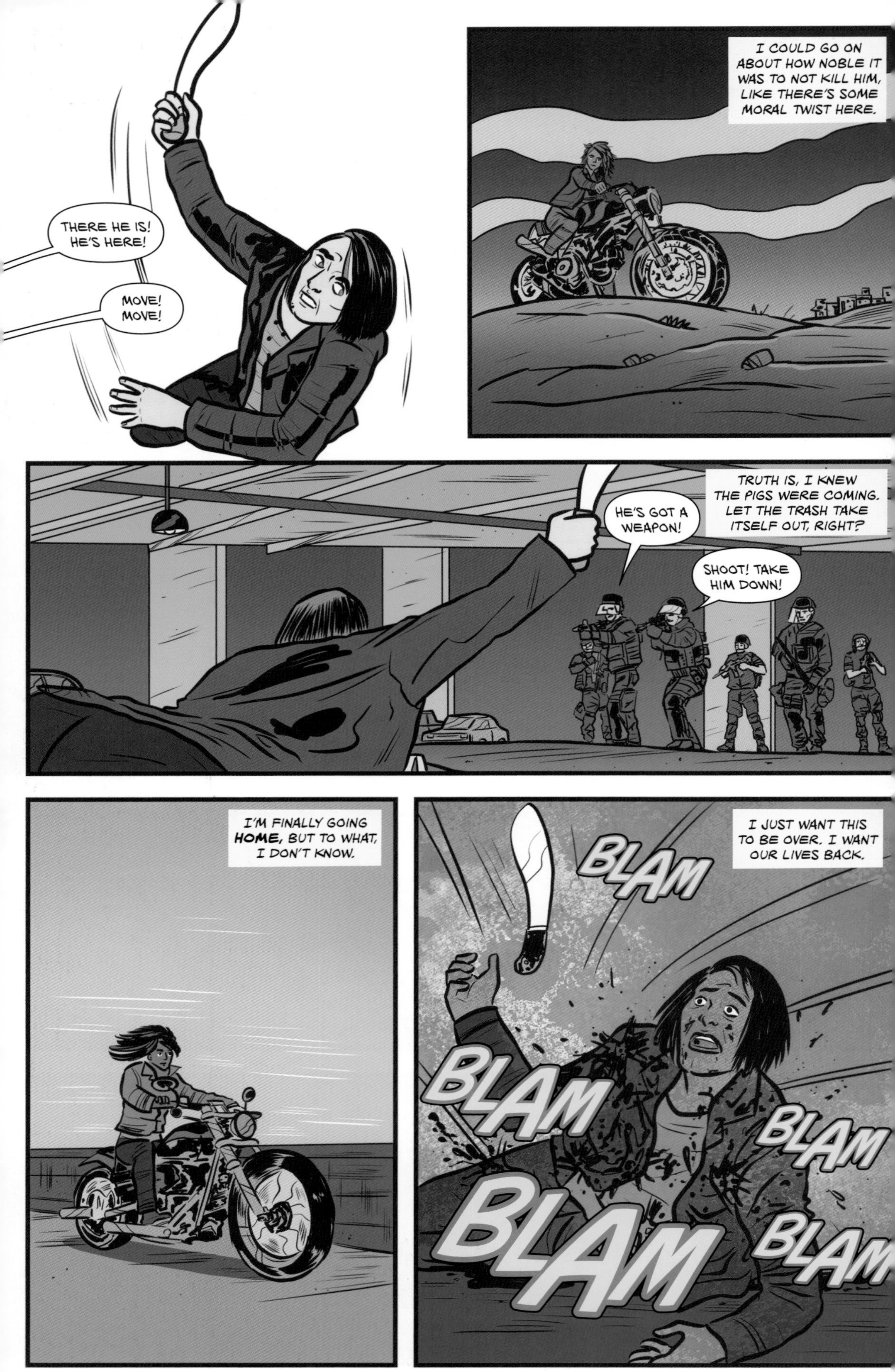

THERE HE IS! HE'S HERE!
MOVE! MOVE!
I COULD GO ON ABOUT HOW NOBLE IT WAS TO NOT KILL HIM, LIKE THERE'S SOME MORAL TWIST HERE.
TRUTH IS, I KNEW THE PIGS WERE COMING. LET THE TRASH TAKE ITSELF OUT, RIGHT?
HE'S GOT A WEAPON!
SHOOT! TAKE HIM DOWN!
I'M FINALLY GOING HOME, BUT TO WHAT, I DON'T KNOW.
I JUST WANT THIS TO BE OVER. I WANT OUR LIVES BACK.
BLAM
BLAM
BLAM
BLAM
BLAM

BETTY, WHAT *HAPPENED?*

SOME PEOPLE TRIED TO TAKE OUR HOME, SUGAR. THEY FAILED.

THIS PLACE LOOKS HOW I FEEL RIGHT NOW.

CAN WE STILL LIVE HERE?

OF COURSE, SWEET PEA. THIS IS YOUR **HOME.**

DAMN, I MISSED HOME.

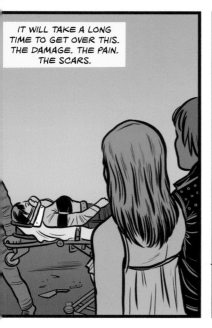

IT WILL TAKE A LONG TIME TO GET OVER THIS. THE DAMAGE. THE PAIN. THE SCARS.

BUT WE CAN CONQUER AND HEAL THE WOUNDS.

WE CAN **REBUILD.**

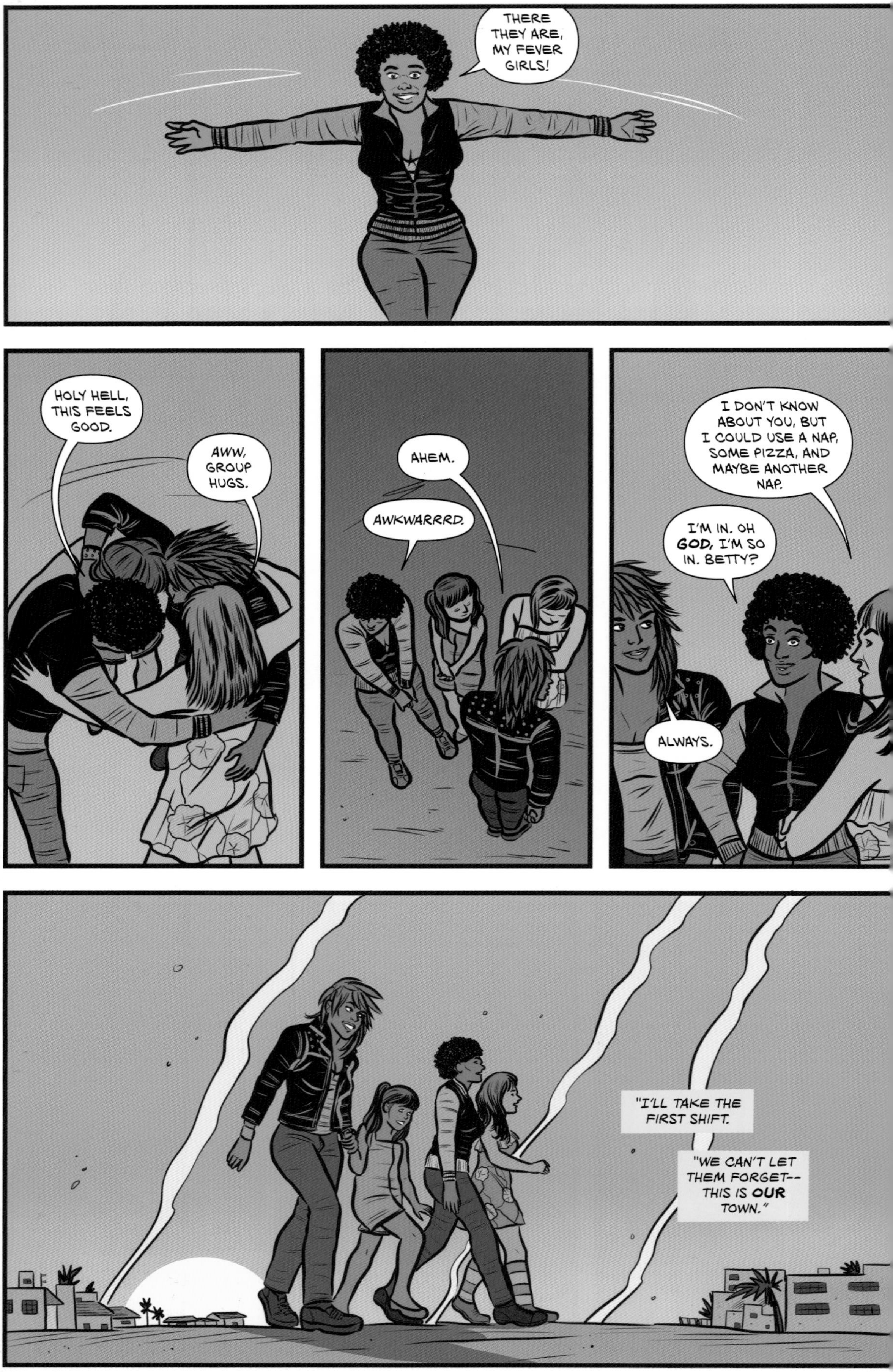
THERE THEY ARE, MY FEVER GIRLS!
HOLY HELL, THIS FEELS GOOD.
AWW, GROUP HUGS.
AHEM.
AWKWARRRD.
I DON'T KNOW ABOUT YOU, BUT I COULD USE A NAP, SOME PIZZA, AND MAYBE ANOTHER NAP.
I'M IN. OH GOD, I'M SO IN. BETTY?
ALWAYS.
"I'LL TAKE THE FIRST SHIFT.
"WE CAN'T LET THEM FORGET-- THIS IS OUR TOWN."

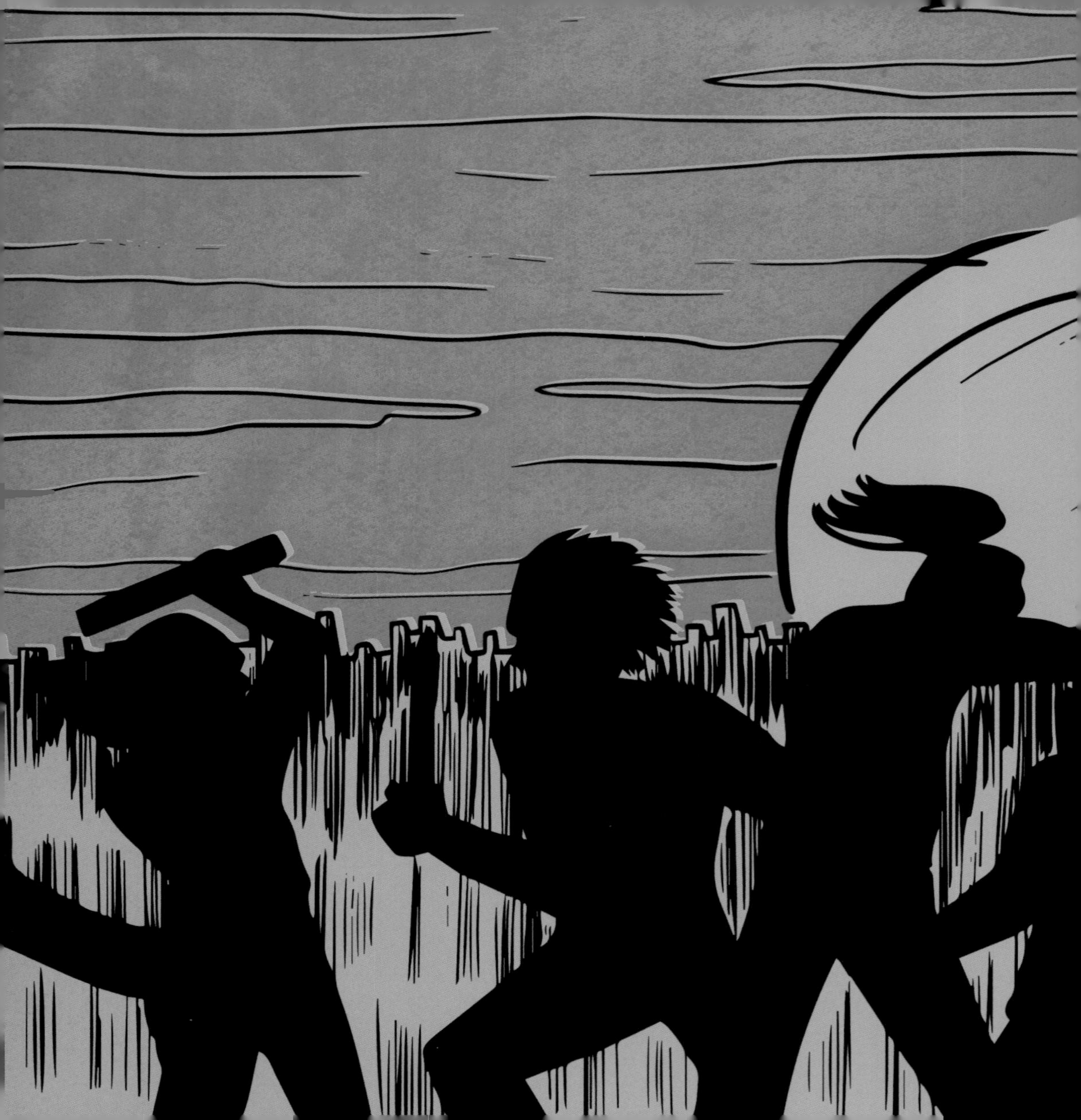

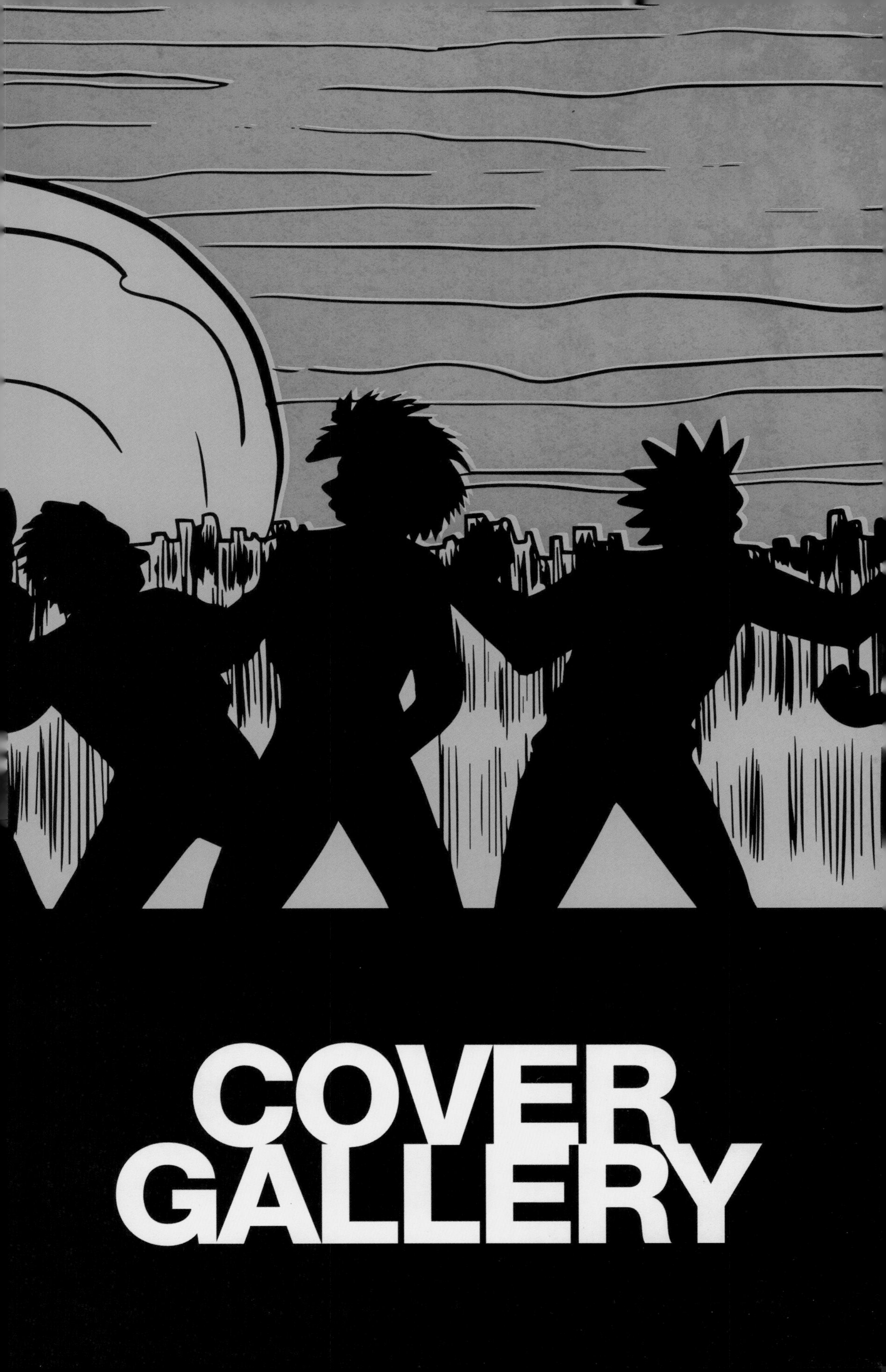

COVER GALLERY

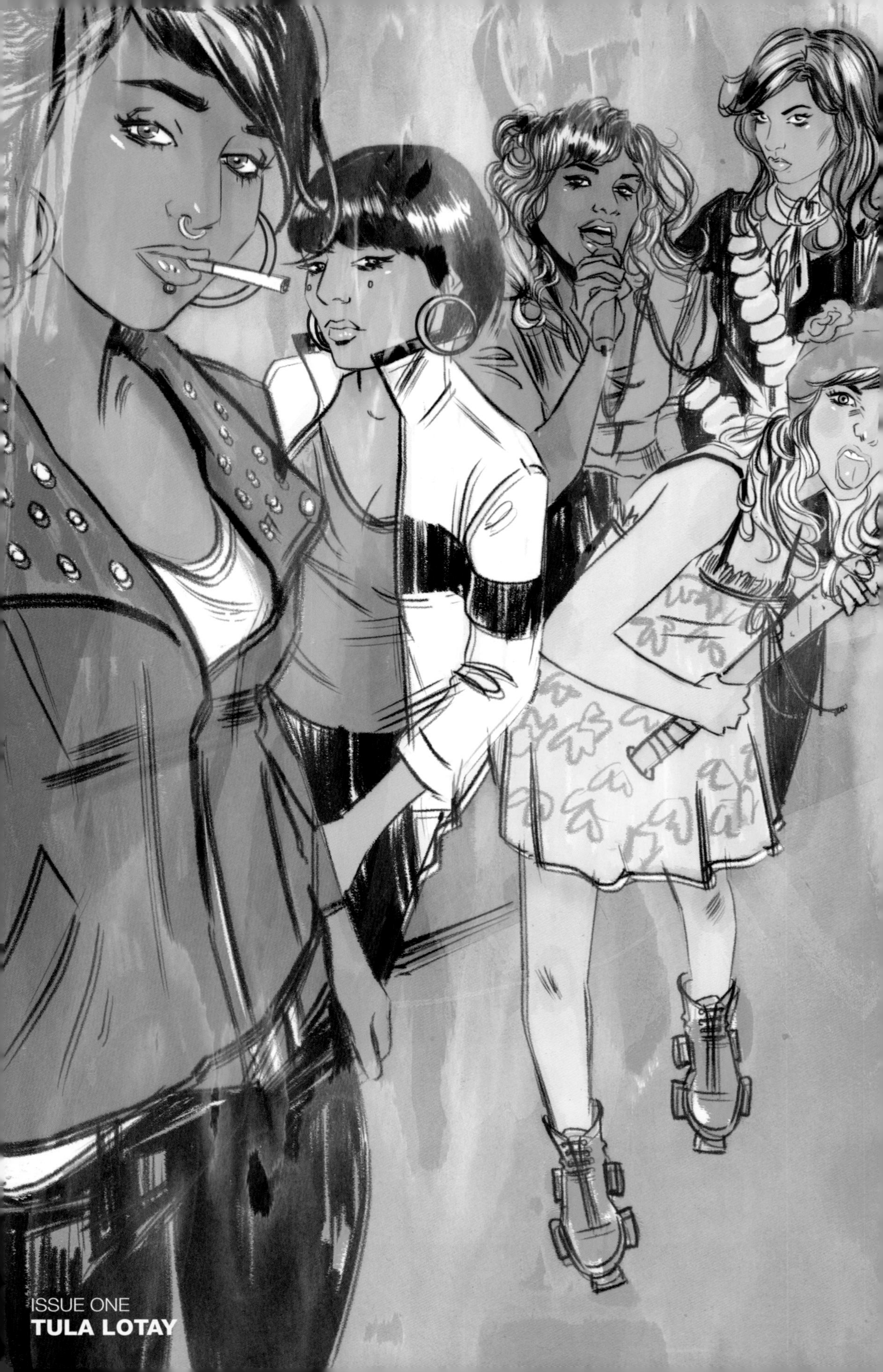

ISSUE ONE
TULA LOTAY

ISSUE ONE VARIANT
MARIE BERGERON

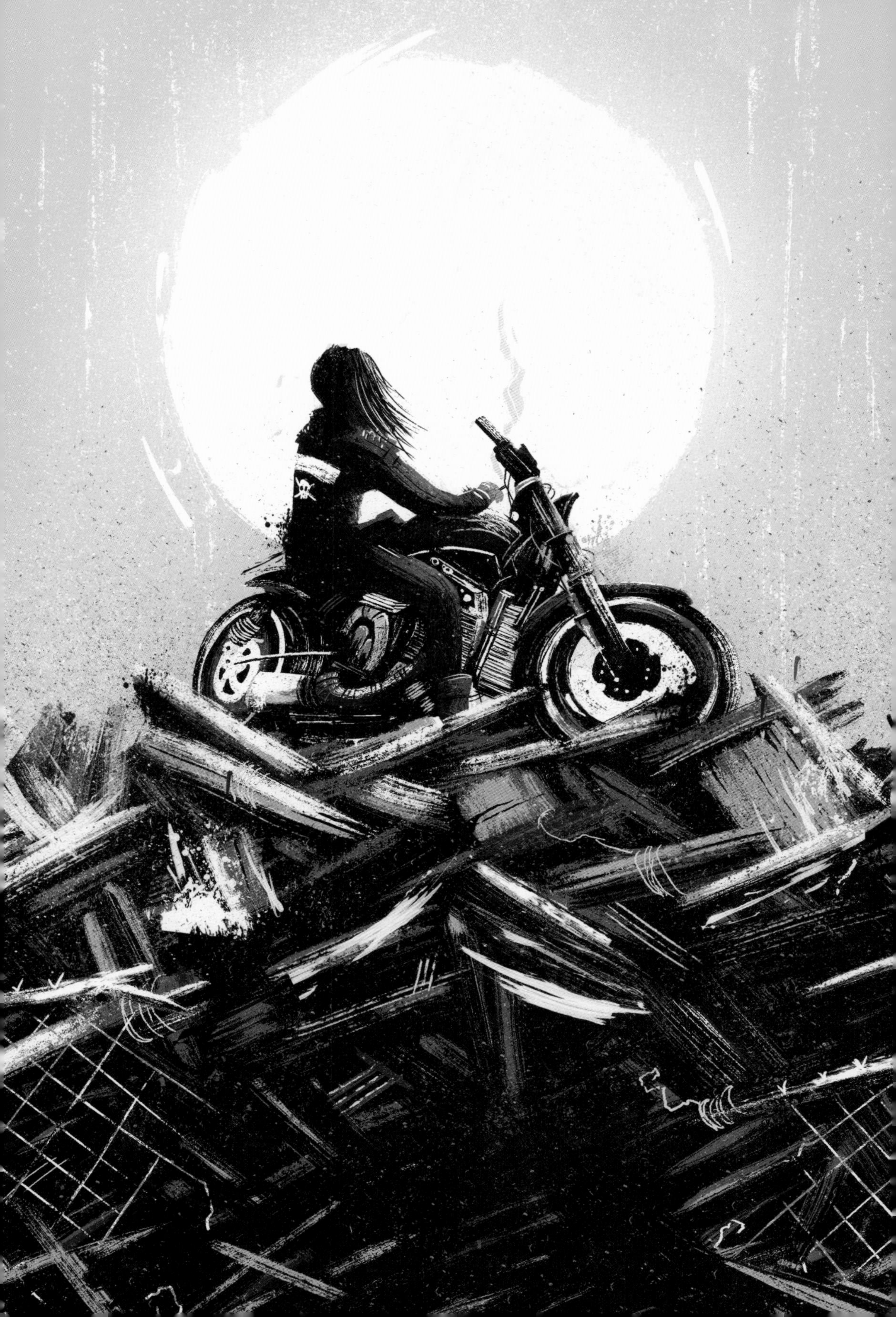

ISSUE ONE SECOND PRINT
DEVAKI NEOGI
COLORS BY **NEIL LALONDE**

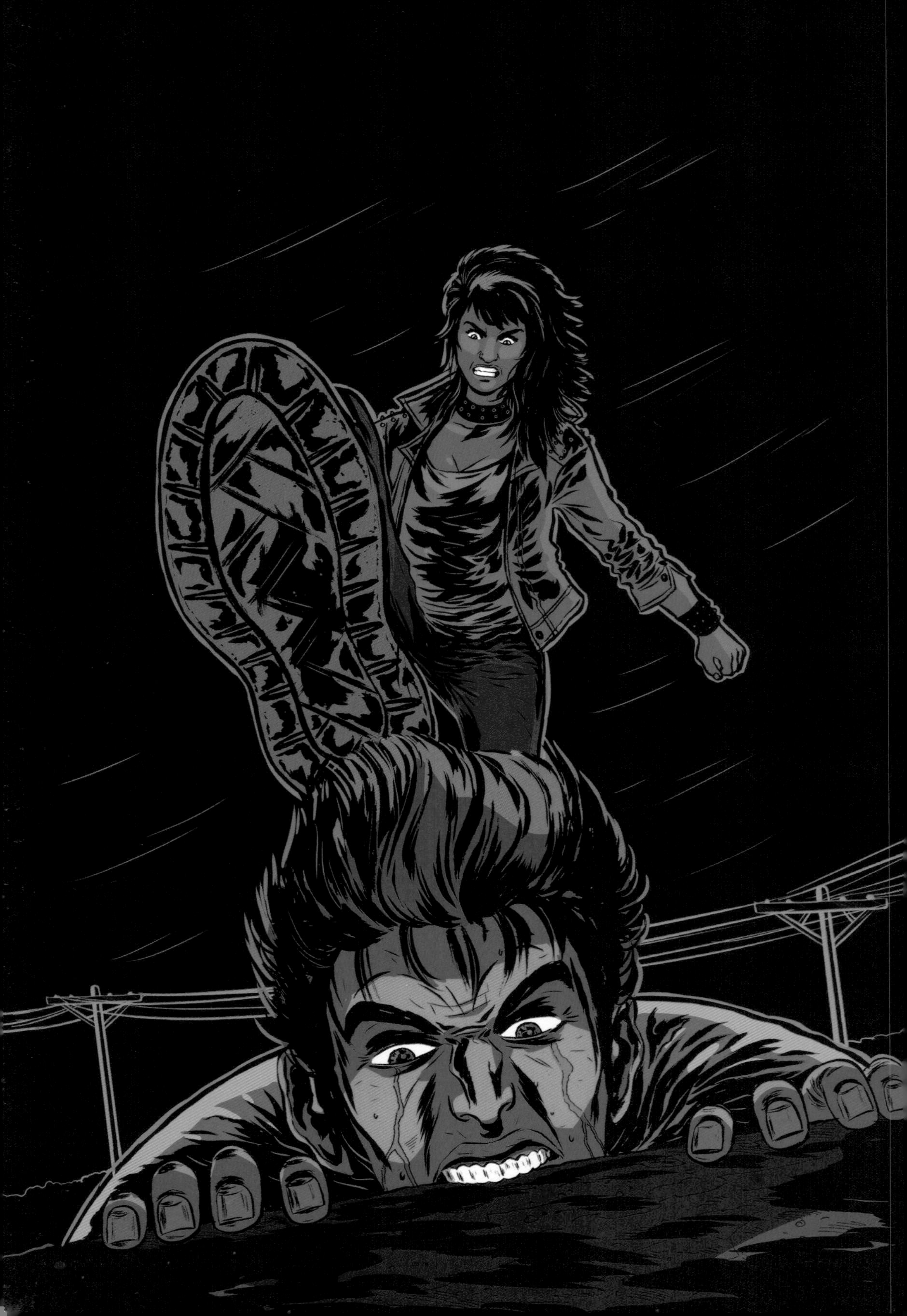

ISSUE TWO
DEVAKI NEOGI
COLORS BY **NEIL LALONDE**

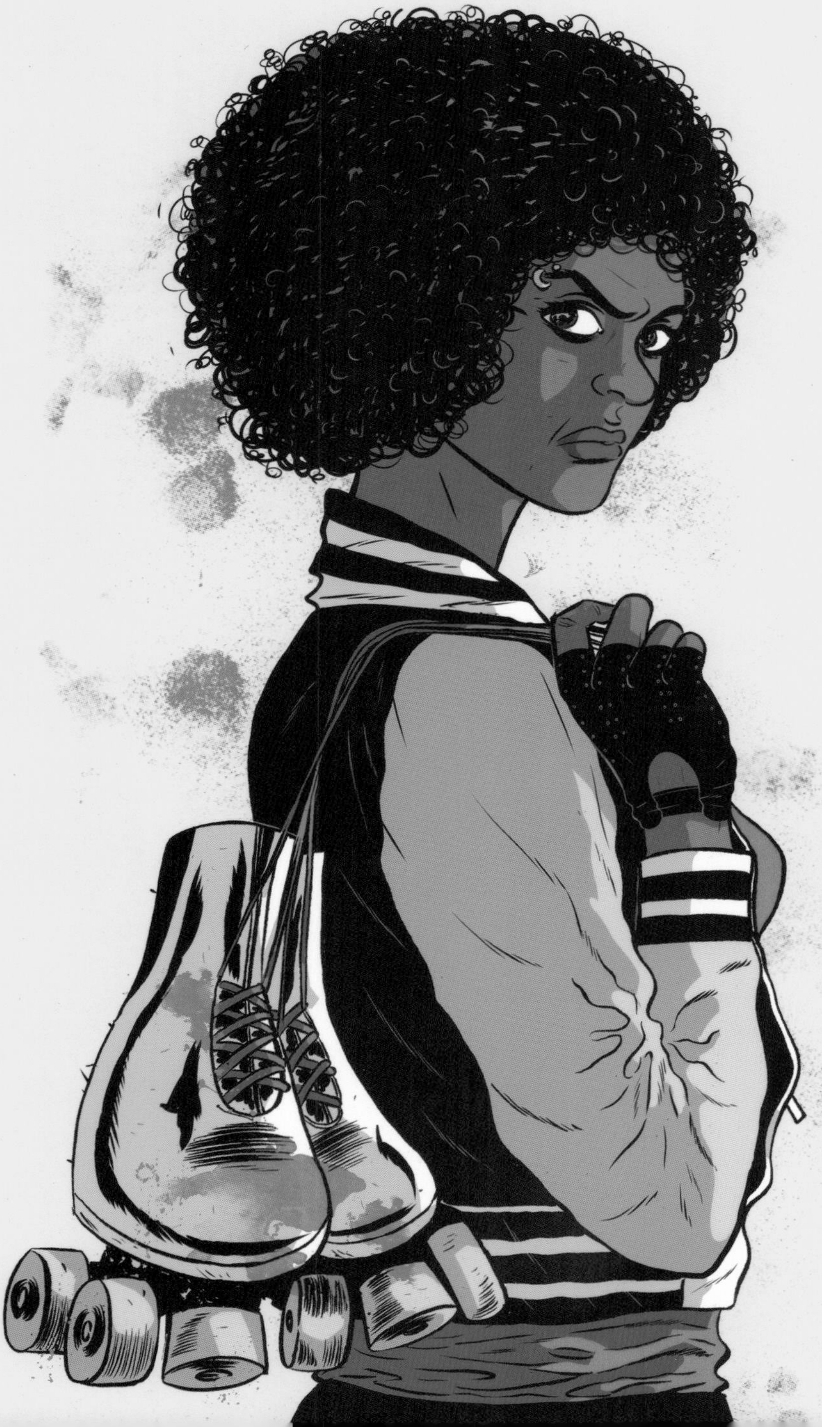

ISSUE THREE

DEVAKI NEOGI

COLORS BY **NEIL LALONDE**

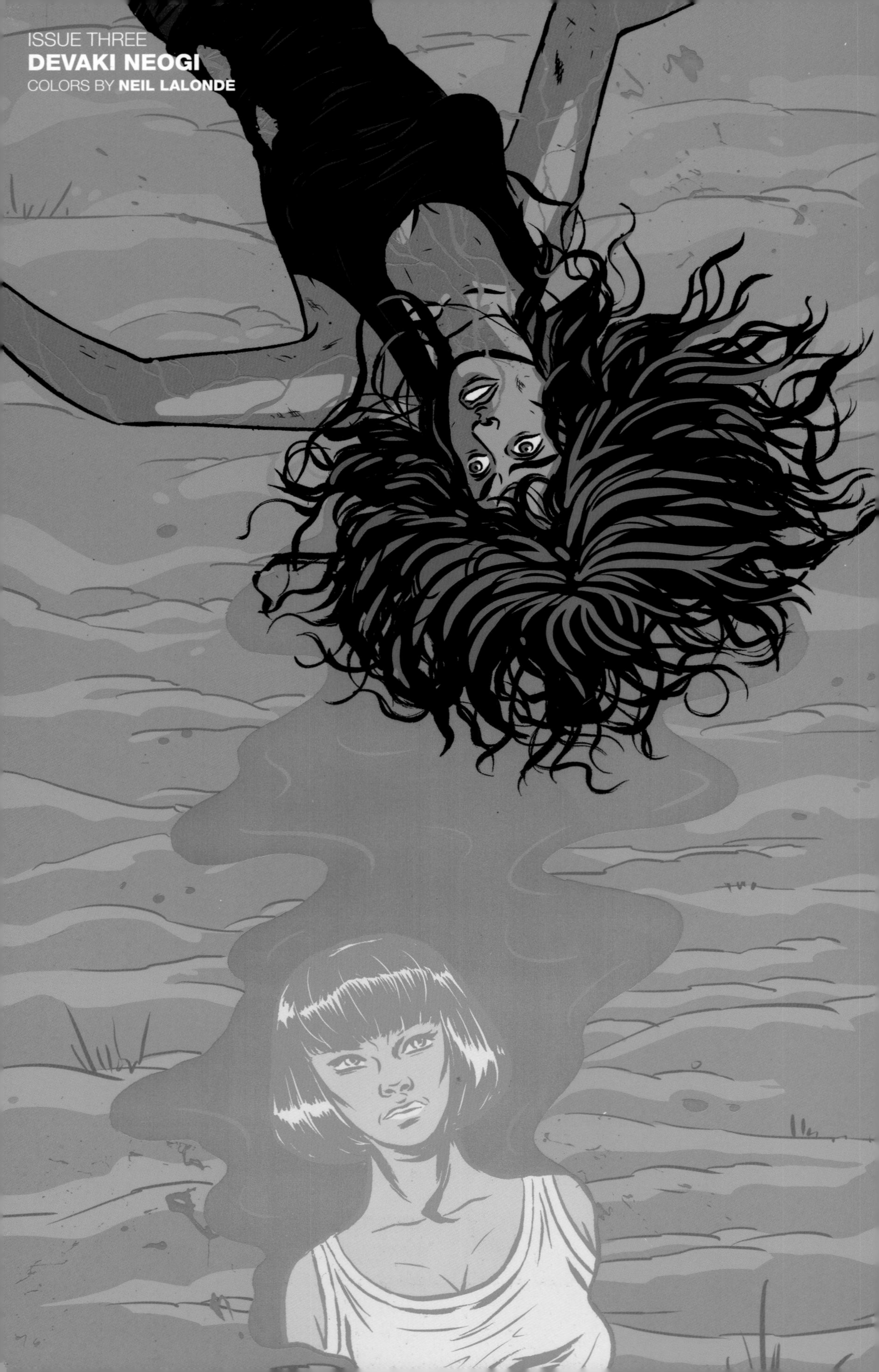

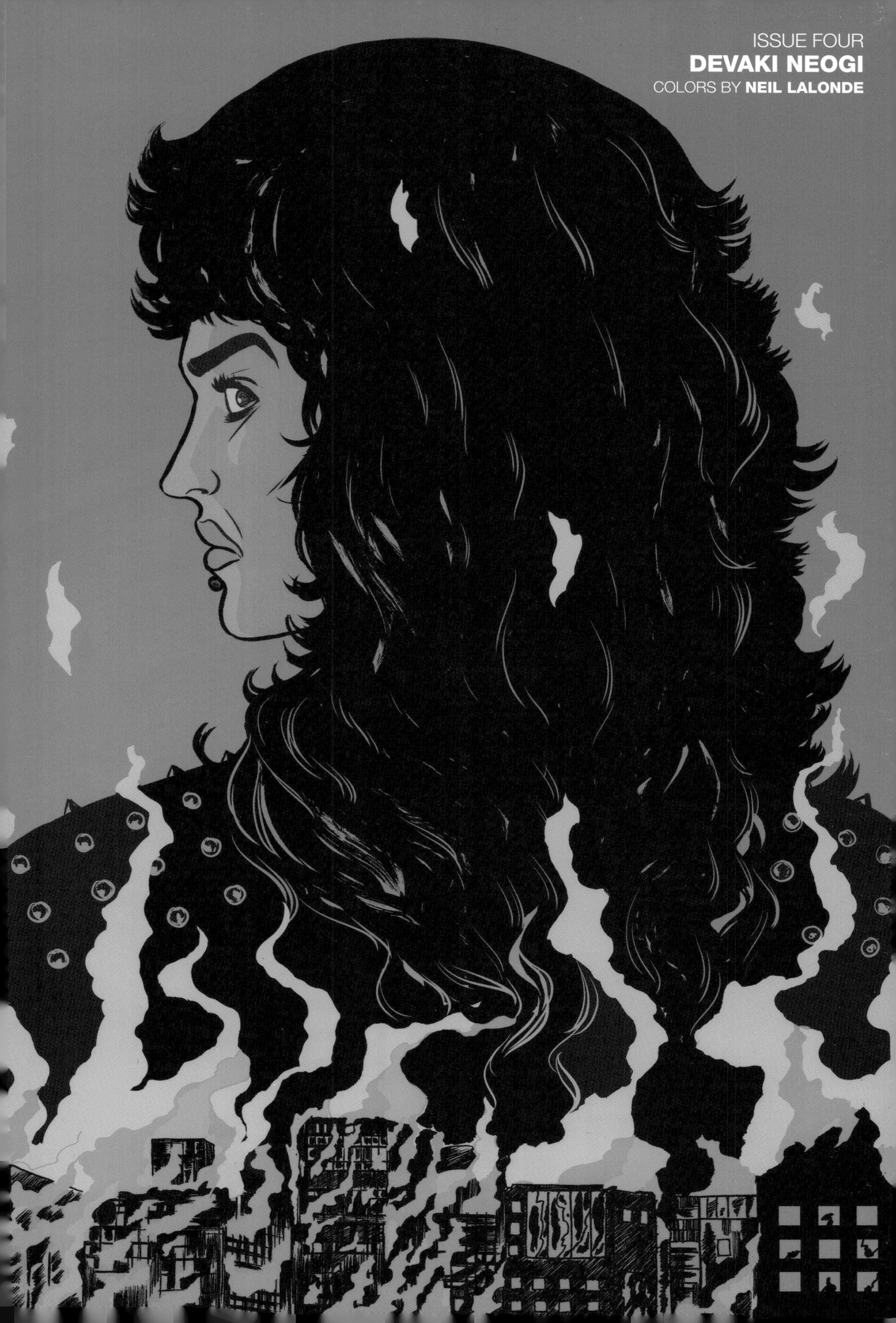
ISSUE FOUR
DEVAKI NEOGI
COLORS BY NEIL LALONDE

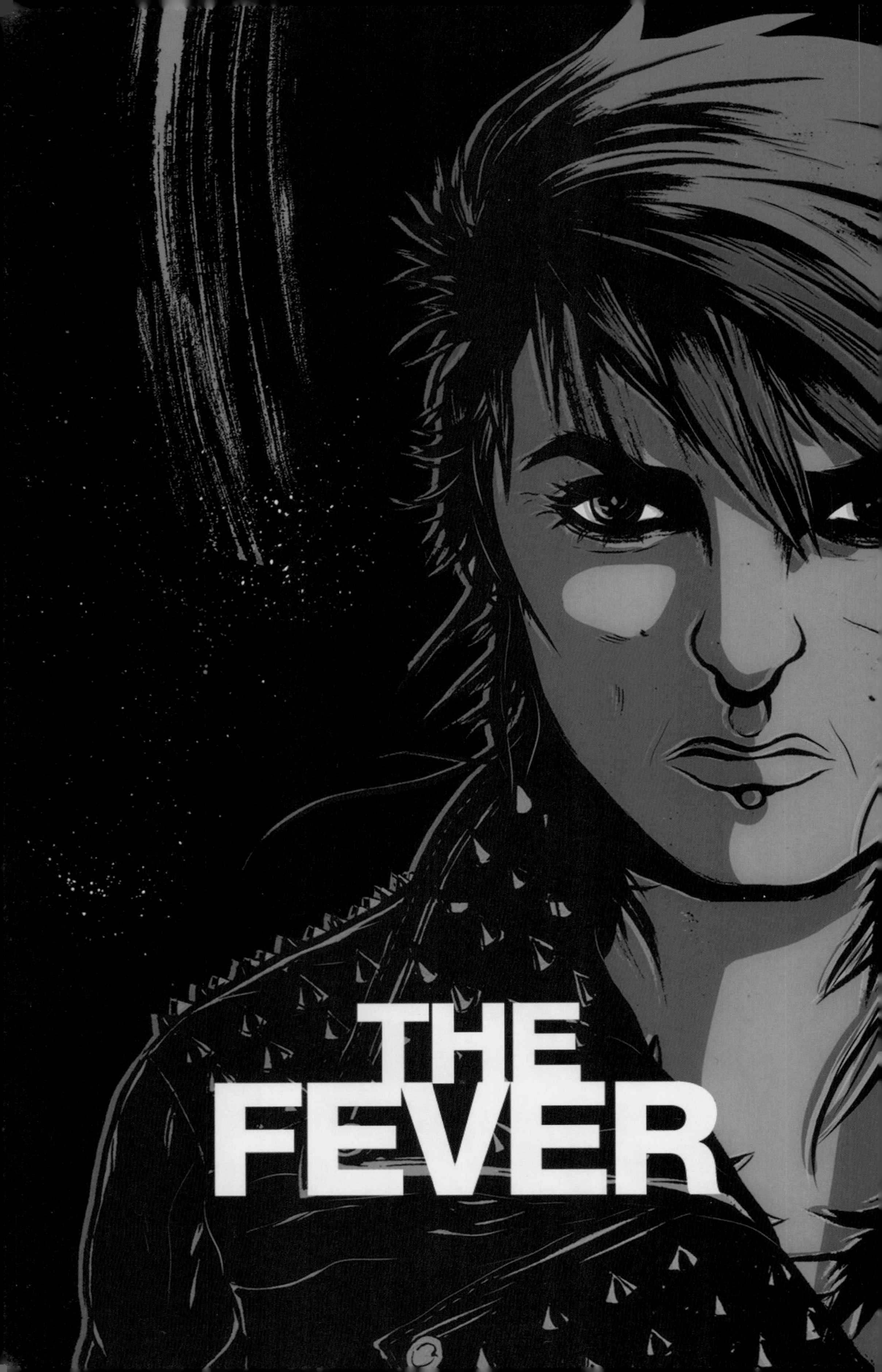
THE
FEVER